HOUSING IN 21ST-CENTURY AUSTRALIA

Housing in 21st-Century Australia
People, Practices and Policies

Edited by

RAE DUFTY-JONES
DALLAS ROGERS
University of Western Sydney, Australia

ASHGATE

© Rae Dufty-Jones, Dallas Rogers and the contributors 2015

All rights reserved. No part of this publication may be reproduced, stored in a retrieval system or transmitted in any form or by any means, electronic, mechanical, photocopying, recording or otherwise without the prior permission of the publisher.

Rae Dufty-Jones and Dallas Rogers have asserted their right under the Copyright, Designs and Patents Act, 1988, to be identified as the editors of this work.

Published by
Ashgate Publishing Limited
Wey Court East
Union Road
Farnham
Surrey, GU9 7PT
England

Ashgate Publishing Company
110 Cherry Street
Suite 3-1
Burlington, VT 05401-3818
USA

www.ashgate.com

British Library Cataloguing in Publication Data
A catalogue record for this book is available from the British Library.

Library of Congress Cataloging-in-Publication Data
Housing in 21st-century Australia : people, practices and policies / [edited] by Rae Dufty-Jones and Dallas Rogers.
       pages cm
    Includes bibliographical references and index.
    ISBN 978-1-4724-3113-4 (hardback) – ISBN 978-1-4724-3114-1 (ebook) – ISBN 978-1-4724-3115-8 (epub)
1. Housing – Australia. 2. Housing policy – Australia. I. Dufty-Jones, Rae. II. Rogers, Dallas.
    HD7379.A3H686 2015
    363.50994–dc23

2015008820

ISBN 9781472431134 (hbk)
ISBN 9781472431141 (ebk – PDF)
ISBN 9781472431158 (ebk – ePUB)

Printed in the United Kingdom by Henry Ling Limited,
at the Dorset Press, Dorchester, DT1 1HD

Contents

List of Figures		vii
List of Tables		ix
Notes on Contributors		xi
Preface		xiii

1   Housing in Australia: A New Century   1
    Rae Dufty-Jones and Dallas Rogers

PART 1   PEOPLE AND PRACTICES

2   Housing Multigenerational Households in Australian Cities: Evidence from Sydney and Brisbane at the Turn of the 21st century   21
    Edgar Liu, Hazel Easthope, Bruce Judd and Ian Burnley

3   Ethnic Discrimination in Private Rental Housing Markets in Australia   39
    Jacqueline Nelson, Heather MacDonald, Rae Dufty-Jones, Kevin Dunn and Yin Paradies

4   Housing and Sustainability: Everyday Practices and Material Entanglements   57
    Chantel Carr and Chris Gibson

5   Indigenous Housing   73
    Daphne Habibis

6   Reshaping Housing Consumption and Production from the Bottom Up: Insights from Interpretivist Housing Research   89
    Wendy Stone

7   Boomer Housing Preferences: Active Adult Lifestyle Communities versus Aging in Place   105
    Caryl Bosman

8   Policy Implications for Governing Australia's Apartment Communities: Tenants, Committees of Management and Strata Managers   121
    Erika Altmann

PART 2 POLICIES

9   Private Rental Housing in Australia: Political Inertia and Market Change   139
       Kath Hulse and Terry Burke

10   Keynes in the Antipodes: The Housing Industry, First Home Owner Grants and the Global Financial Crisis   153
       Elizabeth Taylor and Tony Dalton

11   The Historical Construction of 'The Public Housing Problem' and Deconcentration Policies   173
       Kathy Arthurson and Michael Darcy

12   Reviewing the Social Housing Initiative: Unpacking Opportunities and Challenges for Community Housing Provision in Australia   187
       Kristian Ruming

13   Homelessness, the 'Housing First' Approach and the Creation of 'Home'   205
       Hazel Blunden and Gabrielle Drake

14   21st-Century Australian Housing: New Frontiers in the Asia-Pacific   221
       Dallas Rogers and Rae Dufty-Jones

Index   *237*

List of Figures

3.1	Accommodation situation for new migrants to Australia by stream	42
5.1	Proportion of people living in overcrowded housing, by remoteness area, 2006	78
6.1	Downshifters' characteristics, attitudes and engagement with income/expenditure	94
6.2	Typology of downshifters' housing circumstances	96
7.1	Location map of the case study sites: Halcyon Waters, Helensvale, Golden Crest Manors and Nerang, Gold Coast City Region, Queensland	108
10.1	Dwelling supply and supply-oriented interventions, Australia	155
10.2	First home owner grants, established and new homes, Victoria 2000–2013	158
10.3	First home owner grant expenditure, new and existing dwellings Victoria 2000–2013	159
10.4	Value of first homeowner grant programs and private dwelling commencements	160
10.5	FHOG grants by postcode, 2007–2008, Melbourne	163
10.6	Indicators of housing price trends, Victoria, 2003–2010	166
11.1	Radburn style estate with cul de sacs at Bonnyrigg Estate in NSW	176

List of Tables

2.1	Top ten reasons for living in multigenerational households, multiple responses, Sydney and Brisbane, 2012–2013	27
2.2	Dwelling structure of multigenerational households, Sydney and Brisbane, 2011–2013	30
2.3	Tenure profile of multigenerational households, Sydney and Brisbane, 2011–2013	31
2.4	Challenges of multigenerational co-residence, multiple responses, Sydney and Brisbane, 2012–13	32
3.1	Reported discrimination in housing across 15 EU member states	41
3.2	What makes it hard to find accommodation (Humanitarian entrants only)	46
3.3	Experiences of racism when renting/buying a house (Challenging Racism Project 2001–2008; Ordinariness of Australian Muslims Survey 2011)	47
3.4	Agent flexibility	50
3.5	Provision of information	51
3.6	Interactions with agents	51
3.7	Requirements for renting	52
3.8	Encouragement to rent	52
5.1	Household tenure type, persons aged 15 years and over	74
5.2	Australia's estimated Aboriginal and Torres Strait Islander population by state and territory (at 30 June 2011)	77
5.3	Estimated Resident ATSI Population by Remoteness Areas, 2011	77
7.1	Statistical comparison of the two case study sites (four zones) highlighting key socio-economic characteristics of the different areas	109
10.1	Descriptive statistics, model variables for FHOGs and quarterly new dwelling activity, Victoria 2003–2012	161
10.2	Regression model results: value of new building activity, Victoria ($000s)	161
10.3	Regression model results: new dwelling commencements, Victoria	162
12.1	Interviews conducted	188

Notes on Contributors

Erika Altmann, School of Sociology and Social Work, University of Tasmania, Australia

Kathy Arthurson, Southgate Institute, Flinders University, Australia

Hazel Blunden, School of Social Sciences and Psychology, University of Western Sydney, Australia

Caryl Bosman, School of Environment, Griffith University, Australia

Terry Burke, The Swinburne Institute for Social Research, Swinburne University of Technology, Australia

Ian Burnley, City Future Centre, Faculty of the Built Environment, University of New South Wales, Australia

Chantel Carr, Australian Centre for Cultural Environmental Research, University of Wollongong, Australia

Tony Dalton, Centre for Urban Research, RMIT University, Australia

Michael Darcy, School of Social Sciences and Psychology, University of Western Sydney, Australia

Gabrielle Drake, School of Social Sciences and Psychology, University of Western Sydney, Australia

Rae Dufty-Jones, School of Social Sciences and Psychology, University of Western Sydney, Australia

Kevin Dunn, School of Social Sciences and Psychology, University of Western Sydney, Australia

Hazel Easthope, City Future Centre, Faculty of the Built Environment, University of New South Wales, Australia

Chris Gibson, Australian Centre for Cultural Environmental Research, University of Wollongong, Australia

Daphne Habibis, School of Sociology and Social Work, University of Tasmania, Australia

Kath Hulse, The Swinburne Institute for Social Research, Swinburne University of Technology, Australia

Bruce Judd, City Future Centre, Faculty of the Built Environment, University of New South Wales, Australia

Edgar Liu, City Future Centre, Faculty of the Built Environment, University of New South Wales, Australia

Heather MacDonald, School of Built Environment, University of Technology, Australia

Jacqueline Nelson, Cosmopolitan Civil Societies, Faculty or Arts and Social Sciences, University of Technology Sydney, Australia

Yin Paradies, Centre for Citizenship and Globalisation, Deakin University, Australia

Dallas Rogers, School of Social Sciences and Psychology, University of Western Sydney, Australia

Kristian Ruming, Department of Environment and Geography, Macquarie University, Australia

Wendy Stone, The Swinburne Institute for Social Research, Swinburne University of Technology, Australia

Elizabeth Taylor, Faculty of Architecture Building and Planning, University of Melbourne, Australia

Preface

This book aims to provide a contemporary text on the significant changes, challenges and debates about how housing in Australia is consumed and governed in the 21st century. Housing in Australia is a national obsession. It is rare for a week to go by without a national media outlet producing a piece about housing affordability, housing policy settings, housing finance etc. Through both empirical and theoretical studies, the book builds on established themes in housing studies such as population and economic change, policy shifts, and homelessness, but also introduces new concerns around Indigenous housing and environmental change. In doing so, the text provides original and in-depth insights into some of the contemporary factors shaping the production and consumption of housing in Australia and how they intersect with policy. While the focus of this text is on Australia, many of the issues confronting housing in 21st-century Australia are familiar concerns to other parts of the world. For instance how do suburban-based societies adjust to the realities of aging populations, anthropogenic climate change and the significant implications such change has for housing? How has policy been translated and assembled in different national contexts? Similarly, what policy settings are required to guide the production and consumption of housing in a post-global financial crisis period?

We would like to thank the many contributors who responded with alacrity and enthusiasm to this project. We believe the chapters assembled in this book will contribute to emerging and ongoing housing debates in 21st-century Australia. Finally, we would like to thank Peter Phibbs, Lauren Costello, Michael Darcy, Tim Jones and Jacqueline Nelson for their enthusiasm, encouragement and support of this project.

Rae Dufty-Jones and Dallas Rogers

Chapter 1
Housing in Australia: A New Century

Rae Dufty-Jones and Dallas Rogers

Introduction

> Home is where most of us live more than half our waking hours. It is where we do more than a third of our work, and spend a great deal of our leisure. It's where we suffer or enjoy a great deal of our whole experience of life ... it's an important place. (Stretton 1974: 21)

In 1974 Hugh Stretton, a Professor of History at the University of Adelaide and deputy chair of the South Australian Housing Trust (a post he held for 17 years), delivered a series of five lectures for the Australian Broadcasting Commission (ABC) on the topic of 'Housing and Government' as part of the Boyer Lectures series.[1] Occurring in a period when housing policy in Australia was being radically reshaped, Stretton's talks were pivotal in their timing and their content. The lectures identified the challenges and changes occurring in Australian housing at the time and framed a public research agenda for Australian housing studies.[2] Forty years on, Stretton's 1974 Boyer Lectures provide a unique lens – a time capsule of sorts – on this period in Australian housing history. To gain a sense of present day circumstances and what these mean for the future, an appreciation of where we have been is essential. Stretton's lectures provide a useful frame for orientating ourselves around some of the core issues when considering contemporary housing issues in Australia. Reflecting on the changes to housing in Australia over this 40 year period this chapter introduces the main themes of this collection: people and practices (framed around the areas of economy, society and environment and how housing intersects with these) and policy. The research assembled in this volume and how it advances our knowledges of housing in Australia in the 21st century is outlined throughout each theme.

---

1 The Boyer Lectures were established in 1959 and involve leading public figures delivering a series of lectures on topics of special relevance to the Australian Community. The speakers are selected by the ABC board and are broadcast by ABC in November and December every year.

2 It is important to note however that there were many others also contributing to public debate around housing in Australia during this time and there was (and remains) much debate about Stretton's argument in these lectures.

People and Practices: The Great Australian Dream Then and Now

> ... we have on average comparatively big and well-equipped houses; three quarters[3] of us own one or are buying one; some of the rest are tenants because they want to be tenants, and most of the people in flats are there because they like flats best. So we have the remarkable distinction of giving as many as 90% of our people the type of housing that each wants as his [*sic*] genuine first preference. (Stretton 1974: 13)

1974 was a watershed year in terms of the Australian economy, society, environment and housing. It was the year when the first cracks in the Keynesian economic system, which had served Australia so well during the post-World War II (WWII) 'long boom', began to show. Economics editor for *The Age*, Tim Colebatch (2005) described 1974 as the 'year that the Australian economy went bung ... For the economy, 1974 was the end of the good times'. During this year unemployment increased from 2 to 5 per cent. Those employed during this period were mostly employed full-time and were mostly men (only 36.3% of women were in paid employment compared to 79.1% of men (Australian Bureau of Statistics (ABS) 1972b)). In the early 1970s 23.2 per cent of the labour force were employed in manufacturing, 7.4 per cent were employed in agriculture, forestry and fishing and 6.9 per cent were employed in the finance and business services (ABS 1972b). Inflation rose rapidly in both wages and consumer goods. Rising wage claims were accompanied by increased industrial disputes. The Oil Crisis was beginning to take hold as the OPEC cartel doubled world oil prices. One of Australia's major trading partners, the United Kingdom, joined the European Economic Community (EEC) the year previously and Prime Minister Gough Whitlam commenced what would become a decades-long period of microeconomic reform through the winding back of trade protection. Severe shortages of steel, bricks, timber and other building materials, combined with rising labour costs, saw the post-war housing boom go bust. The productivity limitations of Fordism were also recognised by Stretton (1974: 33) who noted that: 'Once the commercial services have full employment and a limited working week their further growth is severely limited, and mostly depends on getting more housewives back to commercial employment.'

As the opening quote to this section identifies Australian society and the way it was housed was understood as being relatively uniform in 1974. Almost 70 per cent of households were either purchasing or already owned their own home. In comparison, only 22.6 per cent of households rented privately, while even less (5.3%) lived in government owned housing (ABS 1972a). These homes were mostly detached, single story dwellings. The 1971 Census of Population and Housing found that 84 per cent of Australian households lived in a private house while 12 per cent lived in a self-contained flat (ABS 1972a).

The nuclear family reigned supreme in 1974. According to Stretton (1974: 40):

---

3 This figure should be 69 per cent. Following the 1967 Referendum to change the Constitution and a subsequent change in the Aboriginal and Torres Strait Islander question wording in the Census in 1971, the Aboriginal and Torres Strait Islander census count increased by 45 per cent. This change made a contribution to the decrease in the measured proportion of owner occupied private dwellings.

the nuclear family turns out to be more popular than ever, especially where it can get comfortable living space. A higher proportion than ever now live in family households. If they leave home young, or get divorced often, it's usually to form new nuclear households very soon.

Sixty-four per cent of Australians aged over 15 years of age were married, while only 3.5 per cent were either separated or divorced – de facto relationships were not even recognised by the nation's statisticians in the early 1970s (ABS 1972c).

However the diversity that existed within Australian society in the 1970s was also beginning to dawn on the national consciousness. The Whitlam Government had introduced 'no fault' divorce laws. It had also amended the *Migration Act* and, in the following year, it would introduce the *Racial Discrimination Act (1975)*, thereby ending the 'White Australia Policy' that had been in place since 1901. While Stretton still advocated strongly on the universal good derived from the free-standing home on the quarter-acre block he also noted that,

> We are short of housing for many particular needs. Our public authorities have concentrated mostly on housing standard families, and lately pensioners. They are only beginning to do much for childless couples. Most of them still do little or nothing for single women under sixty, or single men at any age. There are shortages and acute problems in aboriginal housing, both where the people do want and where they don't want to be housed in standard white fashion. (Stretton 1974: 17)

Stretton defended the division between work and home ('It's not efficient to smelt steel at home, or on the other hand to bring up children in institutions' (Stretton 1974: 33)). However he did recognise the important economic contribution that work within and around the home space made, as well as the role of the home in the pursuit of social and cultural aspects of Australian lives:

> [Home is] where most people now hear most music, read most books, see and hear most drama, read and see and hear most of the world's news and most of the analysis and commentary on it. (Stretton 1974: 41)

Throughout his lectures Stretton (1974: 49) makes a strong call for the linking of housing to urban and environmental concerns. In 1971, 86.7 per cent of Australian households lived in urban areas (ABS 1972a). According to Stretton suburbanisation was still the best way of delivering a high standard of housing efficiently and equitably. In addition to these distributional benefits, the Fordist technologies that had enabled suburbanisation also provided Australians with the 'gift of … private space' (Stretton 1974: 40). He ferociously defended the suburban house against the discourse of densification that was recommended as a panacea to the diseconomies of scale that had emerged as Australia's housing boom outpaced the delivery of employment and infrastructure in the suburban fringes of the nation's major cities.

> [C]ritics blame that famous Australian quarter-acre for most of the sins of the cities, and they believe that if we built denser housing ... our cities would run more cheaply, efficiently and sociably ... The trouble is not that our gardens are too big, but that two of our cities [Sydney and Melbourne] are too big. (Stretton 1974: 13)

Stretton warned against the creative destructive mentality of 'densification', arguing that the difficulty of retrofitting Australia's cities would be too costly both in terms of resources and time and would fail to supply the market with the level of housing needed. Furthermore, Stretton (1974: 14) argued that densification would amount to 'class robbery' and threatened the egalitarianism inherent in Australian suburban housing ('The middle classes would have the old big houses with gardens, the workers would have the new small flats without [gardens]' (Stretton 1974: 14–15)). Last the demolition involved in densification displaced those least able to resist such planning measures while simultaneously wasting current housing resources and exacerbating housing supply issues.

Suburbanisation was also advocated by Stretton in terms of its socialisation opportunities in the context of an emerging environmentalism during this period. For Stretton (1974: 48), 'our environmental policies will always in the end be determined by our people's values; and houses with gardens are the nursery of most of the best of our environmental values'. Suburbanisation was not the problem; rather it was how Australians used their homes that posed the environmental threat.

> Do generous houses and gardens themselves hurt the environment? They can, if people fill their houses and gardens with machinery and drench them with chemicals, and build them too far from the places where their people work, in over-sized cities that generate too much daily travel. On the other hand generous housing with land around it offers the best scope for good environmental behaviour ... It's in houses with storage space and some land around that it's easiest to collect local energy, or to use more human energy, and to get along with less powered commercial services. It's also easier to adapt to many kinds of environmental and industrial breakdown. People in landless flats suffer most when the rubbish truck doesn't come and the lift and the clothes-dryer stop. (Stretton 1974: 47)

Stretton did recommend some strategies on how to improve Australian suburbanism. In keeping with the planning discourse of the day was the solution of decentralisation (Ruming et al. 2010; Lloyd and Troy 1981). That is, develop satellite cities and make these cities centres of culture and employment. The Australian urban environment would also be improved through the reduction of road transport and less dependence on the car. Planners were urged by Stretton to think of short transportation needs and forms such as pedestrian, bikes and public transport. Sydney was advised to reduce its 'road space and [make] it over for buses and bikes only, instead of increasing it' (Stretton 1974: 47).

The makings of the reformist New Urbanist vision for the Australian suburb is also present in Stretton's critiques. For example in his fourth lecture Stretton (1974: 46) argued that Australian cities and towns should stop building shopping centres to look like television studies in a blasted moonscape of asphalt, which nobody would want to approach any other way than by car. Centres ought to be dense and intricate and villagey. They ought to have people living in them and close around them, instead of being cut off from their living areas by six-lane highways and all that moonscape.

The environment more generally came roaring onto the housing policy scene at the end of 1974 when on December 25 Cyclone Tracy hit the far north city of Darwin. Sixty-six people were recorded as having lost their life due to the cyclone and the city woke up on Christmas Day with 70 per cent of its homes destroyed or severely damaged.

* * *

In 2014 Australia entered its 22nd year of uninterrupted economic growth. To put this in perspective since the turn of the 21st century, despite a global recession that still has many other developed economies struggling, Australia has not experienced two consecutive quarters of negative economic growth. This has been achieved on the back of a confluence of factors ranging from geological good fortune, a stable political and regulatory environment, and a range of microeconomic reforms pursued during the 1980s and 1990s.

In 2011 Australia's unemployment rate was at 5.6 per cent. On the face of it things seem little changed since the figure of 5 per cent recorded in 1974. However these figures belie a four-decade period of change where the fundamentals of the Australian economy have radically shifted. For example 5 per cent of unemployment in 1974 was seen as a major economic problem that needed immediate government response. Today, economists define 5 per cent of unemployment as 'full employment'. The change in the Australian economy also exists in other details. For example the last 40 years has witnessed an unprecedented level of women entering the formal Australian labour force: from 36 per cent in 1971 to 53 per cent in 2011. Stretton's argument that Australia's productivity gains would be achieved through the 'housewife' entering the labour force has seemingly come to pass. However, the restructuring of the Australian economy during the 1980s and 1990s has seen the level of men employed in the formal labour market decline from 79 per cent in 1971 to 63 per cent in 2011. The industry mix of employment in Australia has also shifted. Agriculture, forestry and fishing now only account for 3 per cent of employment (down from 7.4% in 1971) and manufacturing 12 per cent (down from 23.2% in 1971). While finance and business services have increased from 7.9 per cent in 1971 to approximately 15 per cent in 2011 (ABS 2012a).

Australian society has also profoundly changed over the past 40 years. For example the nuclear family is only one of a range of household structures in Australian society. In 2011 48.7 per cent of Australians[4] were married (compared to 64% in 1971). De facto relationships (now recognised by statisticians) were identified by 9.5 per cent of the population. While the proportion of the Australian population who had never been married increased from 15 per cent in 1971 to 34 per cent in 2011. An increase was also observed in the proportion of those individuals who were either separated or divorced: from 3.5 per cent in 1971 to 11.4 per cent in 2011 (ABS 2012a).

---

4   Persons aged over 15 years of age.

The Australian population has also become older. Those aged 65 years old and more made up 16 per cent of the population in 2011, almost double that in 1971 (8.3%). The aging of the population is further exacerbated by the fact that younger generations are having fewer children (the average Australian family had only 1.9 children in 2011). However, through an immigration program that is equal to that which followed WWII, Australians are a more ethnically diverse population with the proportion of the population born in Australia now at 69 per cent (compared to 79.8% in 1971). Not only is Australia's population made up of a higher proportion of immigrants but the countries from which immigrants originate from have also changed. While those from England still account for the largest proportion (4.2%) this is down from the dominance that the United Kingdom and Eire had in 1971 (8.5%). An increasing proportion of immigrants now arrive from New Zealand (2.2%), China (1.5%) and India (1.4%), replacing the role of Southern Europe[5] as a source of immigrants (ABS 2012a).

As a consequence of all these changes Australian households are simply more complex. For example single-parent households now make up 15.9 per cent of all Australian households and single person households now make up 24 per cent of all Australian households (compared to 14% in 1971 (ABS 1972a)). However while some things have radically changed others have remained relatively stable. For instance in 1971 86.7 per cent of the national population were living in urban centres (66% in major urban centres and 20.7% in other urban centres).[6] In 2011 this proportion had only increased to 88.9 per cent (69.4% in major urban centres and 19.6% in other urban centres). Similarly, despite a boom in apartment building in many Australian cities since the turn of the century (see Chapter 8) there are now more households living in private homes (89% compared to 84% in 1971) and the proportion of households living in a flat, unit or apartment has declined (from 12% in 1971 to 10% in 2011). Last, despite the hyperbole that swirls around the topic of housing in Australia, there has been remarkably little change in the rate of homeownership (down from 69% in 1971 to 67% in 2011) and the proportion of the Australian population who rent (up from 27.9% to 29.6%) (ABS 2012b).

There are many measures of this economic and socio-demographic change but few are as pervasive as the measure of housing. Whether it is in the boardrooms of Australia's 'Big Four' banks or in the backyard of a suburban BBQ, housing is a focus for many Australians in a myriad of ways. Key among them is the issue of housing affordability (and the implications of this for the distribution of housing wealth in the form of homeownership – Yates et al. 2007). Since the turn of the 21st century, residential property markets in most of Australia's major cities have gone through a series of booms. The most recent of which (beginning in 2013) has seen Australian house prices increase by 7.4 per cent[7] in the past 12 months (IMF 2014). In the two largest cities, Sydney and Melbourne, this growth has been at 14.6 per cent and 6.9 per cent respectively (ABS 2014). Australia's housing booms have intersected with other economic and social changes. As a consequence, the booms

---

5   In 1971 2.3 per cent of immigrants came from Italy and 1.3 per cent from Greece (ABS 1972c).

6   Major urban centres denote all urban centres with a population of 100,000 or more. Other urban centres include those centres with populations of 1,000 or more.

7   The fourth highest growth rate in the world (IMF 2014).

that have characterised Australian housing in the 21st century have produced a range of responses all pointing to what Wendy Stone (in Power 2013) describes as a 'seachange in the psyche [of] … the Great Australian Dream' of homeownership.

As mentioned earlier there have been relatively small shifts in some of the more basic measures of the distribution of housing wealth in Australia. The 2011 Census of Population and Housing data showed that those households that either own outright or are purchasing a home have only declined from 69 per cent in 1971 to 67 per cent in 2011 (ABS 2012a). Meanwhile those who rent have increased from 27.9 per cent in 1971 to 29.6 per cent in 2011. However, while this change is small it is certainly heading in the wrong direction regarding the distribution of housing wealth and undermines the key tenet of homeownership that sits at the heart of the Great Australian Dream.

Furthermore, lying behind these seemingly benign figures are more subtle, but important shifts, in the concentration of housing wealth in Australia. For instance, the Reserve Bank of Australia (RBA) observed that the proportion of Australian households that owned an investment property had more than doubled from 8 per cent in the early 1990s to 17 per cent in 2005 (Kohler and Rossiter 2005). More recently, the RBA (2014: 49) noted that 'investor housing loan approvals currently account for almost 40 per cent of the value of total housing loan approvals'. As they approach and enter the early years of retirement, the baby boomer generation (those born between 1946 and 1965) are seen as key contributors to the increasing cohort of housing investors in Australia. Compared to younger generations, this generation has benefited the least from the introduction of compulsory superannuation in the 1990s. As life and lifestyle expectancies have increased for the Baby Boomers so has the need to boost retirement savings (see Chapter 7). In a post-Global Financial Crisis (GFC) period a key way to achieving this is on the back of the capital gains that have accrued through residential property in the 21st century (see Chapters 9 and 10).

The fundamentals of those Australian households renting have also shifted. Renting, once considered a short-term step-up into homeownership by most Australians has become the long-term/permanent tenure for an increasing proportion of Australian households (Stone et al. 2013; Chapter 9). As Hulse and Burke (Chapter 9) outline, this tenurial shift has occurred for a variety of reasons including: long periods in education, delays in partnering and having children, and greater labour mobility. Housing affordability is also seen to be a key driver of this shift to rental housing. This exists in both the limited and declining accessibility of social housing, as well as persistently high prices of housing relative to income. 'New economy' jobs are also generally less stable (e.g. contract, part-time etc.) and therefore are unable to provide the surety that financial institutions require for home loans that would allow renters to move into homeownership.

The tenurial shift to long-term renting and the concomitant implications it has for the distribution of housing wealth is falling inequitably between generations. Generation Y (those born between 1981 and 2000) are seen to be locked out of homeownership due to rapidly increasing house prices. Meanwhile, the Baby Boomer generation, as those who are most likely to already own or own a good proportion of their homes, have been able to avail themselves of new housing finance technologies such as equity redraw loans and reverse mortgages without having to sell the principle home (Ong and Wood 2014). At the same time, other families have approached the issue of housing affordability and generational inequality by bringing more than one generation under the same roof (Chapter 2). Lui et al. (Chapter 2) point out that while multigenerational households account for a relatively small proportion of total Australian households (14.5%), they house almost one-fifth of the national population (19.7%). Furthermore such household structures are becoming increasingly popular in a diverse Australian society and are contributing to the densification of Australian urban spaces as 'granny' and 'Fonzie' flats are added to the traditional suburban family home to accommodate multigenerational household structures (Hasham 2013; Wade 2013).

Declining housing affordability in Australia's major cities has also produced heightened concerns around foreign direct investment (Rogers et al.). While there is limited evidence to prove this is the case, there is a prevailing concern amongst many Australians that foreign investment in residential property is further inflating domestic housing prices (Rogers et al.; Chapter 14). For those immigrants who do not have the opportunity of home purchase after settlement there are deeper concerns about ethnic discrimination in the private rental market (Chapter 3). In an Australian first, the study presented by Nelson et al. (Chapter 3) found that for those areas of the private rental process that are regulated in Australia there is little detectable difference in treatment according to perceived ethnicity. However, in those areas that are not regulated (e.g. in informal interaction and quantity of information provided) differences were detected that put those of a non-Anglo background at a disadvantage when it came to renting in Sydney's private rental market.

Housing discrimination is also an issue for Indigenous Australians (Dufty 2009). The inequality of access to secure and suitable housing (let alone the wealth generating opportunities of homeownership which so many Australians consider their birth right) that Indigenous Australians experience has been a perennial feature since European invasion. The dire situation of Indigenous housing in Australia is exemplified by the fact that until the 1967 Referendum, Aboriginal and Torres Straight Islanders were inadequately represented and counted in the nation's quinquennial census. In 1971 when Indigenous Australians were included, the rate of homeownership in Australia declined from almost 75 per cent to 69 per cent. Furthermore this situation has hardly improved in the interceding 40 years. As Habibis (Chapter 5) outlines that, compared with Euro-Australians, few Indigenous Australians own their own home and there remains a heavy reliance on social housing. Worse, a high proportion of Indigenous Australians continue to live in sub-standard housing and are four times more likely to be homeless. In 21st-century Australia this state of Indigenous housing affairs 'diminish[es]' all Australians (Whitlam 1972, in Whitlam Institute 2014). Habibis recommends greater sensitivity to cultural traditions that prioritise social and kin ties and the deep obligations that accompany these. There are also innovative approaches to Indigenous homeownership being pioneered in Australia such as the work of Crabtree et al. (Crabtree 2014; Crabtree et al. 2013) around community land trusts (CLT).

The issue of housing affordability that is so much a feature of housing in Australia in the 21st century has also fed into changes in the way in which housing intersects with the wider urban environment. Since the 1970s there has been a counterurbanisation trend of Australians leaving the major cities in pursuit of a tree or sea change (Burnley 1988; Hugo

1994; Osbaldiston and Picken 2014). High among the reasons for such moves is the need to find affordable housing. Stone (Chapter 6) charts one dimension of this response to worsening housing affordability in Australia through a qualitative investigation of Australian households that voluntarily reduced their income in pursuit of life quality – otherwise known as 'downshifting'. She finds that some Australian households have responded to the issue of housing affordability by grasping the late-modern opportunities that come with diverse household structures, flexible work practices and mobile technologies. By making the household the focus she shows the complex, and often challenging, ways in which some Australian households are carving out an alternative way of producing and consuming affordable housing.

With the price of land in many cities driving up the cost of housing and down its supply the issue of housing affordability has also been tackled through densification. As Altmann (Chapter 8) outlines in her chapter, since the 1990s urban consolidation agendas have become increasingly prevalent as a way of increasing housing supply, making the most of already existing urban infrastructure and reducing the costs of increasing traffic congestion (Randolph 2006; Easthope and Randolph 2008). One way this has been achieved is through the shift to high-rise apartment dwelling. Numerically the number of apartments has grown considerably since 1971 from 453,083 to 1,930,934 in 2011. This represents a more than 400 per cent increase over the past 40 years. Yet, over the same period, the share that flats, units and apartments represent as a total of housing stock has declined from 12 per cent to 10 per cent. However this may be set to change with more recent research by the City of Sydney showing that the number of residential towers completed or proposed since 2010 is already greater than the whole preceding decade (Johnstone 2013). While Australians' housing preferences have diverged – mirroring changes in the ways we work and play – the challenges of what types of housing and where it should be located remain fraught and are only exacerbated through questions of housing affordability.

A significant challenge on the housing affordability front for Australians however is the impact of climate change. Global warming was not an issue when Stretton delivered his lectures. In many ways the relationship between housing and environment that Stretton presented in 1974 has shifted almost 180 degrees. Away from the preoccupation with the environmental effects of urbanisation that emerged during the 19th century and its negative externalities (e.g. pollution and commuting) on the health of the population; to a greater focus on the ways that humanity and the way we consume resources (especially the heightened capacity to produce and consume facilitated through urbanisation) is affecting the health of the environment. Housing is implicated at all scales when considering climate change. For example, the Intergovernmental Panel on Climate Change (IPCC) warns that a quarter of a million Australian homes are at risk from rising sea levels (Hannam 2013). In Chapter 4 Carr and Gibson bring into focus the nexus of housing and environmental sustainability at the micro-scale of the home and household. They point out that the material cultural relations of the home and household are more complex than the reductive catch-phrases of the 'green home'. They argue that a structural shift is required in the way we understand the home space: away from a site of Fordist consumption (Greig 1995) to a space where imperatives of climate change mitigation and adaptation are taken more seriously.

Policy: More Luck than Skill?

> The hard problems of housing are chiefly not technical, they are problems of justice, social values, social and economic understanding; and they are riddled with conflicts of interest. (Stretton 1974: 7)

In 1974 Stretton argued that Australians were one of the best-housed populations in the world. He was at pains to point out however that this was not the product of unfettered market forces. Rather Australia's housing situation in 1974 had been made possible through collective political choice. For Stretton, housing policy in Australia was used primarily (and problematically) as a tool for macroeconomic management. Under the Fordist-Keynesian economic system that characterised post-WWII housing policy, housing had three roles in terms of macroeconomic management (Stretton 1974; Greig 1995; Troy 2012; Badcock and Beer 2000). First, building homes produced an economic boost that trickled throughout the economy. Second, the new homes then had to be filled with capital equipment that was produced elsewhere in the economy. Last, housing was a mechanism for supplying and maintaining a healthy (and compliant) labour force.

This macroeconomic approach to housing was facilitated in the post-war period by an extensive, publicly funded building program – financed by the federal government and implemented by the states. This relationship was established through the Commonwealth State Housing Agreement (CSHA) in 1945. The public housing that was built through the CSHA was targeted towards low-income families. However, after the election of the conservative Menzies Government in 1951, homeownership became the heart of Australian housing policy. While historically Australia had tended to have a relatively high homeownership rate (Troy 2012), the Menzies government reoriented housing policy through amendments to the CHSA in 1956 that encouraged States to sell the public housing they were building and made it easier for tenants to purchase these homes through low-interest loans. Combined with favourable taxation policies (e.g. capital gains exemptions), homeownership rates peaked in the late 1960s at 71.4 per cent – one of the highest rates of homeownership in the world (ABS 2012b).

Despite this apparent success, Stretton (1974: 7) described the policy settings that influenced housing production and consumption in 1974 in Australia as a 'rag-bag of bits and pieces'. With echoes of Donald Hornes' (1964) *Lucky Country* thesis, he provided this damning conclusion on Australian housing policy: 'if we have housed ourselves well in the past, it's more by luck than skill' (Stretton 1974: 8).

From Stretton's perspective there was much to fix regarding housing policy in Australia. Housing supply was a perennial issue and waiting lists for public housing were on the rise ('People are waiting three and four and five years in some places' (Stretton 1974: 17)). Stretton (1974: 16–17) was also critical of the inequalities in government assistance,

> Public tenants usually do better than private ones ... Tax arrangements favour buyers and borrowers more than they favour tenants or savers or lenders. Some of these biases are systematic, usually in favour of richer against poorer, but a lot of them are just chancy and capricious.

When Stretton made these assessments it was the second year of the new Whitlam Government. Having established the Department of Urban and Regional Development (DURD) this government was powering ahead with its plans to reform urban living in Australia. However, while there was much happening in terms of urban and regional development, there was little in the way of housing policy to be found. Stretton's lectures can be seen as staking a claim for DURD to take on housing and housing policy as part of a wider range or urban and regional development policies. For Stretton (1974: 51) the solution to housing policy was simple enough: 'If the [policy] aims are expressed generally enough there need only be two of them: better housing, and more equal shares of it'.

* * *

As both Paris (1993) and Tomlinson (2012) remark, housing policy generally, and Australian housing policy in particular, is a complex beast – chimera-like with its many heads and unintended consequences. Like Australia's housing stock more generally, what is striking about Australian housing policy is how little has changed. This inertia persists despite the social, economic and environmental challenges Australians living in the 21st century face (Chapter 9).

What is perhaps most frustrating for Australian housing researchers is that the same critiques that Stretton (and others) made in the past continue to be repeated, but to all intents and purpose fall on deaf ears. For example, like Stretton (1974), Jane-Frances Kelly (2013), Cities Program Director for the Grattan Institute,[8] contended that government tax and welfare policies problematically favoured homeowners and property investors over Australians who rent. Kelly (2013: 1) argued that in general Australian housing policies were 'worsening the divide between Australians who own housing and those who do not'.

Making the case for how little has changed in Australian housing policy is the chapter by Taylor and Dalton (Chapter 10). Examining the provision of First Home Owner Grants (FHOGs) they find that Keynesian economic approaches to housing policy have not been abandoned in the name of economic rationalism and neoliberalism. Rather, Taylor and Dalton show how FHOG have been revived as a form of housing policy in 21st-century Australia. Initially in response to affordability issues in the first housing boom, and then later as a means of boosting new home builds and the economy more broadly as a response to the GFC. Going beyond the critique of the inflationary effect that FHOGs are argued to produce, they find that as an approach to macroeconomic issues of affordability or cyclical economic change FHOGs are a blunt tool. In Taylor and Dalton's view FHOGs only bring new builds forward and exacerbate the issue of urban sprawl, contrary to the urban plans of many Australian cities.

Hulse and Burke (Chapter 9) also point to the problematic lack of change in Australian housing policy. In particular, they highlight the way that 'many of the institutional settings, policies, practices and cultural norms regarding private renting have not kept pace with market' and social trends – based on the idea the rental properties are for young people

---

8   Established in 2008, the Grattan Institute is an independent think tank making non-partisan interventions as a means of developing high quality public policy.

seeking flexible and short-term housing. This suits rental investors but fails to account for the fact that more and more renters in Australia are seeking to rent over the long-term. Hulse and Burke argue that policies (such as negative gearing, residential tenancy legislation and the Commonwealth Rent Assistance (CRA) payment) work to contrary ends when it comes to the private rental sector. In doing so, these policy settings produce mixed messages for tenants and investors – often to the disadvantage of the tenant. Ultimately, they contend that housing policies need to catch-up to the realities of the private rental housing sector in 21st-century Australia.

Where there has been change in Australian housing policy it has tended to affect a small and vulnerable section of Australian society. For example since the 1970s successive federal governments have progressively withdrawn funding from the CSHA. As public housing has become scarcer it has also become the tenure of 'last resort' and has increasingly focused on housing those in Australian society most in need. However, the historic design and delivery of public housing and current policy settings for its allocation has contributed to a vicious cycle in which public housing has been increasingly constructed as 'problematic'. As Arthurson and Darcy (Chapter 11) show in their chapter, a key consequence of this denigration of public housing has been the conflation with this form of tenure and the production of 'anti-social behaviour' and/or a 'culture of poverty'. Interrogating the policy response of 'deconcentration' to the 'problem' of public housing they find that such programs fail to recognise the structural processes that contribute to 'concentrations of disadvantage'. Their analysis also demonstrates that there was some truth in what Stretton (1974) argued. He presciently pointed out that it would be public housing that would bear the cost of densification experiments and that such experimentation had the potential to further splinter cities and make them more unequal.

As Ruming (Chapter 12) found, where new social housing is built the negative perception of this type of housing tenure now actively works against its development, particularly at the local scale. Reflecting on the Social Housing Initiative (SHI), a program of social housing development that the federal government initiated in response to the threat of the GFC to the Australian economy, he finds the program to have been successful in terms of providing much needed resources to the social housing sector and as part of the broader macroeconomic strategy of stimulating the Australian economy. However numerically this program has been but a drop in the ocean in responding to the demand for social housing, and it has not been able to produce significant reform in the delivery of social housing (although the opportunities are there to be seized). Community housing providers, who make up an increasing proportion of the social housing sector, remain vulnerable due to their rapid growth, relative newness to the sector and a lack of coordination between themselves and state housing authorities. Furthermore – responding to the negative stereotypes that abound around social housing and social housing tenants – resident action groups and local politicians have mounted fierce opposition to the development of new social housing in their neighbourhoods. This is despite evidence showing that such fears are unfounded (Davison et al. 2013)

Another significant change in Australian housing policy since 1974 has been the allocation of government funding to addressing housing need produced through homelessness. The view that homelessness is a product of personal failings has gradually fallen by the wayside. In its place is greater recognition of the structural factors that contribute to individuals and families becoming homeless. While it is questioned whether policies that address homelessness are actually 'housing' or 'social welfare' policies (Paris 1993), the fact that governments have sought to begin to address the issue of house- and home-lessness is an important policy shift nonetheless. Blunden and Drake (Chapter 13) pick up on the most recent government intervention on the issue of homelessness in Australia – the 2008 White Paper on Homelessness – and the subsequent implementation of 'Housing First' approaches to addressing this severe and persistent feature of Australian society. Despite being uncritically imported from the US, they find that 'Housing First' approaches have been relatively successful in terms of retention rates. A key to this success is that such approaches recognise and facilitate the dual purpose of housing – providing both shelter and a sense of home. Blunden and Drake temper such findings by pointing to the need for further longitudinal research on the 'Housing First' programs as well as acknowledging the limitations of such programs in terms of addressing the structural causes of homelessness and the ability of these to serve the vast numbers of those who are homeless in Australia without an increase in funding.

An Australian Housing Research Boom

> there are basic questions about the way people use and value their houses which I think … the experts all tend to neglect. (Stretton 1974: 7)

Earlier in this chapter we argued that Stretton's Boyer Lectures also mapped out a new research agenda for Australian housing studies. This agenda was in Stretton's (1974: 22) words 'a declaration of war … a war of theories'. In his crosshairs were two areas: 1) urban research that neglected housing; and, 2) housing research that drew on classical economic theories. For instance, Stretton (1974: 36) critiqued the millions of dollars' worth of 'road research' that did not spare 'a dime to investigate the personal effects of the social economy' of knocking down hundreds of thousands of homes, 'or the citizens' opinions about [housing demolition for road infrastructure development], or the fortunes of people who have been bulldozed in the past'. Equally problematic were the economists whose 'bad theories' were argued to mislead Australian governments in the best policy settings for the most efficient and equitable delivery of housing to the Australian population. According to Stretton (1974: 36) 'bad [housing] theories' were those theories that narrowly defined 'housing as shelter and the work of the home economy as worthless'. For Stretton (1974) there was too much research on housing production and not enough on housing consumption.[9]

---

9 'There is currently a lot of research into ways of producing houses from factories, but not much of it is asking how people experience the various kinds of industrialized housing … that we … have already' (Stretton 1974: 36). Almost 20 years later, Paris (1993: x) reversed this critique arguing that 'most research has focused on housing consumption at the expense of understanding housing production'.

At a time when Keynesian economic approaches were rapidly going out of policy vogue, Stretton's lectures came at a critical juncture. They were, in essence, a clarion call to social scientists to take back the intellectual agenda driving housing policy. Through this vehement critique Stretton contributed to and further aided the process of carving out a significant space for the social sciences to contribute to housing policy discourse. And to varying extents this call has been heeded.

* * *

Mirroring the 'boom time' in housing in 21st-century Australia, there has been a veritable boom in Australian housing research. One of the key drivers of this research boom has been the re-establishment of the Australian Housing and Urban Research Institute (AHURI) in 2001. Primarily funded by the Australian federal and state and territory governments, AHURI was established to fund and promote high quality independent research into current issues in housing and urban development. The quantum is phenomenal. Since 2001 AHURI has funded the following housing research outputs: 160 Positioning Papers, 246 Final Reports, and 182 Research and Policy Bulletins. Research produced through AHURI has no doubt had a strong policy bent and the organisation has changed significantly since it was first established. However the housing research produced by AHURI has been framed around understanding housing as 'more than shelter', to include the role housing plays in health, community, employment and other non-shelter outcomes. For almost 15 years AHURI has produced housing research that is influenced by key concerns and methodologies in the social sciences. In conjunction with a number of Australian universities, AHURI has built a network of research centres that produce this housing research as well as funded PhD top-up scholarships that have developed a new generation of Australian housing scholars.

Beyond the shear quantitative contribution of research funded through AHURI, Australian housing research in the 21st century is also increasingly critical and theoretical. For a number of years theory seemed to be the weak underbelly of Australian housing research with Paris (1993: x–xi) arguing that

> There have been few attempts to relate the changing nature of the housing question in Australia to wider patterns of social and demographic change, economic restructuring and new political alignments and priorities. Much empirical research has proceeded in a theoretical vacuum, with its agendas determined by bureaucratic or political criteria.

However, since then, theoretically robust Australian housing research has proliferated. Contributions included (but are not limited to) political economic interventions (Badcock and Beer 2000; Berry 1999; Bryson and Winter 1999; Paris 1993), institutional perspectives (Hulse 2003; Burke and Hulse 2010), feminist critiques (Watson 1986; Watson 1988), social constructionist and governmentality analyses (Darcy 1999; Dodson 2006; Dufty 2007; Jacobs et al. 2004; Kemeny 1983; Kemeny 1984; Mee 2004; McGuirk and Dowling 2009; Rogers 2014). Since Stretton's 'call to arms' social science contributions to Australian housing research has not only multiplied but also become increasingly more critical.

New Directions

Nineteen seventy-four marked the beginning of an extended period of economic, social, environmental and policy flux in Australia. Stretton's Boyer lectures captures and reflects this back through the prism of housing. Forty years later, a story of change and stasis can be told.

Since 1974 how we work, who is employed and the kinds of industries we work in have all changed. When Stretton made his call for decentralisation away from the two largest cities – Sydney and Melbourne – he could not have anticipated the digital revolution or the global economic processes that would work to further agglomerate economic activity into the inner-city regions of these major cities. The mining boom precipitated by Japan's demand for our resources was on the wane and there was no real sense of the rise of China as a regional economic and political force. The frequency and size of the booms that have characterised Australian housing throughout most of the 21st century are unprecedented in Australia.

Increasingly flexible work means that, as a population, we are increasingly mobile: a mobility that is further facilitated by digital technologies (Dufty 2012a; 2012b). Who makes up our households and contributes to their collective incomes has also changed. In the 21st century, Australia is facing the demographic squeeze of an aging population with declining fertility rates: a squeeze that has only been temporarily been deferred with an extensive immigration program.

A more troubling aspect of this change is that where some things are changing they have not been for the better. Housing equality in terms of affordability, access and wealth is deteriorating. Commuting times have worsened. Environmentally we face the realities of catastrophic, human induced, climate change.

However, what is also striking looking back over this 40-year period is how little other things have changed. At the end of the first decade of the 21st-century Australian housing policy remains a hotchpotch of taxation, planning and welfare approaches. Some policies inadvertently counteract others. While other policies – relicts designed for a different economy, society and environment in a different century – remain frustratingly sacred cows that governments of all political persuasions are too afraid to touch.

As Australians have changed and diversified so have our meanings of home and what we value in terms of housing. But questions should be asked about whether we have the policy settings that allow markets to deliver affordable housing according to these changed needs and wants. Whether the most vulnerable in our society will be able to access shelter and create homes. And if we have housing that will enable households to respond to climate change and reduce emissions. We need housing policy that responds to the mobilities and flexibilities expected of the 21st-century Australian population. Last Australian housing policies need to improve rather than exacerbate geographical, social and generational inequality. Policy inertia leaves Australians vulnerable. As we have seen over the last 40 years economies and cultural landscapes can change and change quickly, and we should no longer rely on luck to guide us through these increasingly complex times.

Given this context, the time is right for an edited collection that seeks to establish a sense of how Australian housing in the 21st century is sitting. Indeed, the changes in the people, practices and policies influencing housing in Australia, combined with a veritable boom in Australian housing research makes this text essential.

References

Australian Bureau of Statistics (1972a), *Summary of Dwellings, Bulletin 2, Part 9 Australia, Census of Population and Housing, 30 June 1971*. Canberra: Commonwealth Bureau of Census and Statistics.

—— (1972b), *The Labour Force, Bulletin 5, Part 9 Australia, Census of Population and Housing, 30 June 1971*. Canberra: Commonwealth Bureau of Census and Statistics.

—— (1972c), *Demographic Characteristics, Bulletin 3, Part 9 Australia Census of Population and Housing, 30 June 1971*. Canberra: Commonwealth Bureau of Census and Statistics.

ABS (2012a), *2011 Census of Population and Housing*, Canberra: Australian Bureau of Statistics.

—— (2012b), 'Housing', *Year Book Australia, 2012*, Cat. No.1301.0, Canberra: Australian Bureau of Statistics.

—— (2014), *Residential Property Price Indexes: Eight Capital Cities – September Quarter 2014*, Cat. No. 6416.0, Canberra: Australian Bureau of Statistics.

Badcock, B. and Beer, A. (2000), *Home Truths: Property Ownership and Housing Wealth in Australia*, Carlton: Melbourne University Press.

Berry, M. (1999), 'Unravelling the "Australian housing solution": the post-war years'. *Housing, Theory and Society* 16: 106–123.

Bryson, L. and Winter, I. (1999) *Social Change, Suburban Lives: An Australian Newtown 1960s to 1990s*. St Leonards, Allen & Unwin.

Burke, T. and Hulse, K. (2010), 'The Institutional Structure of Housing and the Sub-Prime Crisis: An Australian Case Study.' *Housing Studies* 25: 821–838.

Burnley, I. (1988), 'Population Turnaround and the Peopling of the Countryside? Migration from Sydney to Country Districts of New South Wales'. *Australian Geographer* 19: 268–283.

Colebatch, T. (2005), 'The Year the Economy went "Bung"'. *The Age*. 1 January.

Crabtree, L. (2014), 'Community Land Trusts and Indigenous Housing in Australia – Exploring Difference-Based Policy and Appropriate Housing'. *Housing Studies* 29: 743–759.

Crabtree, L., Blunden, H., Phibbs, P. (2013), *The Australian Community Land Trust Manual*, Sydney: University of Western Sydney.

Darcy, M. (1999), 'The Discourse of "Community" and the Reinvention of Social Housing Policy in Australia'. *Urban Studies* 36: 13–26.

Davison, G., Legacy, C., Liu, E., Han, H., Phibbs, P., van den Nouwelant, R., Darcy, M. and Piracha, A. (2013), *Understanding and Addressing Community Opposition to Affordable Housing Development*, Melbourne: AHURI.

Dodson, J. (2006), 'The "Roll" of the State: Government, Neoliberalism and Housing Assistance in Four Advanced Economies'. *Housing, Theory and Society* 23: 224–243.

Dufty, R. (2007), 'Governing Through Locational Choice: the Locational Preferences of Rural Public Housing Tenants in South-Western New South Wales, Australia'. *Housing, Theory and Society* 24: 183–206.

—— (2009), '"At least I don't live in Vegemite Valley": Racism and Rural Public Housing Spaces'. *Australian Geographer* 40: 429–449.

Dufty-Jones, R. (2012a) *Moving Home: Conceptual and Policy Implications of the Housing-Mobility Nexus*, AHURI Final Report No.189. Melbourne: Australian Housing and Urban Research Institute.

—— (2012b) Moving Home: Theorizing Housing Within a Politics of Mobility. *Housing, Theory and Society* 29(2): 207–222.

Easthope, H. and Randolph, B. (2008), 'Governing the Compact City: Challenges of Apartment Living in Sydney, Australia'. *Housing Studies* 24(2): 243–259.

Greig, A. (1995), *The Stuff Dreams are Made Of: Housing Provision in Australia 1945–1960*, Carlton, Melbourne University Press.

Hannam, P. (2013), 'Australia Vulnerable in a Warming Planet, Leaked IPCC Report Finds', *The Sydney Morning Herald*, 14 October.

Hasham, N. (2013), 'Manor Homes, Fonzie Flats Mooted Under Government Plan to Boost Housing Diversity, Affordability', *The Sydney Morning Herald*, 15 October.

Horne, D. (1964), *The Lucky Country*, Camberwell: Penguin.

Hugo, G. (1994), 'The Turnaround in Australia: Some First Observations from the 1991 Census'. *Australian Geographer* 25: 1–17.

Hulse, K. (2003) 'Housing Allowances and Private Renting in Liberal Welfare Regimes.' *Housing, Theory and Society* 20: 28-42.

International Monetary Fund, *House Prices to Income Ratio: Deviation from Historical Average*, https://www.imf.org/external/research/housing/index.htm, accessed 26 November 2014.

Jacobs, K., Kemeny, J., and Manzi, T. (2004), *Social Constructionism in Housing Research*. Aldershot: Ashgate.

Johnstone, T. (2013), 'Demand for Towers Soars as Sydneysiders Embrace High Life', *The Sydney Morning Herald*, 21 September.

Kelly, J-F. (2013), *Renovating Housing Policy*, Melbourne: Grattan Institute.

Kemeny, J. (1983), *The Great Australian Nightmare: A Critique of the Home-Ownership Ideology*, Melbourne: Georgian House.

—— (1984), 'The Social Construction of Housing Facts'. *Scandinavian Housing and Planning Research* 1: 149–164.

Kohler, M. and Rossiter, A. (2005), *Property Owners in Australia: A Snapshot*, Sydney, Economic Research Department, Reserve Bank of Australia.

Lloyd, C. and Troy, P. (1981), *Innovation and Reaction: The Life and Death of the Federal Department of Urban and Regional Development*. Canberra: ANU.

McGuirk, P. and Dowling, R. (2009), 'Master-planned Residential Developments: Beyond Iconic Spaces of Neoliberalism?' *Asia Pacific Viewpoint* 50: 120–134.

Mee, K. (2004), 'Necessary Welfare Measure or Policy Failure: Media Reports of Public Housing in Sydney in the 1990s' in Jacobs, K., Kemeny, J., and Manzi, T. (eds), *Social Constructionism in Housing Research*. Aldershot: Ashgate, 117–141.

Ong, R. and Wood, G. (2014), 'Your Home as an "ATM": Home Equity a Risky Welfare Tool', *The Conversation*, 5 February.

Osbaldiston, N. and Picken, F. (2014), 'Ongoing and Future Relationships of Second Home Owners with Places in Coastal Australia: An Empirical Case Study from Eastern Victoria', *Tourism Review International* 18: 137–152

Paris, C. (1993), *Housing Australia*, South Melbourne: Macmillan Education.

Power, J. (2013), 'With More People Renting than 30 Years Ago, Change is Needed to Protect Tenants' Rights', *The Sydney Morning Herald*, 13 October.

Randolph, B. (2006), 'Delivering the Compact City in Australia: Current Trends and Future Implications', *Urban Policy and Research* 24(4): 473–490

Reserve Bank of Australia (RBA) (2014), *Finacial Stablity Review: September 2014* Sydney: RBA.

Rogers, D. (2014). 'The Sydney Metropolitan Strategy as a Zoning Technology: Analyzing the Spatial and Temporal Dimensions of Obsolescence'. *Environment and Planning D: Society and Space* 32(1): 108–127

Rogers, D., Lee, C.L. and Yan, D. (2015). 'The Politics of Foreign Investment in Australian Housing: Chinese Investors, Translocal Sales Agents and Local Resistance'. *Housing Studies*. iFirst

Ruming, K., Tice, A. and Freestone, R. (2010), 'Commonwealth Urban Policy in Australia: The Case of Inner Urban Regeneration in Sydney, 1973–75'. *Australian Geographer* 41: 447–467.

Stone, W., Burke, T., Hulse, K. and Ralston, L. (2013), *Long-term Private Rental in a Changing Australian Private Rental Sector*, Final Report No. 209, Melbourne: AHURI.

Stretton, H. (1974), *Housing and Government: 1974 Boyer Lectures*, Sydney: Australian Broadcasting Commission.

Tomlinson, R. (2012), 'Introduction: A Housing Lens on Australia's Unintended Cities', in Tomlinson, R. (ed.), *Australia's Unintended Cities: The Impact of Housing on Urban Development*, Collingwood: CSIRO Publishing.

Troy, P. (2012), *Accommodating Australians: Commonwealth Government Involvement in Housing*, Sydney: The Federation Press.

Wade, M. (2013), 'Home Truths', *The Sydney Morning Herald*, 2 November.

Watson, S. (1986), 'Women and Housing or Feminist Housing Analysis?' *Housing Studies* 1: 1–10.

—— (1988), *Accommodating Inequality: Gender and Housing*, Sydney: Allen & Unwin.

Whitlam Institute (2014), *Indigenous Australians*, http://www.whitlam.org/gough_whitlam/achievements/indigenous, accessed 4 December 2014.

Yates, J., Milligan, V., Berry, M., Burke, T., Gabrielle, M., Phibbs, P., Pinnegar, S. and Randolph, B. (2007), *Housing Affordability: A 21st Century Problem*, Final Report No 105, Melbourne: AHURI..

PART 1
People and Practices

Chapter 2
Housing Multigenerational Households in Australian Cities: Evidence from Sydney and Brisbane at the Turn of the 21st century

Edgar Liu, Hazel Easthope, Bruce Judd and Ian Burnley

Introduction

The global trend towards city living, together with population ageing, has precipitated significant economic, social, political and environmental shifts. Amongst other outcomes, these shifts have led to changes in family configurations and living arrangements. Some changes are directly related to family forms – notably delayed childbearing, increased divorce rates and higher incidence of re-partnering – while others are less directly related, including improved employment opportunities for women, delayed retirement and more complex migration patterns both within and between countries. These changes are also happening in highly urbanised Australia.

Much housing-related research into such changes, however, has focussed on the worldwide increase in the number and percentage share of single person households over recent decades (de Vaus and Richardson 2009). An oft-neglected, though nonetheless significant, living arrangement is that of multigenerational households, where multiple generations of related adults co-reside in the same household. In Australia in 2011, single person households comprised one-quarter of all households (24.3%), while multigenerational households comprised around one-sixth (14.5%). In terms of the total population, however, members of multigenerational households comprised one-fifth of the Australian population (19.7%), while members of single person households comprised around one-eleventh (8.8%; ABS 2012a; 2012b).

This chapter draws on research funded by the Australian Research Council undertaken between 2012 and 2014 to report on the nature and scale of multigenerational households in Australia, their motivations for living together and their experiences of multigenerational living. Through this research, we identified a range of issues that need to be understood by policymakers and industry in order to effectively cater to the needs of a broad range of households, including multigenerational households. We focus on the reasons why and how multigenerational households live together and their implications on suitable housing design, and associated housing and planning policies. Specifically, multigenerational households have a higher propensity to live in owner-occupied detached housing, yet affordable options of these are becoming increasingly rare in areas with good access to employment and services as a result of house price increases and compact city policies. What housing solutions then can developers and policymakers alike offer to this sizeable Australian population?

Multigenerational Households across Nations and Time

Much 21st-century research into people's living arrangements has focussed on shrinking average household size. Indeed, as de Vaus and Richardson (2009: 4) point out, the percentage share of single person households in many western societies worldwide has consistently increased post-WWII, with many (like Australia, Germany and the Netherlands) increasing by threefold or more between 1946 and 2006. Some research connects this rise to the western individualised concept of family formation (e.g. Popenoe 1993) where 'the family' as a social institution has increasingly played a diminishing role, assisted by the onset of 'new individualism' – the individualisation of welfare rights and entitlements (Giddens 1998: 6) – since the late 20th century. Others have suggested an increase in the number and percentage share of single person households is an indirect result of population ageing, with ever increasing numbers of older persons worldwide living alone and a concurrent decline of multigenerational co-residence throughout the 20th century (Grundy 1999; Tinker 2002). Harper (2006: 165) notes that 'the knowledge of demographic ageing is itself impacting on social, economic and political decisions [taken by] both national and international institutions, and individuals themselves', including impacts on important life course transition points (first home-leaving, partnering, and childbirth) and subsequently people's living arrangements.

Since the 1980s, waves of global economic downturn have resulted in uncertain employment conditions and increasing pressure to higher education attainment. As a consequence, these have precipitated changes to the decline in multigenerational co-residence in eastern and western societies alike (Cobb-Clark and Ribar 2009; Yieh et al. 2004). While economic difficulty and increased pressure for tertiary qualification have been noted as primary contributors to young adults' delayed first home-leaving and consequently a return to multigenerational co-residence, there is also evidence to suggest that family background and ethnicity are strong factors that affect the home-leaving motivation and timing of young adults (Flatau et al. 2007).

Recent Australian and international research into multigenerational households has focussed largely on delayed home-leaving amongst the younger generations (e.g. Alessie et al. 2005; Flatau et al. 2007) and the financial dis-benefits experienced by older generations as an unintentional (and to many, undesirable) outcome (e.g. Cobb-Clark and Ribar 2009). Some research has also considered the 'boomerang' phenomenon – where adult offspring return to live in the parental home after periods of independent living (e.g. Parker 2012), which is now also observed in many western societies, including in Australia (Liu et al. 2013). The delayed home-leaving of young adults, however, is only part of the story. There is also evidence to suggest other factors are increasingly influencing the formation of multigenerational households.

An empirical Australian national study by Judd et al. (2010) indicates that high rates of relationship breakdowns have seen older adult 'children' (in their thirties and forties) returning to live with their parents for practical, financial and emotional support. External shocks, notably the global economic downturn as experienced in the late 2000s, have also played a significant role in older adults returning to live in the parental home (Kaplan 2009). In parallel, there is also growing evidence of older parents moving in to reside with their adult children, both in Australia and overseas (Olsberg and Winters 2005; Swartz 2009). Australian studies highlight the increasing incidence of relationship breakdowns amongst older people, with some parents moving in to live with their adult offspring for emotional and practical support but also to provide caring duties for their grandchildren (Judd et al. 2010). These shifts have reconfigured the role that 'the family' plays in care giving (Swartz 2009) in an environment where government policies increasingly encourage older people (and people with disabilities) with low care needs to remain living in the general community, where feasible, rather than relocate to residential care facilities. In Australia, this is reflected in changes to de-institutionalise the aged and disability care sectors (Australian Government 2012; DisabilityCare Australia 2013).

These already complex trends and responses to policy changes are further complicated by Australia's continually changing cultural fabric. Australia's main sources of immigrants have gradually shifted from English-speaking countries (most notably the UK) to Asian and African nations (including China and India) since the introduction of multicultural policies in the 1970s (Burnley 2009). These new migrant sources have resulted in increased diversity in Australia's cultural and ethnic makeup, and many of these more recent migrants had come from societies where multigenerational co-residence is a common arrangement (Billari and Rosina 2005; Chui 2008; Izuhara 2010; Mehio-Sibai et al. 2009). Furthermore, many of those new migrants entering Australia under the family reunion scheme are, for financial reasons, likely to live in multigenerational households. This is significant as the number of applicants to the family reunion scheme, and particularly for their financially non-contributing older parents to migrate to Australia, has been increasing since the mid-2000s (Liu and Easthope 2012). This is already reflected in the changing cultural landscape of multigenerational households in Australia, with a gradual shift away from the more traditional migrant sources from Southern Europe to Asia and Africa, where as much as two-fifths of immigrants from North Africa and the Middle East lived in multigenerational households in 2011 (Liu et al. 2013).

These changes considered, multigenerational households have comprised around one-fifth of all households in Australia since the 1980s. This is despite their numbers having continued to grow and nature of their formation continuing to change. Geographically, the concentration of multigenerational households in Australia has not played out equally across the country, with the majority of multigenerational households in early 21st century living in the outer suburbs of the major cities. The outer suburbs are the main growth centres of these cities (ABS 2013) and offer more affordable housing options for households that require larger dwellings than the inner ring suburbs where there have been notable absolute decreases in the number of multigenerational households since the 1980s. These same inner ring suburbs have also experienced the most intense outcomes of Australia's compact city policies, where lower density housing stock has over time gradually been replaced by higher density housing that is often considered less suitable for multigenerational co-residence (Liu et al. 2013).

Methodology

In this chapter we report on the findings of a multi-year study of multigenerational households in Australia. We used a mixed-methods approach, including a time-series analysis of Australian Census data, a specially designed web-based survey, solicited diaries and follow-up interviews with multigenerational household members in Greater Sydney and Brisbane. This chapter focuses on the results of the web-based survey, with materials from the other methods used to provide supporting evidence.

This research notes Cohen and Casper's (2002: 1) advice that 'conceptually, standard practices for identifying multigenerational living arrangements and their implications remain elusive'. As such, a multigenerational household is defined as any household in which more than one generation of lineally related adults (i.e. of parental-offspring relations) co-reside in the same household, with the oldest of the youngest generation being 18 years or older. This definition is designed to be as broad and as encompassing as possible, though notable multigenerational household forms – e.g. three-generation households where the oldest grandchild is still to turn 18 – are excluded. Compared to other similar studies, however, our definition and its application (especially in the Census analysis) represent the most comprehensive collection of socio-demographic and housing data of these households in Australia.

Census Analysis

Custom cross-tabulations from the six most recent five-yearly Australian Census were purchased following consultations with the Australian Bureau of Statistics (ABS) Census specialists. This allowed for a time-series analysis of key demographic and socioeconomic statistics relating to multigenerational households in Australia spanning a 25-year period between 1986 and 2011. The definition of multigenerational households as described above was applied to the cross-tabulations, which highlighted the age groups, Statistical Local Area of residence, region of birth, dwelling structure, tenure and housing costs (monthly mortgage repayment and weekly rent by quintile) of multigenerational household members.

Web-based Survey

A web-based questionnaire survey was administered via the online portal Key Survey between August 2012 and July 2013, during which time 392 members of 382 multigenerational households in Greater Sydney and Brisbane completed the survey. Participants were recruited via university staff and student online portals, advertisements in local newspapers in local government areas known to have large proportions of people living in multigenerational households (as identified through the Census data analysis), mX (a free daily newspaper available at the city centres) and posters in public libraries in 28 local government areas throughout Sydney and Brisbane. The survey was translated into Arabic, Spanish and simplified Chinese and advertised in migrant newspapers to encourage non-English speakers to participate. As a consequence of these recruitment methods, the survey presents a slight bias towards households with tertiary students who have yet to leave home (or had previously moved out but returned, i.e. boomeranged) compared to the total population living in multigenerational households. The cultural and household makeup and the dwelling structure and tenure profiles of the respondents, however, match closely with the Census analysis. The confidence interval for the survey is 4.95 at 95 per cent confidence, calculated on the basis of individuals living in multigenerational households in Sydney and Brisbane.

Respondents were asked to complete three sections of the survey, focussing on:

1. the dwelling;
2. the living arrangement – including the reasons why they live together – and how it impacts on their personal and family lives; and
3. their personal thoughts on multigenerational living and their likelihood of continuing with this arrangement.

Multiple adult members of the same household were encouraged to complete section three (in confidence) to provide multiple perspectives, and in ten households two members of the same household completed the survey.

The questionnaire included a mix of pre-coded and open-ended questions. Pre-coded questions were analysed using frequency tables and cross-tabulations, while open-ended questions were post-coded and analysed thematically, focussing specifically on why these households co-reside and their likes and dislikes of the arrangement.

Solicited Diaries and Follow-up Interviews

Two qualitative methods – solicited diaries and follow-up interviews – were designed to provide more in-depth data from multigenerational households, especially regarding the day-to-day experiences and interpersonal relationships amongst multigenerational household members. For both of these methods, whole households (instead of individuals) were considered as units, but efforts were made to accommodate household members who wanted to complete the diaries or be interviewed separately. For each participating household, a package containing instructions, a stamped return envelope and two A5 notebooks was provided. The diaries and interviews were conducted between October 2013 and March 2014.

Survey respondents were asked if they would participate in the diary-writing and interviews, and 61 agreed to do so. Attrition was experienced during scheduling, with only 29 households eventually continuing on to the diaries and interviews. Two households chose to skip the diary exercise and partook in interviewing only; members from three households were also interviewed separately due to scheduling difficulty, with the main interviews completed face-to-face at the participant's home and supplementary interviews conducted over the phone, resulting in a total of 21 interviews from 18 households.

In all, 21 completed diaries were returned from 15 households, with each diary comprising between 15 and 30 (often single-page) entries. Interviews lasted between 20 minutes and two and a half hours. All interviews were transcribed professionally, and together with the diary entries these transcripts were analysed using thematic coding.

Case Studies

The major cities of Sydney and Brisbane were chosen as two contrasting case studies for the research. As the main receiving city of many immigrants to Australia, Sydney has long had an ethnically diverse population. Further, since the 1980s it has also had the highest percentage share of its population living in multigenerational households amongst all state capitals. The proportional increase of multigenerational households in Sydney between 1986 and 2011 (43.6%) has also exceeded the overall proportional increase of households in the city over the same period (39.7%). While Brisbane is also experiencing significant recent population growth (especially since 2000) and particularly from overseas and interstate immigrants, the ethnic composition of settlers is different to that of Sydney's (OESR 2011). In terms of increases in multigenerational households, Brisbane had the most rapid proportional growth amongst all state capitals during 1986–2011 (62.5%), though this was dwarfed by the overall increase in households (91.5%). Moreover, Sydney and Brisbane are contrasting case studies as they have different housing market conditions so that each population has distinctive housing demands and constraints (Yates and Gabriel 2006). This is important as housing affordability was highlighted by many survey respondents from both cities as a significant financial factor that influenced their decision to enter a multigenerational co-residence arrangement.

Reasons for Multigenerational Co-residence

Survey respondents were asked to provide reasons behind their decision to live in a multigenerational household in an open-ended question in the survey. Responses to this question were post-coded and analysed thematically. Two-fifths of the respondents provided multiple reasons, suggesting that the formation of multigenerational households in contemporary Australia is the product of complex decision-making of the households, involving a mix of active choice and circumstantial constraints. The ten most commonly nominated reasons for multigenerational co-residence are presented in Table 2.1.

Recent literature suggests that the rise in the number of multigenerational households in western societies has predominantly been due to a delay in young adults' first home-leaving (Cobb-Clark and Ribar 2009; Gee et al. 2003). While there is evidence to suggest this is also true in Sydney and Brisbane – with 'adult children yet to leave home' being the third most common reason for multigenerational co-residence amongst our survey respondents – there is also evidence of other, more significant drivers behind this increase. For Sydney and Brisbane respondents alike, finance appeared to be the main driving force, with two-fifths or more respondents from each city stating this as one of their primary reasons, but as explained below this could encompass a wide range of considerations. Other primary reasons include 'ease in providing care and support', and 'starting and/or continuing education', two factors that may have also limited some respondents' ability to afford independent living. Of note, a much smaller proportion of survey respondents nominated cultural practices as a reason for multigenerational living. This is in contrast to work by Flatau et al. (2007) in Australia and work undertaken in Canada by Gee et al. (2003), which found that cultural practices were an important motivator of multigenerational living.

Table 2.1   Top ten reasons for living in multigenerational households, multiple responses, Sydney and Brisbane, 2012–2013

	Sydney No.	Sydney %	Brisbane No.	Brisbane %
Financial	97	38.0	70	55.1
Care arrangement and support	48	18.8	36	28.3
Adult children yet to leave home	46	18.0	17	13.4
Starting/continuing education	29	11.4	16	12.6
Older (grand)parents moving in	27	10.6	12	9.4
'We're a family'	23	9.0	9	7.1
Convenience/practicality	20	7.8	11	8.7
Cultural practice	20	7.8	3	2.4
Adult children boomeranged	6	2.4	10	7.9
Relationship breakdown	3	1.2	10	7.9
Other	8	3.1	2	1.6
Households stating multiple reasons	99	38.8	67	2.84
Total respondents	255		127	

Source: survey (multiple response question).

These primary reasons given by survey respondents for living in a multigenerational household represent a mix of structural constraints and individual choices, although for most households the line between choice and constraint is blurred.

While finance was the most commonly nominated driver for multigenerational co-residence amongst our respondents, it represents the expression of active choice in:

- sharing household costs – 'share expenses and so parents can support child during a stressful period of time' [Brisbane, survey];
- assisting children in their pursuit of higher qualifications – 'my eldest daughter is working part-time and going to university' [Brisbane, survey]; and

- being able to afford a better home now or in the future – 'I can't afford to rent in areas that provide reliable access to the CBD. Areas I possibly could afford are too far for daily commuting and are poorly serviced by public transport' [Sydney, survey]; 'to help with the cost of living, to have a better quality of life, to support/help each other' [Brisbane, survey].

Concurrently, finance also represents the respondents' constraints in:

- being unable to sustain an affordable housing option on their own – 'my mother-in-law is divorced and she has been a housewife all her life, so can't support herself financially' [Sydney, survey]; and
- affording the high cost of living in Australian cities – 'Sydney is very expensive to rent other than on the outskirts which means family is fragmented and unable to offer support' [Sydney, survey].

Similarly, the second most common reason for co-residence – ease in providing care and support – is a reflection of both active choice and structural constraints, with some households co-residing because:

- older parents and/or young adult children cannot financially afford to, or indeed want to, live independently – 'My mother did not have enough savings or pensions to live alone' [Sydney, survey];
- retired parents have moved in to help take care of young children and to share resources – 'My father assists me with baby sitting and picking up the kids from school. He also helps to pay my mortgage' [Brisbane, survey]; and
- paying for a service/facility to care for their family members is an unacceptable (and often unaffordable) option, whether for cultural or personal reasons – 'culturally, having [my mother] live by herself was unacceptable to me' [Sydney, survey].

While many respondents explained that they decided to live together for pragmatic reasons such as to share resources and provide care for their family, others gave more emotive reasons for multigenerational cohabitation. These included a desire to provide a better future for their children (which may be culturally related, especially with migrants' original migration experience and aspirations; Teunissen 1992) – 'My daughter is a uni student (part time), while I can't pay her fees for her I can at least cover most of the general living expenses like food, electricity and transport. This enables me to feel that I am providing for her and helping her build a better future' [Brisbane, interview]; 'I think that it's just expected that you look after your children until they're ready to fly the coop, as it were, and then they'll look after you when you're in your old age. It's kind of a trade' [Sydney, interview] – or to reciprocate the care they received in the past – 'It is our belief that we should 'give back' or contribute to the older generation who sacrificed much to provide us with our upbringing. It is important to provide that respect and acknowledgement of the older generation' [Brisbane, diary].

Indeed, one-in-twelve respondents nominated family as a primary reason for co-residence. For these respondents, the decision to live with their family was often an easy one to make – 'we're a family – it makes sense for us to live together' [Sydney, survey] – though most acknowledge the complex nature of family, or the familial bond itself, which are often more difficult to articulate clearly – 'the main reason is we cannot live without each other. We are bonded strongly to each other as in family' [Sydney, survey].

Notably, more than two-fifths of the survey respondents nominated multiple reasons for their co-residence, pointing to the complexity that led these households to co-reside. While finance was the most common driver for multigenerational co-residence, it was only the sole reason given by one-third of cases, with 'ease in providing care' and 'starting/continuing education' often precipitating financial constraints. Several respondents also used multigenerational co-residence as a means of achieving life-long goals, with improved financial conditions being an unexpected positive outcome. For example, one diary and interview participant noted that had her family not entered into a multigenerational co-residence situation, her husband would not have been able to leave a career that he had grown to dislike and return to study. As such, the drivers behind multigenerational co-residence are decidedly complex and often multiplicious.

Housing Outcomes of Multigenerational Households

The evidence presented above regarding the reasons for multigenerational co-residence infers some important implications for housing and welfare policies. Many multigenerational households live together at least in part for financial reasons, often influenced by housing (un)affordability. As a result of their household structure, many multigenerational households also have specific space and housing design needs, which include accommodating elderly and disabled household members, young children and students. This raises the question of what type of housing multigenerational households desire and actually live in.

Dwelling Structure and Tenure

The housing consumption patterns of multigenerational households differ to those of most other household types. Reflecting national trends since the 1980s, there is a higher propensity for multigenerational households in Sydney and Brisbane to live in detached houses than in other property types (Table 2.2). Consequently, very few multigenerational households live in medium and higher density dwellings, which tended to have fewer bedrooms and living spaces. This contrast in the types of housing that multigenerational households and all other households occupy is especially stark in Brisbane, with almost all multigenerational households living in detached houses (94.2%), compared to 81.9 per cent of all other households. This observation is a reflection of both the spatial needs of multigenerational households – which on average comprised more members than all other household types – but also the type of housing stock available in each city (a larger percentage share of Brisbane's homes are detached houses compared to Sydney). In 2011, multigenerational households in Sydney had an average household size of 3.7 people (2.7 for all other households) while Brisbane's multigenerational households had an average size of 3.6 people (2.7 for all other households).

Table 2.2   Dwelling structure of multigenerational households, Sydney and Brisbane, 2011–2013

	Multigenerational households (%)				All other households (%)	
	2012–2013 Survey		2011 Census		2011 Census	
	Sydney	Brisbane	Sydney	Brisbane	Sydney	Brisbane
Detached houses*	73.7	87.6	82.9	94.2	65.5	81.9
Semi-detached	4.9	0.9	9.0	3.3	11.4	6.6
Flats	18.3	8.8	7.7	2.3	19.7	8.1
Other**	3.1	2.7	0.3	0.2	0.5	0.5
Not stated	0.0	0.0	0.1	0.0	0.1	0.0

* Survey responses include detached houses with or without a granny flat. For Census outputs, however, granny flats are counted as a separate dwelling; the figures quoted here may therefore be an undercount.

** For the survey, 'other' includes multigenerational households that had the following living arrangements – 'in two detached houses on adjacent lots', 'in two adjoining semi-detached dwellings on the same lot', 'in two adjoining semi-detached dwellings on adjoining lots', 'in two adjoining units/apartments', and 'in separate units/apartments within the same block'.

Source: ABS 2012b; survey.

Aside from a propensity to live in detached houses, multigenerational households are also far more likely to be living in owner-occupied properties than all other household types (see Table 2.3). Around four-fifths of multigenerational households in Sydney and Brisbane were owner-occupiers in 2011, compared to less than two-thirds of all other household types. Multigenerational households were also more likely to own their homes outright, though like most other household types, there has been a downward trend away from outright homeownership amongst multigenerational households since the 1980s (Liu et al. 2013). For the first time in 2011, there were higher percentage shares of multigenerational households living in homes that were mortgaged than fully owned across all state capitals and regional Australia. This reflects rapidly increasing house prices and decreasing affordability in cities Australia-wide (Yates and Gabriel 2006), which, as abovementioned, have prompted some to enter into a multigenerational co-residence situation.

Design and Modifications

As some of the survey and interview participants explained, homeownership was particularly important to many multigenerational households, not only because of the cultural importance placed on homeownership in Australia, but also because of the need to undertake home modifications, which cannot be easily achieved in a private or social rental situation. For many multigenerational households, and especially those who entered into the arrangement with adult children boomeranging or older parents moving in, some level of home modification was required. Some spoke of temporary 'quick fixes' such as using tall bookcases as a dividing wall, while others undertook more substantial extensions and renovations to accommodate the extra household members. The ability to pool resources has also allowed some of these households to enter homeownership, something that they may not have been able to achieve on their own – 'When we first came here we rented, and I didn't have finances to buy a house and it was only in the last year that [my daughter] has saved, so we were able to use her savings and my permanent employment to actually be able to get a mortgage together. Otherwise I still wouldn't be able to buy on my own' [Brisbane, interview].

Table 2.3   Tenure profile of multigenerational households, Sydney and Brisbane, 2011–2013

	Multigenerational households (%)				All other households (%)	
	2012–2013 Survey		2011 Census		2011 Census	
	Sydney	Brisbane	Sydney	Brisbane	Sydney	Brisbane
Fully owned	41.5	33.6	35.6	30.8	25.5	22.0
Under mortgage	42.4	59.6	42.4	45.2	39.5	41.0
Rented*	16.1	16.8	19.5	22.2	27.9	31.1
Other	0.0	0.0	0.9	0.6	1.5	1.3
Not stated	0.0	0.0	1.6	1.3	5.6	4.6

* Include both private and social rentals.
Source: ABS 2012b; survey.

While many households spoke of sharing resources as one benefit of multigenerational co-residence, the sharing of space was noted as a common drawback of such a living arrangement. This is despite the fact that many of the homes that multigenerational households occupy comprise multiple bedrooms and living spaces.

In particular, many participants spoke about how modern houses have not been designed with multigenerational co-residence in mind, and as such they have had to 'make do' and find alternative uses of bedrooms and living spaces. This was especially the case for households with adult children who boomeranged back to the family home after experiencing life shocks such as relationship breakdowns and therefore returned suddenly. Households in this situation spoke of turning living spaces into bedrooms or the rumpus becoming an off-limit storage area:

> We had to modify our home, which is only a small home, to accommodate – changing the front sun room into a bedroom to accommodate children sleeping over, their children

coming here, changing another bedroom into our eldest son's room that we used before for an office, sewing room sort of thing. [Brisbane, interview]

As a result, shared living space is often limited, and with multiple users this can create tensions. Some households spoke of spending more time in their own bedrooms when all members of the household were home as the only solution for enjoying some level of privacy, whether it was the freedom of watching their own TV program or enjoying a hobby:

I think you need two living rooms and that might just be in our situation but my father is almost completely deaf so you can't watch TV with him, because the TV has to be at 400 decibels and so it would be challenging for all of three generations to share one TV or one living space. [Brisbane, interview]

Indeed, the ability to maintain some level of privacy in a shared home was the most common challenge faced by multigenerational household residents (see Table 2.4).

Table 2.4   Challenges of multigenerational co-residence, multiple responses, Sydney and Brisbane, 2012–13

	Sydney		Brisbane	
	No.	%	No.	%
Privacy/interference	102	60.0	60	57.7
Impact on intra/interfamilial relationships	32	18.8	20	19.2
Chores/Not pitching in	20	11.8	18	17.3
Space	13	7.6	11	10.6
Lack of flexibility/compromises	6	3.5	14	13.5
Nothing	15	8.8	1	1.0
Financial constraints	5	2.9	5	4.8
Noise	4	2.4	3	2.9
Generational contract/expectations	3	1.8	3	2.9
Stigma of living at home	2	1.2	3	2.9

Source: survey (multiple response).

The ability to make modifications is limited by a number of factors. Finance is often a top consideration for many multigenerational households wanting to modify their homes, where the high cost means that compromises were often made. Bedroom space is regularly prioritised, with kitchen and bathroom renovations to accommodate more adults (larger pantry, repairs and replacements of appliances due to additional users) less likely to be carried out.

Some households that considered their multigenerational living arrangement to be long-term opted to design and build their own detached home to suit their household's needs. This is often a rather costly option, and some of these households also admitted to not knowing how best to design a dwelling for multigenerational co-residence, even though some of the families had lived together for several years prior. This partly comes down to the ability of architects, home builders and interior designers to fully understand these households' less common needs, but also the fact that the needs of these households are constantly changing, with young children growing up and older household members' ability to negotiate stairs being common considerations. One three-generation household that had their current dwelling specially designed for multigenerational co-residence admitted to changing their living arrangements five times in the seven years since first moving in because they simply did not (and could not) have anticipated some of the changes to their household – 'we've changed the configuration of our living arrangements a number of times' [Brisbane, interview].

Other households had opted not to create the 'ideal home' for their family, because they were concerned that it would limit potential resale opportunity of the property and their ability to recoup investment spent on the home – 'you'd never get the money back when you sell' [Brisbane, interview].

Implications on Housing and Planning Policies

A large proportion of multigenerational households live in detached houses in the outer suburbs because of their relatively larger household size and because this is where the larger and more affordable properties are. Despite living in larger properties, for many people living in a multigenerational household raises challenges in respect to sharing space and the (lack of) privacy that the 'traditional' detached family home in the suburbs offers. This has important implications for housing design and housing and planning policies.

At the scale of the dwelling, the design of many existing larger properties is not conducive to multigenerational living, partly because of changed housing needs (e.g. home offices, hobby rooms for the retired) but also the heightened need to provide spaces within the multigenerational home where some level of privacy can be maintained. The majority of larger project homes have open planned living areas with little ability to close off areas for different groups of users. Some developers have begun to respond to the market demand for multigenerational living in Sydney by providing custom-built houses for this market (Madigan and Vonow 2014), but this does not necessarily overcome the dilemma of re-sale value and the high cost involved in constructing these multigenerational homes raised by some of our research participants. Another solution may be to encourage the adoption of universal design principals in all new properties and major refurbishments (Beer and Faulkner 2009: 11). While the principles of universal design has been around since the 1960s (Follette Story et al. 1998), they are seldom put into practice outside of custom-designed homes. The introduction of the Livable Housing Design Guidelines

(Livable Housing Australia 2013) with its three levels of universal/adaptable design application is a step in this direction, but as it is a voluntary code it is unlikely to overcome resistance in the housing industry due to cost. Policies should encourage the adoption of these design principles in all new housing that would facilitate not only houses that are suitable to people of all ages, but also housing that can be more easily modified to suit a wider range of living arrangements, including multigenerational households. As suggested by some of our interviewees, better information and guidelines on housing design and modification for multigenerational living could also be helpful to consumers, designers and the housing industry.

At the city scale, the push for more compact cities has facilitated smaller households to live closer to employment and service centres, but affordable housing options for larger households with similar accessibility are rare. Based on evidence from this research, it seems likely that many young adults will continue to remain living in the family home and delay their first home-leaving. If these multigenerational households continue to be concentrated in the outer suburbs of major cities, with poor access to employment, higher education and service centres, this will negatively disadvantage these young adults and also impact the quality of these households' family live, a main reason why some of the multigenerational households co-reside in the first place. Urban planners and policymakers will need to take into account the resulting demand for affordable larger dwellings with good access to such services. This might include promotion of the provision of larger dwellings, or more flexible options, in multi-unit developments that are closer to service centres. There is some evidence that this is already occurring at the high-end of the Sydney development industry, with recent high-profile multi-unit developments including a large number of 3–4 bedroom (1 Australia Avenue n.d.) and duel-key apartments (Central Park n.d.). Such developments could be promoted throughout the market, to provide similar options at the more affordable end of the property scale. The relaxation of the rules regarding building secondary dwellings on the same title (e.g. granny flats), as has been the case recently in NSW (NSW DPI 2011), may also be beneficial in providing more housing options for multigenerational households.

Conclusions

Multigenerational households form a relatively small proportion of households in Australian cities, and as a result academic and policy concerns have moved towards the needs of single-person and other smaller households. In spite of this, multigenerational households contain a relatively large proportion of our population, and those numbers are growing rapidly in Australian cities. In Sydney, the largest of all of Australian cities, the growth in the number of people living in multigenerational households has far outpaced the growth of the population as a whole. It is important therefore that the needs of these households are not overlooked in policies and discourses focused on the compact city and the need to house smaller households.

The nature of multigenerational living means that many multigenerational households have particular housing needs that are not necessarily well-served by the type of housing they are currently living in – predominantly detached houses in the outer suburbs of cities – which can disadvantage these households in regards to access to employment, education and services and in regards to the suitability of the design and layout of these properties for multigenerational living. The solutions lie in recognising multigenerational families as a common and important household form and in developing suitable planning and housing design. This does not necessarily mean the development of custom built 'multigenerational housing', but instead suggests that housing design and planning policies need to be flexible enough to accommodate many different household forms. Suggestions include better information and guidelines for multigenerational dwelling design and modification, the wide adoption of universal design principles, planning policies to facilitate the provision of larger dwellings in multi-unit developments and the building of secondary dwellings on the same property title.

Acknowledgement

This chapter is based on research funded by the Australian Research Council's Discovery Project program during 2012–2014, DP120100956.

References

1 Australia Avenue (n.d.) *Apartments*, http://1australiaavenue.com.au/design/apartments, accessed 28 January 2014, Colliers International, ecove and Sydney Olympic Park.
ABS (2012a) *2011 Census of Population and Housing*, Australian Bureau of Statistics, Canberra.
—— (2012b) customised tables of the *2011 Census Population and Housing*, Australian Bureau of Statistics, Canberra.
—— (2013) *Regional Population growth, Australia, 2012*, Cat. No. 3218.0, Australian Bureau of Statistics, Canberra.
Alessie, R., Brugiavini, A. and Weber, G. (2005), 'Saving and Cohabitation: The Economic Consequences of Living with One's Parents in Italy and the Netherlands', *NBER Working Paper 11079*, National Bureau of Economic Research.
Australian Government (2012), *Living Longer. Living Better*, Commonwealth of Australia, Canberra.
Beer, A. and Faulkner, D. (2009), *21st Century Housing Careers and Australia's Housing Future*, AHURI Final Report No. 128, Australian Housing and Urban Research Institute, Melbourne.
Billari, F. and Rosina, A. (2005), *'Mamma' and the Diffusion of Cohabitation: The Italian case*, Population Association of America 2005 Annual Meeting, Philadelphia Pennsylvania, USA.
Burnley, I. (2009), 'Immigration II', in N. Thrift and R. Kitchen (eds), *International Encyclopaedia of Human Geography*, Elsevier, Oxford: 308–316.
Central Park (n.d.), *The Mark*, http://www.centralparksydney.com/live/the-mark, accessed 28 January 2014, Sekisui House and Frasers Property.

Chui, E. (2008), 'Ageing in Place in Hong Kong – Challenges and Opportunities in a Capitalist Chinese City', *Ageing International* 32(3): 167–182.

Cobb-Clark, D. and Ribar, D. (2009), 'Financial Stress, Family Conflict, and Youths' Successful Transition to Adult Roles', *Centre for Economic Policy Research Discussion Paper No. 627*, Australian National University, Canberra.

Cohen, P. and Casper, L. (2002), 'In Whose Home: Multigenerational Families in the United States, 1998–2000', *Sociological Perspectives* 45(1): 1–20.

de Vaus, D. and Richardson, S. (2009), *Living Alone in Australia: Trends in Sole Living and Characteristics of Those Who Live Alone*, ASSA Occasional Paper CS#4, Academy of Social Sciences in Australia.

DisabilityCare Australia (2013), *One Big Difference to Lots of Lives: An Introduction to DisabilityCare Australia*, Department of Families, Housing, Community Services and Indigenous Affairs, Canberra.

Flatau, P., James, I., Watson, J., Wood, G. and Hendershott, P. (2007), 'Leaving the Parental Home in Australia over the Generations: Evidence from the Household, Income and Labour Dynamics in Australia (HILDA) Survey', *Journal of Population Research* 24(1): 51–71.

Follette Story, M., Mueller, J. and Mace, R. (1998), *The Universal Design File: Designing for People of All Ages and Abilities*, NC State University, Center for Universal Design.

Gee, E., Mitchell, B. and Wister, A. (2003), 'Home Leaving Trajectories in Canada: Exploring Cultural and Gendered Dimensions', *Canadian Studies in Population* 30(2): 245–270.

Giddens, A. (1998), *The Third Way*, Polity Press, Cambridge.

Grundy, E. (1999), 'Changing Role of the Family and Community in Providing Support for the Elderly', in R. Cliquet and M. Nizamuddin (eds), *Population Ageing: Challenges for Policies and Programmes in Developed and Developing Countries*, United Nations Population Fund/Population and Family Study Centre, New York: 103–122.

Harper, S. (2006), 'The Ageing of Family Life Transitions', in Vincent, J., Phillipson, C. and Downs, M. (eds), *The Futures of Old Age*, SAGE, London: 164–171.

Izuhara, M. (2010), 'Housing Wealth and Family Reciprocity in East Asia', in M. Izuhara (ed.), *Ageing and Intergenerational Relations: Family Reciprocity from a Global Perspective*, Policy Press: 77–94.

Judd, B., Olsberg, D., Quinn, J., Groenhart, L. and Demirbilek, O. (2010), 'Dwelling, Land and Neighbourhood Use by Older Home Owners', *AHURI Final Report No. 144*, Australian Housing and Urban Research Institute, Melbourne.

Kaplan, G.H. (2009), 'Boomerang Kids: Labor Market Dynamics and Moving Back Home', *Working Paper 675*, Federal Reserve Bank of Minneapolis Research Department.

Liu, E. and Easthope, H. (2012), 'AHURI Essay: Multi-generation Households in Australian Cities', *AHURI Final Report No. 181*, Australian Housing and Urban Research Institute, Melbourne.

Liu, E., Easthope, H., Burnley, I. and Judd, B. (2013), 'Multigenerational Households in Australian Cities: Evidence from Sydney and Brisbane at the Turn of the Twenty-first Century', *7th Australasian Housing Researchers' Conference*, Fremantle Western Australia, 6–8 February 2013.

Livable Housing Australia (2013), *Livable Housing Design Guidelines*, Sydney.

Madigan, M. and Vonow, B. (2014), 'Queensland Architect Gabriel Poole Designs Home to House Three Generations of One Family', *Courier-Mail*, Brisbane, 10 January.

Mehio-Sibai, A., Beydoun, M. and Tohme, R. (2009), 'Living Arrangements of Ever-Married Older Lebanese Women: Is Living with Married Children Advantageous?', *Journal of Cross-Cultural Gerontology* 24(1): 5–17.

NSW DPI (2011), *Supporting Secondary Dwelling (Granny Flats)*, NSW Department of Planning and Infrastructure.

OESR (2011), *Queensland Government Population Projections to 2013: Local Government Areas, 2011 edition*, Queensland Treasury Office of Economic and Statistical Research, Brisbane.

Olsberg, D. and Winters, M. (2005), 'Ageing in Place: Intergenerational and Intrafamilial Housing Transfers and Shifts in Later Life', *AHURI Final Report No. 88*, Australian Housing and Urban Research Institute, Melbourne.

Parker, K. (2012), *The Boomerang Generation: Feeling OK about Living with Mom and Dad*, Social and Demographic Trends Series, Pew Research Center, Washington D.C.

Popenoe, D. (1993), 'American Family Decline, 1960–1990: A Review and Appraisal', *Journal of Marriage and Family* 55(3): 527–542.

Swartz, T. (2009) 'Intergenerational Family Relations in Adulthood: Patterns, Variations, and Implications in the Contemporary United States', *Annual Review of Sociology* 35(1): 191–212.

Teunissen, F. (1992) 'Equality of Educational Opportunity for Children from Ethnic Minority Communities', in E. Reid and H. Reich (eds), *Breaking the Boundaries: Migrant Workers' Children in the EC*, Multilingual Matters: 88–111.

Tinker, A. (2002), 'The Social Implications of an Ageing Population', *Mechanisms of Ageing and Development* 123(7): 729–735.

Yates, J. and Gabriel, M. (2006), *Housing Affordability in Australia. National Research Venture 3: Housing Affordability for Lower Income Australians Research Paper*, Australian Housing and Urban Research Institute, Melbourne.

Yieh, K., Tsai, Y.-F., Kuo, C.-Y. (2004), 'An Exploratory Study of 'Parasites' in Taiwan', *Journal of Family and Economic Issues* 25(4): 527–539.

Chapter 3
Ethnic Discrimination in Private Rental Housing Markets in Australia

Jacqueline Nelson, Heather MacDonald, Rae Dufty-Jones,
Kevin Dunn and Yin Paradies

Introduction

Housing represents more than just a physical dwelling; it is central to our social, psychological and cultural security (Abramsson et al. 2002). Housing inequality, in terms of access to appropriate housing, to the locational amenities that come with housing, and the housing experience, is responsible for considerable social disadvantage across the world. For recently arrived international migrants, finding adequate, affordable housing has been demonstrated to be important for their adjustment, particularly during the initial settlement period (Murdie and Teixeira 2003: 8).

Differential access to housing has a range of deleterious effects, including on health and wellbeing (Access Alliance Multicultural Community Health Centre 2005). This is in line with research that finds experiences of discrimination are linked to poor health, particularly mental health (Paradies 2006; Pascoe and Smart Richman 2009; Williams and Mohammed 2009). In the United States, differential access to housing is strongly associated with residential segregation (Polikoff 2006). Galster (1990) argued that housing discrimination and the neighbourhood segregation that results means that minority groups, including African and Hispanic Americans, are deprived of access to neighbourhoods with higher levels of services, esteem and quality of life. Housing discrimination reduces employment and educational opportunities and puts pressure on commuting. It is also associated with higher housing costs as segregated groups compete for a limited amount of housing and as minorities spend more energy and resources on their search for their housing preference (Gabriel and Rosenthal 1996; Massey and Denton 1993; Myers 2004; Yinger 1998).

In Australia, both anecdotal and survey reports suggest Australians from migrant and Indigenous backgrounds experience discrimination in the private rental housing market. Among these groups, as many as a quarter report that they have experienced discrimination on the basis of ethnicity when seeking accommodation (see Table 3.3). This chapter reflects on recent paired testing experiments of actual behaviour by real estate agents in the Sydney metropolitan area. These experiments confirm the existence of uneven treatment across ethnicity. It was found that real estate agents provided greater levels of service, advice and encouragement to Anglo-Australians, and less to Indian-Australians and those from a Muslim Middle-Eastern background. This lesser service would add to the costs of the housing search for these minorities, reproducing inequality across ethnicity and therefore constituting a form of racism. Increased regulation, and more testing to expose racism in private rental markets, are two suggested remedies for this unnecessary burden experienced by ethnic minorities.

What is known about Housing Discrimination?

Housing discrimination has been most extensively studied in the United States, where the Department of Housing and Urban Development (HUD) undertakes regular large-scale national research on the issue. The HUD studies use the paired testing method. In the housing context, paired (or audit) testing involves sending sets of trained actors or 'testers' (of varied ethnic backgrounds) to rental property inspections and recording their experiences during the rental inspection process. Testers are carefully selected to ensure that they 'match' on as many relevant characteristics as possible. Over a large number of 'tests', discrimination is determined based on the relative treatment of each of the ethnic minority testers. HUD studies were conducted in 1977, 1989, 2000 and 2012 (Turner et al. 2002; Turner et al. 2012; Turner et al. 1991; Wienk et al. 1979). This method inspired a host of community organisations to run their own audits. Galster (1990) reviewed 71 of these in the US in the 1980s. The HUD studies found significant levels of discrimination in the first two studies (1977 and 1989), with reductions in discrimination against African-Americans in the 2000 study and further reductions in 2012. In 2012, the study encompassed 28 metropolitan areas and involved some 8000 tests, examining discrimination experienced by black, Hispanic and Asian Americans. In the 2012 study black renters were told about 11.4 per cent fewer units and shown 4.2 per cent fewer units than matched White renters. The technique has been adapted for use in other countries, where it has generated evidence of discrimination encountered by immigrant ethnic minorities in Canada (cited in Dion 2001), Sweden (Ahmed and Hammarstedt 2008) and Spain (Bosch et al. 2009). Looking to Europe, a 2005 study of discrimination in housing across 15 member states of the European Union (EU) found that across the EU immigrants and ethnic minorities are 'subject to persistent, extensive and varied forms of ethnic, racist and national discrimination' (Harrison et al. 2005: 59). As can been seen in Table 3.1, almost every state reports the presence of housing discrimination. Another key theme of Table 3.1 is the paucity or weakness of the data in Europe. This information is based on data compiled from various sources, depending on the member state, and includes sources such as official reports of housing discrimination received by the government as well as experiences documented by non-government organisations.

Murdie and Teixeira (2003) reported that for some ethnic minorities in Toronto, Canada, factors such as source of income, family size, skin colour and family type can produce discriminatory barriers. Dion (2001: 533) describes a 'hierarchy of perceived discrimination' in Toronto that operates according to the visibility of minority status.[1] Accordingly, when

---

[1] Visibility is a term used to denote skin colour and other physical features as a identifier of ethnic minority status in Canada.

Table 3.1 Reported discrimination in housing across 15 EU member states

Country	Discrimination in housing
Belgium	Case-level evidence of discrimination in both the private and social housing sectors (Harrison et al. 2005: 18).
Denmark	Individuals experience direct discrimination, both in terms of access to housing and experiencing harassment once having secured housing (Harrison et al. 2005: 18).
Germany	Underdeveloped legislation, no national monitoring system that documents cases of discrimination. Evidence of unchecked discriminatory practices, such as quota systems to prevent non-German households from accessing housing (Harrison et al. 2005: 19).
Greece	Very limited state intervention in housing and very little information available about the housing situation of migrant/ethnic groups in Greece (Harrison et al. 2005: 20).
Spain	Discrimination 'quite extensive and in some cases very overt' (Harrison et al. 2005: 20).
France	Evidence of direct, indirect and institutional discrimination (Harrison et al. 2005: 21). However, limited statistical data available.
Ireland	Systematic data unavailable. Available qualitative data suggests experiences of both direct and indirect discrimination, particularly in access to private rental market (Harrison et al. 2005: 21).
Italy	Discrimination in both public and private housing sectors (Harrison et al. 2005: 22).
Luxembourg	No information about systematic effects of discrimination because appropriate data not collected (Harrison et al. 2005: 22).
Netherlands	Authors of national report claim 'there is little or no discrimination taking place in the Netherlands' (Harrison et al. 2005: 23) but Harrison et al. are sceptical of this claim.
Austria	'Third country nationals' experience discrimination and restricted access to parts of the private housing sector (the better quality accommodation) (Harrison et al. 2005: 23).
Portugal	Systematic data scarce, but evidence of discrimination against some groups, including Roma and people of African origins (Harrison et al. 2005: 24).
Finland	Qualitative evidence of discrimination against minorities in housing (Harrison et al. 2005: 24).
Sweden	Ombudsman complaints document racism in housing.
United Kingdom	Social housing sector 'subject to extensive guidance, performance measurement, and control, so that overt racist practices are now hard to find'. Regulation less well developed in private sector and not much information available on discrimination (Harrison et al. 2005: 25).

Source: Compiled from (Harrison, et al. 2005)

seeking housing in Toronto, Somali Canadians perceived the most discrimination followed by Jamaican and then Polish Canadians. The difficulties of Somali Canadians points to how some minority groups are exposed to multiple axes of discrimination, which can be linked to skin colour, visa status, mode of arrivals (e.g. refugees), employment status, age, marital status etc. Applicants for mortgages whose financial credentials are marginal are especially exposed to this cumulative disadvantage (Hunter and Walker 1996). Paired testing misses these intersectionality effects because it makes the non-ethnicity characteristics of the testers' equivalent. Nonetheless, reports in Australia have observed that Indigenous Australians, Australians from non-white backgrounds and refugees will be particularly

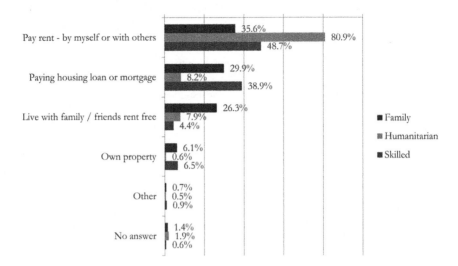

Figure 3.1 Accommodation situation for new migrants to Australia by stream
Source: Australian Survey Research Group 2011: 36.

exposed to discrimination when seeking housing. The European findings in Table 3.1 also point to the difficulties of recent immigrants, non-citizens and racialised minorities (e.g. Roma, people of African ancestry).

The international literature indicate that there is insufficient quality data on housing discrimination, that certain groups endure a higher burden of this discrimination, and that state regulation and intervention is crucial for challenging this form of racism. Our argument is that the collection of high quality data on the prevalence and impact of ethnic discrimination in housing is a forceful tool for anti-racism.

Housing Discrimination in Australia

Discrimination in rental housing is a significant issue for both new migrants to Australia, members of established ethnic minority groups and Indigenous Australians. Most new arrivals to Australia spend a substantial period of time in rental housing after arrival. Figure 3.1 shows the type of accommodation new migrants to Australia hold after their arrival,[2] a large majority of humanitarian entrants to Australia in particular are reliant on rental housing (including both public and private sectors). A range of policy-relevant research has identified the difficulties some recent migrants experience in finding decent affordable housing (Dhanji 2010; Ethnic Communities Council of Victoria 2008; Foley and Beer 2003). Aboriginal Australians have also been identified as suffering from unfair treatment when seeking housing.

---

2 Participants in this study were surveyed at a point in time between their arrival and 60 months thereafter.

The anecdotal evidence available in Australia strongly suggests that ethnic minority groups experience discrimination when seeking accommodation. A handful of official inquiries found that Australians complained of ethnic discrimination in their dealings with real estate agents and Department of Housing officers. The issue of housing discrimination has only received formal government attention in Western Australia and in Victoria (Equal Opportunity Commission of Western Australia (EOCWA) 2004, 2009; Human Rights and Equal Opportunity Commission (HREOC) 1991; Victorian Equal Opportunity and Human Rights Commission (VEOHRC) 2012). In 1999 the then national Race Discrimination Commissioner advocated improvement to 'compliance with Commonwealth and State anti-discrimination legislation throughout the real estate industry' (HREOC 1999: 21). Most official inquiries into the links between ethnic discrimination and accommodation have focused on certain localities, and specifically public housing estates, and tensions between racist tenants and members of minority ethnic groups (Dufty 2009; EOCWA 2004; HREOC 1991: 162–163, 337–343).

Historically, there has been some scholarly and policy interest in Australia in discrimination in public housing, particularly experiences of Aboriginal public housing tenants. Dufty (2009) found discussions of public housing in rural Australia to be highly racialised. Participants in Dufty's Griffith based study (in south-western NSW) referred to the 'unfair privileges' Indigenous Australians enjoyed, both in access to housing as well as to desirable alterations or types of housing stock. Indigenous public housing tenants were seen to violate expected behaviour in relation to their housing, particularly around housing maintenance. Contrary to these perceptions of privilege, at the turn of the 21st century Beresford (2001) reported that Aboriginal Australians experienced discrimination in access to public housing and reported that racist attitudes of neighbours affected their experiences while living in government owned housing. Between 1996 and 2004, the West Australian Equal Opportunity Commission (EOCWA) received more than 400 complaints alleging discrimination from Aboriginal public housing tenants against the Department of Housing and Works (DHW), also known as 'Homewest'. This led to the *Finding a Place Inquiry*, which examined direct or indirect 'discriminatory treatment of Indigenous persons in Western Australia in the provision of accommodation and/or services, because of their race or characteristics of their race' (EOCWA 2004: 16). A number of recommendations relevant to housing discrimination were made, including:

- 'All Homewest policies are to be reviewed to ensure that they do not directly or indirectly disadvantage Aboriginal tenants or prospective tenants in their content or their practice' (EOCWA 2004: Recommendation 5).
- 'Reference to any other irrelevant matters to be discontinued and ultimately deleted from the file. For example ... racial background of neighbours and their preferences regarding the racial makeup of the tenants in nearby properties' (EOCWA 2004: Recommendation 28).
- ' ... many submissions referred to the existence of racist attitudes in the private rental market and the effect this has on the capacity of Aboriginal prospective tenants to gain housing. The Inquiry recommends that DHW conduct training sessions to raise awareness of this' (EOCWA 2004: Recommendation 52).

- 'In view of the frequency with which Aboriginal people report race based discrimination in accessing the private housing rental market, the DHW to cease the practice of requiring that Aboriginal prospective tenants make multiple attempts to access the private rental market before the DHW will list these tenants for priority housing' (EOCWA 2004: Recommendation 53).

Recommendation 53 is particularly pertinent for this chapter. Prior to the *Finding a Place* Inquiry, individuals wishing to access public housing in Western Australia needed to demonstrate they had attempted, and failed, to access housing in the private rental market. This requirement was abolished after the inquiry, because 'it was humiliating for [Aboriginal people] to face often blatant discrimination from agents or owners' (EOCWA 2009: 24).

> The very real fear of rejection leads many homeless Indigenous clients to not even try for private rental .... Agency Submission 17 (EOCWA 2009: 63)

Six years on from *Finding a Place*, the West Australian Equal Opportunity Commission reported on progress in five areas of reform: staffing; communication and consultation with Aboriginal people, review of the Department of Housing's policies and practices, provision of housing and maintenance services and appeals mechanisms (EOCWA 2011).

The *Finding a Place* inquiry in Western Australia led to an inquiry into discrimination in the private rental housing market, *Accommodating Everyone* (EOCWA 2009). Although the Inquiry stated that 'very few formal complaints of race discrimination in the private housing rental market [had] been received by the EOC or other similar jurisdictions in Australia' (EOCWA 2009: 5), it found 'substantial evidence of racial discrimination in the private housing rental market' (EOCWA 2009: 6). The Inquiry found that discrimination commonly took the form of an agent telling a prospective renter that a property was available during an initial contact over the phone, but when the individual arrived in person they were told the property was no longer available. The Victorian Immigrant and Refugee Women's Coalition (in EOCWA 2009: 6) reported that Lily, a 31-year-old international student from Taiwan, had a similar experience,

> I went to a house inspection. I didn't know the street and rang the real estate office to say I was going to be late. When I arrived, the woman said, 'I don't know what you're talking about'. I was already there. She never looked at me, just on her computer screen. I don't think people care about me. I'm like air because I can't speak English properly.

Experiences of discrimination can lead to negative experiences once in private rental housing, as those who have experienced discrimination are forced to take on properties in poor condition, requiring significant maintenance,

> Many CaLD and Aboriginal tenants are reluctant to pursue their right to have urgent maintenance issues attended to. They will accept poor living conditions in order to secure some form of accommodation (Agency Submission 9: 4 in EOCWA 2009: 70).

The Inquiry found a strong reluctance amongst Aboriginal and Culturally and Linguistically Diverse (CaLD) individuals to make formal complaints about discrimination in rental housing or to seek statutory forms of remedy, such as those available for residential tenancy matters through the Magistrates Courts.

The Accommodating Everyone inquiry identified international students as another group at risk of housing discrimination in Australia, as the submission below demonstrates.

> This agency believes that international students are treated less fairly than tenants of non-CaLD backgrounds. In particular, international students regularly approach the agency in regard to bond issues. These clients often state that owners/agents cause delays in bond arrangement because they are aware that the student is leaving the country and will have trouble pursuing their claim from their home country once they leave Australia ... Additionally, international students who intend to return to Australia to work or live can be unwilling to challenge contentious bond disposals for fear of a prejudicial tenant database listing (Agency Submission 9: 6 in EOCWA 2009: 75).

In the wake of the controversies over attacks on international students in 2009, there was a series of stakeholder consultations and fora that included student representatives. International students from non-English speaking backgrounds identified discrimination in the seeking of rental housing as a key issue, though it has received little media attention and little policy response (see Australian Human Rights Commission and New Zealand Human Rights Commission 2009). Delegates to the 2009 Australasian Race Relations Roundtable were told of exploitative and discriminatory treatment of international students in the rental market, reported by both student representatives and by the state-level Human Rights Commissions (see VEOHRC 2008).

In addition to those coming to Australia as international students, humanitarian entrants experience a range of difficulties finding accommodation once they arrive in Australia (Australian Survey Research Group 2011). As can be seen in Table 3.2 below, according to one survey just over three per cent reported discrimination, with a further two per cent indicating they faced a difficult real estate agent. However, it is likely that these figures underestimate the rate of discrimination. As we will show, discriminatory treatment in the private rental markets can take subtle, difficult to perceive, forms. Similarly, some of the reasons identified in Table 3.2 could be considered a form of discrimination, or may be linked to it, for example, lack of rental history/referees, poor English and large family size.

Using data from the second Longitudinal Survey of Immigrants to Australia of 1999/2000[3] Forrest et al. (2012) found differences in the types of housing refugee migrants secured according to country of origin. The study found that 18 months after migration, home ownership was higher for Bosnians, Croats and Serbs. West Asians and East Africans were more likely to be accommodated in private rental housing, while staying with family members was more common amongst Sudanese arrivals. In the Forrest et al.

---

3   Survey only includes offshore refugee immigrants, who made up 75 per cent of those admitted under the Refugee and Humanitarian Program in 1999. The total sample of refugee immigrants who participated in both waves was 2649.

Table 3.2   What makes it hard to find accommodation (Humanitarian entrants only)

Primary reason	Number	Percentage
Too expensive to rent/buy home	700	36.6
Hard to find appropriate accommodation	400	20.9
Difficult to find a place due to lack of employment or low income	254	13.3
Difficult application process inc. lack rental history/referees and ID points	161	8.4
Poor English / not able to communicate	161	8.4
Large family size	88	4.6
Experience discrimination	61	3.2
Competition	48	2.5
Lack of knowledge, technology, transport, friends, support in how to apply, where to go	41	2.1
Difficult real estate agent	39	2.0
TOTAL	1914	

Source: (Australian Survey Research Group 2011: 41).

(2012) analysis, reports of discrimination were higher than those found by the Australian Survey Research Group (2011). One third of refugees reported some intolerance towards them in seeking housing, while 8 per cent experienced 'a lot' of intolerance. Real estate agents were again mentioned as a barrier to finding appropriate accommodation, with 13 per cent of refugees mentioning this problem (Forrest et al. 2012).

The Challenging Racism Project undertook a series of surveys between 2001 and 2008 on Australians' racial attitudes and experiences of racism. The survey suggested that experiences of racism are elevated amongst those who speak a language other than English at home or in their community, with just over 10 per cent reporting they 'sometimes', 'often' or 'very often' experience racism when renting/buying a house. Reports of racism are common amongst Indigenous Australians, for whom 18 per cent 'sometimes', 'often' or 'very often' encounter racism in the housing market. Indian and Sri Lankan born respondents reported similarly high rates of racism (17%) in this sphere, as did Muslim Middle Eastern Australians (20%), suggesting that these groups are targets of differential treatment in housing.

The willingness of the real estate industry to address the issue of ethnic discrimination in private rental housing is as yet unclear. Engagement with the *Accommodating Everyone* inquiry by the real estate industry in WA was minimal. No submissions from real estate industry representatives were received, in spite of their attendance at information briefing sessions and a concerted effort of the Commission to engage the Real Estate Institute of Western Australia. A study of real estate agencies and the role risk plays in the rental decision-making process provides some insight into potential drivers of housing discrimination (Short et al. 2008). In the Short et al. (2008) study two aspects of risk were

Table 3.3 Experiences of racism when renting/buying a house (Challenging Racism Project 2001–2008; Ordinariness of Australian Muslims Survey 2011)

	English only speakers (non-Indigenous)[a]	Speaks language other than English (non-Indigenous)[a]	Indigenous Australians[a]	TOTAL[a]	Sri-Lanka and India born Australians[a]	Muslim Australians[b]
Number of respondents	10150	1955	186	12290	143	501
Never	95.5%	81.9%	76.9%	93.0%	72.8%	59.5%
Hardly Ever	2.3%	7.6%	4.8%	3.1%	9.5%	19.8%
Sometimes, Often, Very Often	2.3%	10.4%	18.3%	3.8%	17.5%	20.8%

NB: Figures may not add to exactly 100% due to rounding.
Sources: [a] Challenging Racism Project 2001–2008; [b] Ordinariness of Australian Muslims Survey 2011.

pertinent: financial risk and risk of litigation. Rental applications are assessed using a range of formal, informal and intuitive assessments of risk. The primary focus of Short et al. (2008: 4) study was 'the moment of allocation', or 'the events and interactions entailed in the acceptance or rejection of tenancy applications'. Real estate agents give primary importance to the 'ability to pay' and the 'ability to care' for the property, and construct these criterion as 'objective, fair and reasonable' (Short et al. 2008: 34).

Short et al. (2008) identified a four stage process of assessing the likelihood that a prospective tenant will be able to pay and care for a rental property:

1. 'Sorting out' – prospective tenants assessed according to income and prior records/presence on residential tenancy databases. If the rent is over one third of a prospective tenant's income they are classified as 'high risk'.
2. 'Ranking' – applicants that pass previous assessment are ranked from most desirable to least desirable on the 'ability to pay' and 'ability to care' criterion.
3. 'Discriminating' – discrimination is characterised by Short et al. as an implicit process, with real estate agents being fully aware that they must comply with legislation when they select and recommend prospective tenants.
4. 'Handing over' – the owner is given the responsibility for making a final decision about tenancy. This is characterised as a risk avoidance strategy. Short et al. noted that both owners and agents feel no social responsibility to offer housing to applicants that have historically been disadvantaged in housing markets.

The risk factors associated with Aboriginality and other ethnic minorities were said to be family size, cultural practices and housekeeping. However, agents and owners could also invoke the financial vulnerability of these groups to justify their exclusion. This reinforces the American findings on the cumulative effects associated with an intersectionality of issues around financial capacities and cultural characteristics. A final observation from Short et al. (2008: 36) is that the 'tension between lawful and unlawful discrimination is palpable in the talk of property managers; the bottom line of business profitability is also evident'. This suggests that while agents may attempt to avoid visible or *direct* discriminatory practices, *indirect* discrimination nonetheless occurs. Again, this links to recent American data that affirms the rising importance of subtle discrimination, and the demise of the blatant forms of racist 'door slamming' in the 1960s and 1970s (Turner et al. 2012: 68).

This brief review reveals a relative lack of specific research on housing discrimination in Australia. Reported experiences of discrimination have often been mentioned in studies of the housing search. Also, the broader housing experiences of several ethnic or racial minority groups have been studied. However, there has been little methodologically rigorous investigation of ethnic discrimination in Australia.

Paired Testing for Housing Discrimination in Australia

The Equal Opportunity Commission of Western Australia (2009: 39) concluded their inquiry by stating that while there is lots of evidence to suggest race discrimination exists in access to private rental housing, there has been 'very little systematic research investigation of the issue'. They explicitly stated that paired testing in the Australian context would be helpful to test perceptions of discrimination. Paired testing involves matched pairs of 'testers' attending rental property inspections and observing their relative treatment during the process. Perceptions of discriminatory treatment are an unreliable basis for conclusions about the extent of discrimination, because individuals cannot compare their own experiences to those of others. Complaint-based estimates of the problem are thus unlikely to accurately reflect actual experiences. This chapter describes the first large-scale application of paired testing to the rental housing market in Australia. The paired testing method has been used to study discrimination in two other spheres in recent Australian research. Booth et al. (2011) examined discrimination in Australian employment by sending sets of matched CVs to employers in response to advertised job vacancies and found 'ethnic penalties' for job applicants with Italian, Chinese, Middle Eastern and Indigenous sounding names. Applicants with 'ethnic' sounding names had to apply for more jobs than those with Anglo-Saxon sounding names to get the same number of interviews. However, a similar approach would not work in the Sydney rental housing markets, given the competition for rental housing, and the prevailing practice of applying for housing after an inspection. Real estate agents are unlikely to respond to email inquiries. The second example involved an examination of treatment on public buses in Queensland, Australia (Mujcic and Frijters 2013). Research assistants of varied ethnic appearance told bus drivers that their travel pass was faulty and requested a free ride on the bus. White and Asian (mainly Chinese) research assistants were granted a free ride on 72 per cent and 73 per cent of occasions respectively. Indian and black research assistants fare less well, with Indian research assistants allowed to catch the bus 51 per cent of the time and black research assistants only 36 per cent of the time.

This study took place across the Sydney metropolitan area between August and November 2013. We recruited 29 'testers' or Research Assistants (RAs), as we will refer to them here, of Anglo, Muslim Middle Eastern and Indian appearance. Research Assistants were allocated two rental properties each week and were required to inspect, or attempt to inspect, each property they were allocated and record details of their experience during the rental inspection process. RAs were organised into pairs (Anglo-Indian; Anglo-Muslim Middle Eastern). In order to create the pairs, RAs were matched on as many relevant characteristics as possible, including, for example, age, gender, level of extroversion and education level. Each member of the pair was allocated the same rental properties, to allow a direct comparison of treatment to be made. Rental properties were selected from a widely used real estate database, using a stratified random sample of properties available in major regions of the metropolitan area. When RAs were allocated a rental property, they were also allocated equivalent occupations and family characteristics appropriate for the allocated property. For example, for a studio apartment in the Sydney CBD, RAs may have been asked to role-play as a single professional (with varied but equivalent status occupations) looking for a studio or one bedroom apartment in central Sydney.

The testing process had two stages. First, testers were allocated an advertised rental property and called the agency to set up an inspection. During this call they communicated their ethnically identifiable name (Anglo, Muslim Middle Eastern or Indian) to the agent. The second stage involved the testers attending the rental property inspection in person, either at an individual appointment or an advertised open house. Each stage was scripted to approximate equivalent behaviour by each tester. Testers independently recorded their experience on a detailed questionnaire as soon as possible after each stage of the process.

RAs attended a half-day training session before fieldwork commenced. Key elements of the training included:

1. A discussion of the importance of objectivity: RAs were asked not to *interpret* behaviour or treatment but, so far as is possible, to objectively report or describe their experiences.
2. Role playing with scripts: RAs worked with their matched pair in order to ensure that their behaviour/use of the script felt natural to them, but was equivalent within the group.
3. Sample surveys: A set of surveys were developed for RAs to complete at each stage of the process (allocation of property; phone call; inspection; contact before/after inspection). Training involved detailed explanation of these materials and practice using sample properties.

Paired testing provides data that are more reliable than survey reports of retrospective experiences. The paired testing method is more reliable because of the training RAs undertake about observation and the timing of observations, being recorded immediately after each stage of the process. By this method 'observations avoid contamination by possible memory lapses, biases, and confabulations by being detailed and recorded shortly after the discrimination has occurred' (Dion 2001: 527).

Overview of Findings

Five composite variables were created in order to look broadly at how RAs of different ethnic appearances were treated during the rental inspection process. The composites summarised a variety of related response items from the surveys; thus, the composite 'provision of information' summarised responses to 19 different questions about different types of information the agent might have provided. By analysing composite variables as well as individual questions, we were able to identify broader patterns of interaction where differential treatment might have occurred. Composite questions also offered a more meaningful picture of the entire rental interaction, which occurred over three stages.

Agent Flexibility

Agent flexibility included two items: the offer of an individual appointment (over the phone) and the offer of alternative inspection times (outside the advertised time). These items were scored '1' if the offer was made and '0' if the offer was not made. The composite variable was created by adding scores on these two items together to give a score out of 2. Thus higher scores indicate greater agent flexibility. Table 3.4 compares level of agent flexibility for Anglo RAs compared with Indian RAs, and Anglo RAs compared to Muslim Middle Eastern RAs. Offers for personal inspections and alternative booking times dramatically impact the length and depth of the housing search. This process can have a substantial personal and opportunity costs for renters. Unfairly exacerbating the process for members of minority groups places an unnecessary ethnic penalty upon them.

Table 3.4   Agent flexibility

	Anglo RAs	Indian RAs	Anglo RAs	MME RAs
Agent flexibility	0.41**	0.26**	0.46	0.43
Number of cases	228		90	

** Significant at $\alpha = .01$ level.

There were no significant differences in agent flexibility for Anglo and Muslim Middle Eastern pairs. However, Anglo RAs scored significantly higher than Indian RAs on the flexibility variable, suggesting Anglo RAs were offered more flexibility in attending inspections than Indian RAs in this initial, telephone based phase. This was a moderate effect (eta-squared=0.075).

Provision of Information

Information provided to RAs by real estate agents either over the phone and at the inspection itself was compiled in this composite variable. This variable included a total of 18 items, each of which was scored '1' if an RA was provided with that piece of information and '0' if they were not. Hence higher scores indicate provision of more information. The variable includes items such as being told about alternative properties available (over the phone), being given information about the application process (over the phone or at the inspection), being told about features/details of the property (over the phone) and comments on aspects of the neighbourhood during the inspection, such as the availability of schools or public transport. This is another set of items that are critical to the housing search. Information provision to all groups was relatively low – on average RAs reported being provided with between two and three of the 18 possible pieces of information we gathered data on. However, provision of information was nonetheless uneven among the groups. As Table 3.5 indicates, Indian and Muslim Middle Eastern RAs were provided with significantly less information than their matched Anglo RAs. These were small effects (eta-squared=0.045 (Indian-Anglo comparison); eta-squared=0.031 (Muslim Middle Eastern-Anglo comparison)).

Table 3.5 Provision of information

	Anglo RAs	Indian RAs	Anglo RAs	MME RAs
Provision of information	3.02**	2.56**	2.85*	2.48*
Number of cases	362		147	

** Significant at α = .01 level; * Significant at α = .05 level.

Interactions with Agents

The extent to which the RAs were given opportunities to interact with the real estate agent managing a rental property is captured in this composite variable. A total of nine items were included; for each item '1' indicates that a form of contact was made/requested and '0' indicates it was not. The types of items included were: did the agent request your contact details over the phone, did the agent inquire about your housing needs during the inspection, did the agent greet you on arrival or farewell you on departure from the inspection, and did the agent initiate a conversation with you during the inspection. Table 3.6 shows that for both the Anglo-Indian and the Anglo-Muslim Middle Eastern pairs, Anglo RAs had more extensive interactions with agents. There was a stronger effect when comparing Muslim Middle Eastern and Anglo pairs (eta-squared=0.061) than Indian Anglo pairs (eta-squared=0.016).

Table 3.6 Interactions with agents

	Anglo RAs	Indian RAs	Anglo RAs	MME RAs
Interactions with agents	3.51*	3.29*	3.59**	3.11**
Number of cases	379		157	

* Significant at α = .05 level; ** Significant at α = .01 level.

Requirements for Renting

Requirements for renting included eight items, five of which related to the terms of occupancy of the tenancy (e.g. restricted number of occupants, pets allowed), the rental bond requested, points of ID needed to apply for the property and whether or not there was a fee to apply. Again, each of these items was scored '1' if the tenant was told that this restriction/fee applied or '0' if there was no restriction/fee or it was not mentioned. Rental bond required was scored '1' if the RA was asked to pay more than the equivalent of four weeks rent, '0' for four weeks rent, and '-1' for less than four weeks/no bond. As can be seen in Table 3.7 RAs were rarely told about restrictive terms of occupancy and there were no statistically significant differences in the requirements for renting for either of the matched groups. This likely reflects the very high demand, and busy, Sydney private rental market.

Table 3.7   Requirements for renting

	Anglo RAs	Indian RAs	Anglo RAs	MME RAs
Requirements for renting	0.30	0.34	0.36	0.45
Number of cases	287		118	

Encouragement to Rent

There were 18 items included in the variable encouragement to rent, and they included the availability of a 12-month lease, inclusions in price (e.g. gas, water, pay TV), positive comments about the neighbourhood and negative comments about the neighbourhood (reverse scored). These questions, and the composite, measure the more subtle manifestations of housing discrimination (see Table 3.8). While there were no differences in the encouragement given to Anglo and Indian RA pairs, there was a significant difference in the encouragement given to Anglo RAs compared to their matched Muslim Middle Eastern RAs. This was a moderate effect (eta-squared=0.062).

Table 3.8   Encouragement to rent

	Anglo RAs	Indian RAs	Anglo RAs	MME RAs
Encouragement to rent	1.20	1.16	1.39**	1.08**
Number of cases	366		152	

** Significant at $\alpha = .01$ level.

Conclusion

These results suggest that Anglo, Indian and Muslim Middle Eastern renters in Sydney do experience differential treatment that would be consistent with ethnic discrimination. A limitation of this study is that the interactions reported ended before the point of submitting a rental application. The experiences studied here relate to the earlier stages of the rental process, where subtle differences in treatment (for instance, in the provision of information about documents to bring to an inspection) may nevertheless have significant impacts, resulting in some prospective renters being able to submit an application earlier than others, thus having the chance to be offered the dwelling before others and having shorter rental searches. For most of the interactions on which testers reported, it would have been almost impossible for an individual renter to determine whether other prospective tenants were receiving different sorts or amounts of information. In the focus groups conducted following the conclusion of fieldwork, to debrief the RAs and receive their feedback, several RAs expressed surprise at the differences between their experiences and those of teammates. This suggests that the paired testing method of investigating differential treatment offers a robust evidence base, more so than surveys of individuals' experience or a reliance on complaints received.

A closer look at the results offers some insights into where, when and how differential treatment may occur. For those elements of the rental process that are regulated in Australia, such as the amount of security bond required, we did not detect any significant differences. Differences were more likely to be related to informal interaction and the quantity of information provided, which are not regulated (and would be very difficult, if not impossible, to regulate). We have not addressed the policy implications of these findings in this chapter, but our findings suggest that education and awareness campaigns may be the most useful way to address the subtle discrimination that exists in the formal rental market. Also, paired testing research has been shown to have a dramatic influence on real estate agent practice in the United States. The HUD surveys have been stimulus for reducing racism within housing allocation processes, and that has been associated with a further professionalisation of that industry (Turner et al. 2012: xxiii). State endorsed and targeted paired testing has meritorious effects: 'if housing providers know that testing is ongoing, they are more likely to comply with the law'. In the US context, paired testing is used as enforcement testing, where unfair treatment can be basis for legal action. The US case suggests that in Australia ongoing monitoring using paired testing methods could reduce the differential treatment observed here.

Our study findings should also be considered within the broader context of the entire Sydney rental market. The sample of properties we chose was drawn from what we might describe as the 'formal' rental market: they were chosen from one of the most widely used internet advertising sites and thus excluded a range of properties advertised very locally or by word of mouth. While our study did not investigate differences between formal and informal segments of the market, we might expect properties in the 'informal' rental market to be of different quality, to include more managed by owners directly, and possibly to include more opportunities to evade regulations. The experiences of people of different ethnicities in other segments of the rental market may thus be quite different to those we summarise here.

References

Abramsson, M., Borgegård, L.-E. and Fransson, U. (2002). Housing Careers: Immigrants in Local Swedish Housing Markets. *Housing Studies* 17(3): 445–464.

Access Alliance Multicultural Community Health Centre. (2005). *Racialised Groups and Health Status: A literature review exploring poverty, housing, race-based discrimination and access to health care as determinants of health for racialised groups*. Toronto, Ontario: Access Alliance.

Ahmed, A.M. and Hammarstedt, M. (2008). Discrimination in the Rental Housing Market: A Field Experiment on the Internet. *Journal of Urban Economics* 64: 362–372.

Australian Human Rights Commission, and New Zealand Human Rights Commission. (2009). *Communique: Human Rights of International Students a Major Issue: Australian and New Zealand Race Relations Roundtable* 2009. Retrieved from www.hreoc.gov.au/about/media/media_releases/2009/107_09.html

Australian Survey Research Group. (2011). *Settlement Outcomes of New Arrivals: Report of Findings*. Canberra: Department of Immigration and Citizenship.

Beresford, Q. (2001). Homeswest versus Aborigines: Housing Discrimination in Western Australia. *Australian Aboriginal Studies* 2001 (2): 40–46.

Booth, A., Leigh, A. and Varganova, E. (2011). Does Ethnic Discrimination Vary across Minority Groups? Evidence from a Field Experiment. *Oxford Bulletin of Economics and Statistics* 74(4): 547–573.

Bosch, M., Carnero, M.A. and Farre, L. (2009). *Discrimination against Immigrants in the Spanish Rental Market: Evidence from Field Experiments*. Paper presented at the European Association of Labour Economists, Tallinn, Estonia.

Dhanji, S. (2010). Social or Unsocial? The Linkage between Accommodation, Health and Well-being among Former Horn of Africa and Sudanese Refugees Living in Australia. *Australasian Review of African Studies* 31(1): 106–136.

Dion, K.L. (2001). Immigrants' Perceptions of Housing Discrimination in Toronto: The Housing New Canadians Project. *Journal of Social Issues* 57(3): 523–539. doi: 10.1111/0022-4537.00227.

Dufty, R. (2009). 'At Least I Don't Live in Vegemite Valley': Racism and Rural Public Housing Spaces. *Australian Geographer* 40(4): 429–449.

Equal Opportunity Commission of Western Australia. (2004). *Finding a Place: An Inquiry into the Existence of Discriminatory Practices in Relation to the Provision of Public Housing and Related Services to Aboriginal People in Western Australia*. Perth: Equal Opportunity Commission of Western Australia.

—— (2009). *Accommodating Everyone*. Perth: Equal Opportunity Commission of Western Australia.

—— (2011). *Finding a Place: Final Report for the Section 80 Implementation and Monitoring Committee of the Inquiry into the Existence of Discriminatory Practices in Relation to the Provision* of *Public Housing to Aboriginal People in Western Australia*. Perth: Equal Opportunity Commission of Western Australia.

Ethnic Communities Council of Victoria. (2008). *Availability, Affordability, Accessibility: Housing Victoria's New Migrant and Refugee Communities* (Vol. ECCV Policy Discussion Paper No. 4). Carlton, Victoria: Ethnic Communities Council of Victoria.

Foley, P. and Beer, A. (2003). *Housing Need and Provision for Recently Arrived Refugees in Australia*. Melbourne: Australian Housing and Urban Research Institute; Southern Research Centre.

Forrest, J., Hermes, K., Johnston, R. and Poulsen, M. (2012). The Housing Resettlement Experience of Refugee Immigrants to Australia. *Journal of Refugee Studies* 26(2): 187–206.

Gabriel, S.A. and Rosenthal, S.S. (1996). Commutes, Neighborhood Effects, and Earnings: An Analysis of Racial Discrimination and Compensating Differentials. *Journal of Urban Economics* 40: 61–83.

Galster, G. (1990). Racial Discrimination in Housing Markets During the 1980s: A Review of the Audit Evidence. *Journal of Planning Education and Research* 9(3): 165–175.

Harrison, M., Law, I. and Phillips, D. (2005). *Migrants, Minorities and Housing: Exclusion, Discrimination and Anti-Discrimination in 15 Member States of the European Union*. European Monitoring Centre on Racism and Xenophobia.

Human Rights and Equal Opportunity Commission. (1991). *Racist Violence, Report of the National Inquiry into Racist Violence in Australia*. Canberra: Australian Government Publishing Service.

—— (1999). *New Country, New Stories: Discrimination and Disadvantage Experienced by People in Small and Emerging Communities*. Canberra: Race Discrimination Commissioner.

Hunter, W.C. and Walker, M.B. (1996). The Cultural Affinity Hypothesis and Mortgage Lending Decisions. *Journal of Real Estate Finance and Economics* 13(1): 57–70.

Massey, D.S. and Denton, N.A. (1993). *American Apartheid: Segregation and the Making of the Underclass*. Harvard University Press.

Mujcic, R. and Frijters, P. (2013). *Still Not Allowed on the Bus: It Matters If You're Black or White!* Bonn: The Institute for the Study of Labour (IZA). DP No. 7300.

Murdie, R.A. and Teixeira, C. (2003). Towards a Comfortable Neighbourhood and Appropriate Housing: Immigrant Experiences in Toronto. In P. Anisef and M. Lanphier (eds), *The World in a City*. Toronto: University of Toronto Press, 132–191.

Myers, C.K. (2004). Discrimination and Neighborhood Effects: Understanding Racial Differentials in US Housing Prices. *Journal of Urban Economics* 56(2): 279–302.

Paradies, Y. (2006). A Systematic Review of Empirical Research on Self-Reported Racism and Health. *International Journal of Epidemiology* 35(4): 888–901.

Pascoe, E.A. and Smart Richman, L. (2009). Perceived Discrimination and Health: A Meta-analytic Review. *Psychological Bulletin* 135(4): 531–554

Polikoff, A. (2006). *Waiting for Gautreaux: A Story of Segregation, Housing, and the Black Ghetto*. Evanston: Northwestern University Press.

Short, P., Seelig, T., Warren, C., Susilawati, C. and Thompson, A. (2008). *Risk-Assessment Practices in the Private Rental Sector: Implications for Low-Income Renters*. Melbourne: Australian Housing and Urban Research Institute.

Turner, M.A., Struyk, R. and Yinger, J. (1991). Housing Discrimination Study Synthesis. Washington DC: US Department of Housing and Urban Development.

Turner, M.A., Ross, S., Galster, G. and Yinger, J. (2002). *Discrimination in Metropolitan Housing Markets: Phase 1*. Washington DC: US Department of Housing and Urban Development.

Turner, M.A., Santos, R., Levy, D.K., Wissoker, D., Aranda, C., Pitingolo, R. and The Urban Institute. (2012). *Housing Discrimination Against Racial and Ethnic Minorities 2012*. Washington DC: US Department of Housing and Urban Development.

Victorian Equal Opportunity and Human Rights Commission (2008). *Submission to Victorian Overseas Taskforce*. Melbourne: Victorian Equal Opportunity and Human Rights Commission.

—— (2012). *Locked Out: Discrimination in Victoria's Private Rental Market*. Melbourne: Victorian Equal Opportunity and Human Rights Commission.

Victorian Immigrant and Refugee Women's Coalition (2009). *A Survey Report on Female International Students*. Melbourne: Victorian Immigrant and Refugee Women's Coalition.

Wienk, R.E., Reid, C.E., Simonson, J.C. and Eggers, F.J. (1979). *Measuring Discrimination in American Housing Markets: The Housing Market Practices Survey*. Washington DC: US Department of Housing and Urban Development.

Williams, D. and Mohammed, S. (2009). Discrimination and Racial Disparities in Health: Evidence and needed Research. *Journal of Behavioral Medicine* 32(1): 20–47.

Yinger, J. (1998). Evidence on Discrimination in Consumer Markets. *The Journal of Economic Perspectives* 12(2): 23–40.

Chapter 4

Housing and Sustainability: Everyday Practices and Material Entanglements

Chantel Carr and Chris Gibson

Introduction

The home and the household is a key scale to interpret problems of climate change and environmental sustainability. An expanding research literature considers the home as a site of social organisation for pro-environmental behaviour (Reid et al. 2009; Lane and Gorman-Murray 2011; Tudor et al. 2011). Matters of housing are central. There are important questions of household size, lifestyle, comfort and cultural norms that plug into the bigger picture of resource use and carbon emissions (Shove 2003; Keilman 2003), as well as socio-technical considerations of home design, materials use and interactions with Big Infrastructure systems (Kaïka 2004; Horne and Hayles 2008). Australian researchers across planning, geography, design, architecture and cultural studies have been among a global vanguard advancing inter-disciplinary understanding of such issues (e.g. Hobson 2003; Allon and Sofoulis 2006; Crabtree 2006; Lane et al. 2008; Lane and Gorman-Murray 2011; Horne and Hayles 2008; Strengers and Maller 2012; Head et al. 2013), focused on housing, the household as social and material assemblage, and on homes as loci of complex socio-cultural dynamics.

Considerable technical developments have been forthcoming on passive design for minimising energy use, for rainwater capture and storage, retrofitting and construction materials recycling technologies, as well as new low-carbon and insulating materials for home construction, and photovoltaic cell technologies for home energy generation (Wright et al. 2009). Yet even with significant advancements in technology, we still know relatively little about the complexities of household life within the home or how families interact with materials and wider networks of infrastructure and economy (Head et al. 2013). What happens within the home are not small details that might prove useful after materials technology and 'big systems' have been improved, but rather the mundane, and yet utterly pervasive, everyday decisions, practices and behaviours that pattern human life. The infinitesimal details that make up home life matter enormously: they are the cellular activity fuelling climate change; they are the lifestyles, relationships and emotions that most people care and worry about.

And yet, research funding and resources for social science research on sustainability within the home has paled in comparison with that directed towards the 'hard' sciences, materials and engineering disciplines. It has been estimated, for instance, that for every dollar spent on social sciences and humanities research into energy use, 35 are spent on infrastructural and supply systems (Sovacool 2014). But without truly understanding what people think and do within their homes (and how these things might change) much of that investment may prove fruitless – especially if, as ethnographic research has shown (Moy 2012), householders regularly transgress rules and confound practices expected of them by governments, finding ways to repurpose materials and 'get around' regulations as a matter of course.

Compounding this, understanding the contributions households make to greenhouse gas emissions in the affluent world is a slippery undertaking. In Australia, gross statistical calculations are subject to a varying range of assumptions about responsibility. Figures are relatively low (13%) if only direct energy use within the household is included, but rise to 56 per cent if the embedded energy of goods and services consumed in the household is included (Head et al. 2013). While such variations indicate issues of clarity around data measurement and scale, they also signal a need to better understand how social and ecological relations are configured within households.

In developing environmental policy that targets the scale of the home, a critical question is how to better account for the diverse and shifting ways in which people interact with each other and engage with the material world of the home, as they move through the ebb and flow of everyday life. This chapter surveys Australian contributions towards answering this question. The home space is a co-production, where sustained material, emotional and embodied work between inhabitants, technologies, materials and practices go into home-making (Jacobs 2003) – all with implications for resource use and environmental sustainability. We seek to break down categorical distinctions between houses as the physical structures of accommodation, and homes as the lived cultural spaces of dwelling. As Jacobs and Smith (2008: 518) point out, 'to talk only of housing is insufficient to understand the complexity of what home is, both emotionally and materially'.

Understanding housing in this broader sense – as a socio-technical achievement – assists in decoding much of the complexity surrounding household sustainability. To this end, our chapter is structured in four parts. First, we consider the policy context for environmental sustainability and housing, and chart moves away from a behaviour change model premised on universal price mechanisms, regulation and information and marketing campaigns towards a recognition of the complexity of household practices. Second, we draw on conceptual and empirical work (much of it Australian) that recommends moving beyond assumptions of households as mere passive consumers to recognise home spaces as productive and contested sites of sustainability actions. Third, we discuss the socio-demographic diversity and complexity of households, focusing especially on lifecourse transitions and how this influences resource use. Finally, we survey work on the material realm that pushes researchers to consider entanglements between humans and a range of nonhuman actors in and around the home. Households encompass more than just housing, and are instead socio-technical achievements within which physical materials, human and nonhuman actors jostle, in ways that shape sustainability outcomes.

Policy Context: From Behaviour Change to Sustainability Dilemmas

In Australia, the home and households have become important sites of policy intervention aimed at reducing environmental burdens. Technological programs have included significant subsidy campaigns around items such as water tanks, insulation and solar panels. Macroeconomic approaches have seen attempts – frequently highly politicised – to tax carbon pollution or to introduce price triggers for reducing consumption. Social programs encouraging changes in behaviour such as composting or recycling, or initiatives promoting public transport and growing food have also become more common.

Nevertheless, such efforts towards transforming everyday practices have been met with varying degrees of success. Despite a growing enthusiasm within households for contributing to broad sustainability goals, such policies have not always solicited the intended outcomes. Smart meters do not challenge practices that householders consider non-negotiable (Strengers 2011). Water tanks do not save as much water as predicted (Moy 2012). Education programs emphasising that 'it's easy being green' understate the amount of domestic labour involved, and sidestep the question of who does the work (Organo et al. 2012). Residential energy consumption continues to rise, due to a combination of bigger homes containing more appliances and computer equipment, a growing population and a declining number of people per household (Australian Bureau of Statistics 2011). Often, the inherent complexity of the household – and the ways households make decisions to incorporate new technologies, routines and practices – is smoothed over by the top-down process of delivering solutions to perceived issues of consumption. Ironically, one effect is that often these policies serve to maintain – and even reinforce – existing levels of consumption (Moy 2012). The more sustainability becomes mainstreamed, the less it signifies a genuine alternative to the high throughput model of resource extraction and consumption, and the more it shares with consumerism, as products become coded as the 'right' green choices.

The landscape for sustainability policy for housing has accordingly become much less straightforward in recent years. An initial focus on behaviour change, centred around use of social marketing campaigns to educate, raise awareness and trigger alterations in personal actions (*a la* road speeding or quitting cigarette smoking), has proven everywhere to be ineffective in the absence of significant systemic change (Moloney et al. 2009). The result has been the emergence of a significant 'value-action gap' whereby levels of awareness of the importance of climate change and what constitutes more sustainable actions are high, without accompanying shifts in everyday practice or reductions in carbon emissions (Kollmuss and Agyeman 2002). The 'distinction between knowing and doing' (Davidson 2012: 14) persists: we know that climate change requires substantial action, but we continue to do unsustainable things.

Moreover, one-dimensional policy constructs simply do not match with the complexities, contrasts and contradictions of households. People are stubbornly fixated on some things – such as what it means to be 'clean' (Shove 2003; Waitt 2014), the need for automobility (Dowling 2000; Harada 2014), and for privacy within household spaces when watching television (Klocker et al. 2012) or urinating or defecating (Gibson et al. 2013) – and yet are not necessarily so stubborn others, such as water frugality (Head and Muir 2007) or heating and cooling practices (de Vet 2013). Households are not uniform or passive, and are unlikely to 'play ball' when governments or corporations might wish them to.

Nor are households homogenous, socially or geographically. The family with children, the student shared household, the extended family or the retired couple will all experience and respond to climate change and sustainability policies differently, as will home-owners, private and public renters, and unit and house dwellers. Patterns of resource use, sharing and frugality are refracted through underlying demographic and socio-economic variables such as age, family composition and income (Liu et al. 2003; Klocker et al. 2012). In our quantitative research on household practices in Wollongong (Gibson et al. 2013), the wealthiest households were twice as likely to install solar power (although still in very small numbers) as the poorest, but were also the most prevalent users of air-conditioning. The poorest households were most likely to say that they were 'uninterested' in climate change as an issue, but they were also the least likely to own LCD or plasma screen televisions or clothes dryers. The poorest households, often retirees, were also the most likely to repair clothing, to use toilet paper made from recycled paper; to buy 'environmentally-friendly' detergents; to reuse glass bottles and jars; and to save water by taking shorter showers. Those with higher levels of educational qualifications were equally likely to use air-conditioning habitually during summer, as were those with basic high school education. Baby boomers were the least likely to be sceptical about climate change, but the most likely to fly five times or more annually. Such contradictions repeated themselves across a myriad of other forms of consumption within households, and the introduction of sustainability social marketing campaigns and price measures to reduce consumption has done little to resolve them.

There are contradictions in household sustainability policy too. Much government policy has been directed towards low-income families (for instance, the Federal Government's Low Income Energy Efficiency Program, which provided funds to retrofit low-income homes), upon the noble premise that marshalling resources to reduce water and energy costs with that socio-economic stratum will deliver a much-needed social justice outcome. And yet, quantitative and ethnographic research by social scientists has shown that low-income households are already doing most of the 'work' of being sustainable (Waitt et al. 2012), with already lower overall carbon and energy footprints (an outcome of having to be frugal just to make ends meet). Those households who ought to reduce their environmental burden most urgently – middle class and wealthy households – have by and large evaded academic scrutiny or targeted government policy initiatives.

Nevertheless, the policy landscape is itself shifting in ways that provide glimmers of hope. Government agencies are showing belated, but growing interest in what cultural researchers have to say about everyday practices within homes, acknowledging more of the messiness, dilemmas and contradictions. The National Water Commission, for instance, commissioned cultural studies academic Zoe Sofoulis (2011) to produce a report on linking engineering and science approaches to understanding water provision and consumption with humanities and social science researchers who specialise in analysing everyday cultural interactions with water. Ralph Horne has developed similar ties around energy and residential home renovations in Victoria, and in NSW the Office of Environment and Heritage has through its sustainable households and communities division co-funded projects and entered into partnership agreements with cultural researchers at the University of Wollongong to link sustainability initiatives to an ethnographic evidence base. The challenge will be to evolve a 'second phase' of household sustainability policy making in coming years, beyond sustainable technologies and education campaigns, and focused on local community capacities and more sophisticated understandings of social and cultural life.

Beyond Consumption: The Home as a Productive Space

Where housing policy and sustainability issues have intersected, there has tended to be an overarching focus on consumption, particularly in official and corporate programs that have sought to change household behaviour on environmental grounds. For Slocum (2004) climate change programs operate within the neoliberal state, assuming citizens are mere passive 'consumers'. Sustainability however relies on the notion of the 'responsible, carbon-calculating individual' (Dowling 2010: 492), constructed in climate change campaigns as the new ideal citizen-consumer (Rutland and Aylett 2008). Promotion campaigns risk treating people merely as consumers rather than citizens or active subjects negotiating everyday lives.

The assumption is that many households are, through their consumption, 'doing the wrong thing' vis-à-vis sustainability. Homes and households are *problematised* as sites of excessive consumption, urban sprawl, and overuse of energy and water – exemplified in the typecasting of large new-build homes as unsustainable 'McMansions' (Nasar et al. 2007; Dowling and Power 2012). Ideal sustainable citizens in contrast transform themselves in response to the problematisation of being an excessive consumer – weaning themselves off resource intensive lifestyles. Smuggled into this narrative is however a subtle shift that sees consumption, rather than production, as the problem, and that places the burden of responsibility for change onto householders, rather than onto governments or corporations.

Campaigns framed around everyday technologies such as recycling bins, energy-saving lightbulbs and shower timers trigger discussions of environmental ethics within households. In turn they 'produce' sustainable citizens who buy the 'right' things and install new green technologies around the home, reduce car dependency, lower heating thermostats or raise air-conditioning settings (Hobson 2006). Such concerted policy efforts have codified and normalised certain 'acceptable' types of actions required to become a 'good environmental citizen' at the expense of other practices, that perhaps require more skill and time' (Maller and Horne 2011: 66; see also Hobson 2006). Moreover, as Davidson (2010) argues, this keeps intact the institutions of capitalist democracy – markets, corporations, governments – and emphasises that households must govern their own actions in order to become 'proper' sustainable citizens.

How households react to governmental imperatives within the spaces of the home is, nevertheless, unpredictable. As Scerri's (2011: 175) survey work with households in Melbourne demonstrates, 'householders are rejecting official claims that 'rational' sustainable consumption choices and self-regulatory approaches will achieve the kinds of changes that sustainable development necessitates'. Humans are social beings acting in the contexts of communities and landscapes, not atomised individuals driven solely by rational economic or environmental preferences (Hobson 2002; 2003). Household sustainability is more than an amalgam of individuals' 'energy-minimising' actions (Gibson et al. 2011), and environmental gains may be forthcoming inadvertently as a result of other changing priorities (Hitchings et al. 2013). Environment is just one line of responsibility being juggled in acts of consumption, which necessarily serve different anticipated needs.

Moreover, policy focus on consumption alone frequently falls victim to a placeless character that neglects that sustainability is as much an integrated *urban* problem as a national one (Bulkeley and Betsill 2005), encompassing infrastructure provision, industry, and regional cultural inheritances. Geographical context and social and cultural meanings vary, thus altering the entire landscape of what sustainability might mean for households. We, for instance, work within a team across a number of interrelated projects on households, sustainability and cultural practices in Wollongong, 80 kilometres to the south of Sydney. Here, understanding and acting on the imperative to be sustainable is refracted through a number of contingencies. Wollongong's industrial heritage (steel, coal) means that it has been 'carbon central'. That these industries are still active means that a substantial proportion of the city's population are employed in industries that may be affected by future legislative attempts to reduce national carbon emissions. Additionally, within households in Wollongong individuals are also producers of carbon emissions in an industrial sense (Gibson et al. 2011). Legacies of coal and steel dwell in the present. Employed in coalmines, steelworks and associated industries, people are implicated as producers of greenhouse gas emissions, with all the dependencies, commitments and outlooks that this entails.

At the same time, the household is a key productive space within which improvements in sustainability are being made. In households where frugality is a necessity rather than choice, creativity and adaptability is needed to make ends meet (Waitt et al. 2012). Families find ways to achieve quality of life without the stockpiling of material things, without air-conditioners or SUVs. From clothes to televisions, furniture to Christmas presents, people continue to privilege the usefulness of things (Klocker et al. 2012; Farbotko and Head 2013). They keep, store and gift because usefulness still resonates as a core human value. This is an enormous potential source of traction. There are those who grew their own food or mended clothes during periods of wartime rations – a reminder that there are effective systems of provision beyond the industrial capitalist system and individuals with stocks of knowledge not yet lost. Migrant families bring with them other ways of knowing how to provision energy, food and water (Strengers and Maller 2012), and how to relate to nonhuman nature (Klocker and Head 2013). Knowledge of microclimates, materials and the spatiality and rhythms of home-spaces, accumulated over time (de Vet 2013), illustrate that households are more than mere spaces for passive consumption of resources, but rather a key productive site in which human capacities to respond to the challenge of reducing resource intensity develop and unfurl.

Lifecourse Transitions

If homes are to be considered as socially diverse, productive spaces, what kinds of complexities matter most for sustainability? One vector consistently identified in empirical research is generational difference (Klocker et al. 2012; Menz and Welsch 2012; Strengers and Maller 2012; Hitchings et al. 2013). Opportunities for gaining traction on sustainability issues emerge as households encounter transition points in lifecourse. Having a baby, expanding the nuclear unit to accommodate extended family, accommodating the privacy demands of teenagers and young adult children, migrating, losing a job, retirement and divorce are all examples of transitions or events that precipitate a disruption to existing practices and routines. Such moments open up a space for new decisions and behaviours to develop, that in turn impact on housing needs, home-making, and household sustainability. What happens when familial, economic or material circumstances change? Policies designed to address issues of household sustainability needs to attend to the changing spatial, social and material needs of generational cohorts, and of households as they undergo demographic shifts.

Households are, fundamentally, social assemblages with demographic qualities including the formation of family units and their attendant dynamics (Klocker et al. 2012), as well as the many axes of social identity and inequality, such as gender, age and class (Organo et al. 2012; Waitt et al. 2012). Different ways households are constructed and how these constructs change over time – through major, life-changing events – affect both the physical home and interactions within it, with environmental sustainability implications. People moving in and out require different levels of connection or privacy, alter internal home designs and patterns of resource use, and bring different information across the border of the household as their outside connections (with schools, workplaces, community organisations) change. Shifts in resource use may emerge out of lifecourse transitions less as a result of environmental motivations, but through the desire to keep families harmonious or safe (Dowling 2000; Farbotko and Head 2013), or to care for elderly parents, or poor or recently divorced siblings and relatives (Klocker et al. 2012). In our quantitative survey work (see Waitt et al. 2012 for details of method and sampling), where households recorded a change in energy use in the previous 12 months, among the more common reasons cited were 'changing household dynamics/patterns', 'changing numbers of people in the household' and 'having a baby', while climate change and environmental concern barely rated a mention.

Retirement is an especially decisive lifecourse transition with implications for sustainability as people change their work, consumption and often, residential circumstances. Consumption expenditure has been shown to decrease substantially on retirement, even when that transition has been well-planned financially (Lundberg et al. 2003; Davies and James 2011). Current retirees who were born between the two world wars and retired at the end of the 20th century – known in popular culture as the 'Silent Generation' – often have a strong heritage of living frugally, and provide a benchmark of 'making do'. In this cohort we see the ways age and low socioeconomic status interact to shape practices of frugality and thrift. In our quantitative survey work (see Waitt et al. 2012), retirees/pensioners were more likely than other employment status groups to 'always': save water in the bathroom by taking short showers; buy environmentally-friendly detergents whenever possible; switch off lights in unoccupied rooms; buy products with as little packaging as possible; use their own bag when shopping rather than one provided; and compost kitchen and garden waste. They were most likely (along with the unemployed) to 'always' repair clothing and to have a water-saving device fitted to their shower. Those born after World War II – the 'Baby-Boomer' generation, now coming into retirement – have by contrast grown up in more affluent circumstances. They are also living longer, with expectations of an active retirement. It is unclear whether they will inherit frugal practices in retirement as with the Silent Generation before them.

Meanwhile, urban morphology is encountered at different stages of life, with house size and material construction important considerations. Households who can afford it may want to increase their house size at retirement, or improve it in other ways, because they will spend more time there (Gobillon and Wolf 2011). In other contexts elderly people move in with extended family members, such as adult children and their families. Increasing household size is one way to reduce the high overall ecological footprints associated with low numbers of people per dwelling (Keilman 2003). Nevertheless, as Klocker et al. (2012) demonstrate, such living arrangements require complex negotiations. They describe a phenomenon of *living together but apart*, in which the different generations create and maintain their own spaces – kitchens and bathrooms in particular – to maintain independence and privacy (see also Chapter Two). Decisions are not made in a straightforward way but are rather 'informed by competing desires to care for and support relatives, to maintain a sense of nuclear family, and an individualist predilection for privacy and space' (Klocker et al. 2012: 17). Such negotiations of domestic space across and between generations are made more complex again beyond the boundaries of the home, as different modes of governance become more or less important during life stage transitions. Ownership and agency to make material changes are not evenly distributed at lifecourse stage, or within generational cohorts, and a predominantly private rental system in Australia all but precludes incorporation of sustainable technologies (Gabriel and Watson 2010). Housing needs, alterations and sustainability practices combine with financialisation and processes of buying property at different life stages.

Material Entanglements: Towards a Relational Approach

While generational difference constitutes a key social variable influencing household sustainability, there are other complexities that emerge from the manner in which humans interact with other living things and inorganic materials within and surrounding home spaces. The household, as a social-geographical scale, is entangled relationally with other nonhuman actors within domestic space, and at 'larger' geographical scales. Relationality challenges the idea that we can 'identify discrete scales from which causes originate and at which effects are felt' (McGuirk 1997: 482). Thinking of households as discrete entities forces 'processes, outcomes, and responses ... into distinct "boxes"' (McGuirk 1997: 482). In contrast, relational thinking encourages analysis a variety of actors, big and small, human and non-human, intertwined in patterns of power relationships (Bennett 2010). Multiple materialities and networks make up the family home (Kaika 2004; Blunt 2005; Head and Muir 2007).

This sort of thinking alters where one might go looking for the root causes of problems, and how one might subsequently trace actions and responses. For instance, are gatekeepers – educators, newspaper editors, carbon offset retailers, energy-saving websites, solar hot water installers, electrical switches – as important as individual household actors? Gatekeepers mediate relationships and flows between scales and things. Arguably, institutional problems with gatekeepers along production and consumption chains have been more important than a lack of uptake of sustainability technologies within homes. According to Crabtree and Hes (2009: 203), these include 'the disaggregation and piecemeal nature of innovation within the building industry ... unfamiliarity with new technologies, a lack of consistent legislation and pricing and unclear channels of communication'. The relationships between scale and order, or scale and causation, should not be assumed but be the subject of empirical enquiry.

What exactly constitutes a 'household' is increasingly contested, as demographic and physical definitions (based on family units and/or buildings) are supplanted by notions of the household as networks of connections that mediate relations with other publics, with industries, with nature, with flows of materials and resources, and with outside institutions (Reid et al. 2010: 318; see also Kaika 2004; Power 2005). The black box is revealed to contain humans and diverse nonhumans, its own cohabiting things, complex politics and practices. The challenge is, to quote Ruth Lane and Andrew Gorman-Murray (2011: 2), 'to consider the operations of the household in terms of interactions between different animate and inanimate entities'. Homes are containers for appliances, pets, stuff – none of which we should take for granted as inanimate or powerless, or as disconnected from wider movements and flows (Power 2012). The black box is porous. Home spaces and the people and things that live in them are inextricably linked into the social, technological, ecological and regulatory networks that make up suburbs, cities, regions and nations. Granularity is therefore needed to disentangle the complex assemblage that is the household.

Moreover, viewing the material things around the home as inert, or the nonhuman living things in our homes and gardens as inconsequential, merely 'feeds human hubris and our earth-destroying fantasies of conquest and consumption' (Bennett 2010: ix). The assumption of intrinsically inanimate matter 'may be one of the impediments to the emergence of more ecological and more materially sustainable modes of production and consumption' (Bennett 2010: ix). The social and symbolic place we call home is enmeshed within a scaffold of materials: bricks, concrete, timber and steel, grass, glass and plaster. The sheer physicality of these materials – their weight, bulk or fixing – can often imply stability, in the context of the cultural ideals, social relations and everyday practices with which they intersect (Blunt and Dowling 2006). And yet, materials contribute to both the acquisition and performance of environmental knowledge. Specifically, materials influence how we 'learn' our immediate environmental context, and how we operate our houses accordingly (Hitchings and Lee 2008). Gathering knowledge about the performance of materials leads to changes in the ways homes are occupied spatially and temporally. As people grow to inhabit their homes, they become intimately aware of the ways particular materials perform in, and mediate, different weather conditions. This knowledge is somewhat analogous with the training in contextual assessment acquired by architects, and is, we argue, critical to managing the microclimate of the house passively, without resorting to mechanical means of heating and cooling.

Nevertheless, households committed to the concepts of environmental sustainability face challenges in reducing their resource consumption during home renovations (Maller et al. 2012). Altering dwelling fabric through renovation opens up possibilities for social and material change within households in which tangible environmental change can be realised, but these possibilities for change jostle with imperfect information and limited availability of low-impact or recycled materials (Crabtree and Hes 2009), the performance of 'homeyness' (Dowling and Power 2011), and the power of the domestic imaginary (Pink 2004). Actual improvements in energy and water use have, even in purportedly 'green' renovations, proven to be ineffective because they 'intersect with aspirations of the ideal home and the accommodation of existing and future daily routines' (Maller et al. 2012: 255). Watson and Shove (2008) have similarly considered interventions to the fabric of the home, examining the way materials, tools and competence come together in undertaking DIY renovations, in the process noting that renovation and customisation of the home has become normalised and legitimate as both work and leisure.

It is important not to assume that households in the affluent West are powerless, or to underestimate trust and power sharing issues, in favour of physical design considerations (Crabtree 2006). The issue is how power is exercised in relationships between actors. Some of these actors include the state, infrastructure providers and planners; while in other directions relationships exist with appliances (and their manufacturers), retailers, corporations, communities – with even water and energy itself. Households have capacities and can generate traction along diverse pathways – sometimes informal and unheralded. Some such pathways are gradual, opening possibilities for change where immediate overhaul is unlikely, such as with norms of toileting (Gibson et al. 2013) or Christmas (Farbotko and Head 2013). Other pathways depend on capacities to adapt quickly – as with responses to financial hardship (such as finding cheap ways to heat bodies in winter without need for electric heaters – Collier 2012). In certain circumstances resisting change can be productive – as when ignoring fashion cycles in clothes or furniture or not turning on the air-conditioner. In this understanding, the 'local' – which can include the household – does not just feed into pre-existing scales of something bigger in accumulative fashion, but rather can itself be a generative site of creative possibilities.

Conclusions

As the hub of domestic consumption, households are increasingly encouraged to consider and reduce their greenhouse gas emissions. Yet as Maller and Horne (2011) point out, the maintenance, operation and lived experience of housing remains somewhat uncharted territory in policy settings. As we have sought to show here, the home and household as a site of material cultural relations is far more complex than policy sound bites about the 'green home' might suggest. The burdens and the productive possibilities associated with such reductions are unevenly distributed spatially into future times and places. Any changes that a household makes are limited unless connected to larger scale movements. Furthermore, as Hinchliffe (1997) argued, homes are understood as a refuge or haven from the problems of the world, confounding its potential role as a site of climate change mitigation via changes in household practices. Boundless consumption remains ever possible for the wealthy, inviting the ready exercise of scepticism by the less well off. Options to consume remain largely open – freedom and choice are themselves barriers of sorts.

Nevertheless, ethnographic research has shown that households are simply not mere passive consumers caught up in excessive lifestyles, but rather dynamic social units negotiating competing demands within the constraints of daily rhythms and needs (Lane and Gorman-Murray 2011; Klocker et al. 2012; Maller et al. 2012). Households will argue within themselves over the best courses of action, over clothes wash temperatures, how to keep warm in winter, and what stuff to keep or to throw out. Households are homes in which social relations are the core human concern (Blunt and Downling 2006); in which families bond, people invest emotions and undertake all kinds of identity work beyond the putatively 'environmental'.

Across Australian ethnographic studies, households have been shown to have developed more constructive and reflective modes of interaction and stewardship – clothes swapping, handing down furniture, reviving dormant water and energy harvesting methods from memories of rural and migrant childhoods, repurposing materials, opening windows to catch the late afternoon breeze, putting up with the smell of family urine so that toilets were flushed less often (Lane et al. 2008; Strengers and Maller 2012; Gibson et al. 2013). Everyday understandings of home materials are more sophisticated than might be assumed, and interactions with them are a part of daily life, through the occupation and operation of the home. Material interactions and decisions are being negotiated on a daily basis within the existing fabric of the home. Nevertheless, gains made in some areas are contradicted by losses in others, and levels of consumption can ratchet up for reasons that have nothing to do with lack of environmental commitment within households.

Such complexities are important, for a number of reasons. First, they illustrate the intertwining of different kinds of demographic, socio-economic and material entanglements across forms of consumption, household types and income groups. Reductions in resource use and intensity are being made within Australian households, but not in a predictable fashion that correlates with singular socio-economic variables. Rather, improvements are held in tension, are traded-off against other imperatives, and are constrained and contradicted by other circumstances and tendencies. If housing policy is to adjust in light of the imperatives of climate change mitigation and adaptation, it will need to take such entanglements much more seriously. Second, there is much more to sustainable housing than considerations of design, new technologies and materials. Advances in low-impact construction must be matched by more funding for documenting and analysing the everyday social and cultural practices within households that are the key determinants of resource use. Third, such complexity confounds assumptions that concern over climate change or sustainability itself drives altered practices, as well as challenging the presumption that cost is the single and most significant universal factor influencing household consumption. While price triggers for reducing consumption underpin such whole-of-economy initiatives as carbon taxes and trading schemes, cultural research within the home illustrates how everyday practices, social assemblages, governance, power, materiality and wider systems of provision influence environmental outcomes.

References

Allon, F. and Soufoulis, Z. 2006. Everyday water: Cultures in transition. *Australian Geographer* 37(1): 45–55.

Australian Bureau of Statistics 2011. *Environmental Issues: Energy Use and Conservation: March 2011*. Canberra: Australian Bureau of Statistics.

Bennett, J. 2010. *Vibrant Matter: A Political Ecology of Things.* Durham, NC: Duke University Press.

Blunt, A. 2005. Cultural geography: Cultural geographies of home. *Progress in Human Geography* 29: 505–515.

Blunt, A. and Dowling, R. 2006. *Home.* London: Routledge.

Bulkeley, H. and Betsill, M. 2005. Rethinking sustainable cities: Multilevel governance and the 'urban' politics of climate change. *Environmental Politics* 14(1), 42–63.

Collier, K. 2012. Hot-water bottles are a must in cold times. *Daily Telegraph*, 16 August 2012.

Crabtree, L. 2006. Sustainability begins at home? An ecological exploration of sub/urban Australian community-focused housing initiatives. *Geoforum* 37(4): 519–535.

Crabtree, L. and Hes, D. 2009. Sustainability uptake in housing in metropolitan Australia: An institutional problem, not a technological one. *Housing Studies* 24(2): 203–224.

Davidson, M. 2012. Sustainable city as fantasy. *Human Geography* 5(2): 14–25.

Davies, A. and James, A. 2011. Environmental implications of an aging population, in *Geographies of Ageing: Social Processes and the Spatial Unevenness of Population Ageing*, edited by A. Davies and A. James. Farnham: Ashgate, 159–173.

de Vet, E. 2013. Exploring weather-related experiences and practices: Examining methodological approaches. *Area* 45(2): 198–206.

Dowling, R. 2000. Cultures of mothering and car use in suburban Sydney: A preliminary investigation. *Geoforum* 31: 345–353.

—— 2010. Geographies of identity: Climate change, governmentality and activism. *Progress in Human Geography* 34: 488–95.

Dowling, R. and Power, E. 2011. Beyond McMansions and green homes: Thinking household sustainability through materialities of homeyness, in R. Lane and A. Gorman-Murray (eds), *Material Geographies of Household Sustainability*, Farnham: Ashgate, 75–88.

Dowling, R. and Power, E. 2012. Sizing home, doing family in Sydney, Australia. *Housing Studies* 27(5): 605–619.

Farbotko, C. and Head, L. 2013. Gifts, sustainable consumption and giving up green anxieties at Christmas. *Geoforum* 50: 88–96.

Gabriel, M. and Watson, P. 2010. *The Environmental Sustainability of Australia's Private Rental Housing Stock*, AHURI, Online, (145) EJ ISSN 1445-3428 (2010).

Gibson, C., Farbotko, C., Gill, N., Head, L. and Waitt, G. 2013. *Household Sustainability: Challenges and Dilemmas in Everyday Life.* Cheltenham, UK: Edward Elgar.

Gibson, C., Head, L., Gill, N. and Waitt, G. 2011. Climate change and household dynamics: Beyond consumption, unbounding sustainability. *Transactions of the Institute of British Geographers* 36: 3–8.

Gobillon L. and Wolff, F-C. 2011. Housing and location choices of retiring households: Evidence from France. *Urban Studies* 48: 331–347.

Harada, T. 2014. Driving Cultures, PhD Thesis, University of Wollongong, http://ro.uow.edu.au/theses/4058/.

Head, L., Farbotko, C., Gibson, C., Gill, N., Waitt, G. 2013. Zones of friction, zones of traction: The connected household in climate change and sustainability policy. *Australasian Journal of Environmental Management* 20(4): 351–362.

Head, L. and Muir, P. 2007. Changing cultures of water in eastern Australian backyard gardens. *Social and Cultural Geography* 8: 889–906.

Hinchliffe, S. 1997. Locating risk: energy use, the 'ideal' home and the non-ideal world. *Transactions of the Institute of British Geographers* 22: 197–209.

Hitchings, R. and Lee, S.J. 2008. Air conditioning and the material culture of routine human encasement. *The Journal of Material Culture* 13: 251–265.

Hitchings, R., Collins, R. and Day, R. 2013. Inadvertent environmentalism and the action-value opportunity: Reflections from studies at both ends of the generational spectrum. *Local Environment*, DOI:10.1080/13549839.2013.852524

Hobson, K. 2002. Competing discourses of sustainable consumption: Does the 'rationalisation of lifestyles' make sense? *Environmental Politics* 11: 95–120.

—— 2003. Thinking habits into action: The role of knowledge and process in questioning household consumption practices. *Local Environment* 8: 95–112.

—— 2006. Bins, bulbs, and shower timers: On the 'techno-ethics' of sustainable living. *Ethics, Place and Environment* 9: 317–336.

Horne, R.E. and Hayles, C. 2008. Towards global benchmarking for sustainable homes: An international comparison of the energy performance of housing. *Journal of Housing and the Built Environment* 23: 119–130.

Jacobs, J. 2003. Editorial: Home rules. *Transactions of the Institute of British Geographers* 28: 259–63.

Jacobs, J. and Smith, S. 2008. Guest editorial: Living room: rematerializing home. *Environment and Planning A* 40: 515–19.

Kaïka, M. 2005. *City of Flows: Modernity, Nature and the City*. London: Routledge.

Keilman, N. 2003. The threat of small households. *Nature* 421: 489–490.

Klocker, N. and Head, L. 2013. Diversifying ethnicity in Australia's population and environment debates. *Australian Geographer* 44(1): 41–62.

Klocker, N., Gibson C. and Borger, E. 2012. Living together but apart: Material geographies of everyday sustainability in extended family households. *Environment and Planning A* 44: 2240–59.

Kollmuss, A. and Agyeman, J. 2002. Mind the Gap: Why do people act environmentally and what are the barriers to pro-environmental behaviour? *Environmental Education Research* 8(3): 239–260.

Lane, R. and Gorman-Murray, A. 2011. *Material Geographies of Household Sustainability*. Farnham: Ashgate.

Lane, R., Horne, R. and Bicknell, J. 2008. Routes of reuse of second hand goods in Melbourne households. *Australian Geographer* 40(2): 151–168.

Liu, J., Daily, G., Ehrlich, P. and Luck, G. 2003. Effects of household dynamics on resource consumption and biodiversity. *Nature* 421: 530–533.

Lundberg, S., Startz, R. and Stillman, S. 2003. The retirement-consumption puzzle: A marital bargaining approach. *Journal of Public Economics* 87: 1199–1218.

Maller, C. and Horne, R. 2011. Living lightly: How does climate change feature in residential home improvements and what are the implications for policy? *Urban Policy and Research* 29(1): 59–72.

Maller, C., Horne, R. and Dalton, T. 2012. Green renovations: Intersections of daily routines, housing aspirations and narratives of environmental sustainability. *Housing, Theory and Society* 29(3): 255–75.

McGuirk, P.M. 1997. Multiscaled interpretations of urban change: The federal, the state and the local in the Western Area Strategy of Adelaide. *Environment and Planning D* 15: 481–498.

Menz, T. and Welsch, H. 2012. Population aging and carbon emissions in OECD countries: Accounting for life-cycle and cohort effects. *Energy Economics* 34: 842–849.

Moloney, S., Horne, R.E. and Fien, J. 2009. Transitioning to low carbon communities – from behaviour change to systemic change: lessons from Australia. *Energy Policy*, doi:10.1016/j.enpol.2009.06.058.

Moy, C. 2012. Rainwater tank households: Water savers or water users? *Geographical Research* 50: 204–216.

Nasar, J.L., Evans-Cowley, J.S. and Mantero, V. 2007. McMansions: The extent and regulation of super-sized houses. *Journal of Urban Design* 12: 339–358.

Organo, V., Head, L. and Waitt, G. 2012. Who does the work in sustainable households? A time and gender analysis in New South Wales, Australia. *Gender, Place & Culture* 20(5): 559–77.

Pink, S. 2004. *Home Truths: Gender, Domestic Objects and Everyday Life*, Oxford: Berg.

Power, E. 2005. Human-nature relations in suburban gardens. *Australian Geographer* 36(1): 39–53.

—— 2012. Domestication and the dog: Embodying home. *Area* 44(3): 371–378.

Reid, L., Sutton, P. and Hunter, C. 2010. Theorizing the meso level: The household as a crucible of pro-environmental behaviour. *Progress in Human Geography* 34: 309–24.

Rutland, T. and Aylett, A. 2008. The work of policy: Actor networks, governmentality, and local action on climate change in Portland, Oregon. *Environment and Planning D* 26: 627–646.

Scerri, A. 2011. Rethinking responsibility? Household sustainability in the stakeholder society, in R. Lane and A. Gorman-Murray (eds), *Material Geographies of Household Sustainability*. Farnham: Ashgate.

Shove E. 2003. *Comfort, Cleanliness and Convenience: The Social Organization of Normality*. Oxford: Berg.

Slocum, R. 2004. Consumer citizens and the cities for climate protection campaign. *Environment and Planning A* 36: 763–782.

Sofoulis, Z. 2011. Cross-Connections: Linking Urban Water Managers with Humanities, Arts and Social Science Researchers. Waterlines Report Series, No. 60, National Water Commission, Canberra, http://archive.nwc.gov.au/__data/assets/pdf_file/0009/18396/60-Cross-connections.pdf.

Sovacool, B.K. 2014. Diversity: Energy studies need social science. *Nature* 511: 529–530.

Strengers, Y. 2011. Negotiating everyday life: The role of energy and water consumption feedback. *Journal of Consumer Culture* 11(19): 319–338.

Strengers, Y. and Maller, C. 2012. Materialising energy and water resources in everyday practices: Insights for securing supply systems. *Global Environmental Change* 22: 754–763.

Tudor, T., Robinson, G.M., Riley, M., Guilbert, S. and Barr, S.W. 2011. Challenges facing the sustainable consumption and waste management agendas: Perspectives on UK households. *Local Environment* 16: 51–66.

Waitt, G. 2014. Bodies that sweat: The affective responses of young women in Wollongong, New South Wales, Australia. *Gender, Place & Culture* 21(6): 666–682.

Waitt, G., Caputi, P., Gibson, C., Farbotko, C., Head, L., Gill, N. and Stanes, E. 2012. Sustainable household capability: Which households are doing the work of environmental sustainability? *Australian Geographer* 43: 51–74.

Watson, M. and Shove E. 2008. Product, competence, project and practice. *Journal of Consumer Culture*, 8, 69–89.

Wright, J., Osman, P. and Ashworth, P. 2009. *The CSIRO Home Energy Saving Handbook*. Sydney: Pan Macmillan.

Chapter 5
Indigenous Housing

Daphne Habibis

Introduction

Indigenous Australians share with the First Nations peoples of the United States of America and Canada the unenviable location at the bottom of their nation's distribution of economic goods. On many health and well-being indicators, the gap between Indigenous and non-Indigenous Australians is even wider than between their overseas counterparts with housing exclusion one of the factors implicated in this (Productivity Commission 2009). Compared with Euro-Australians,[1] few Indigenous Australians own their own home; there is a heavy reliance on social housing and a high proportion live in substandard housing (Flatau et al. 2004). Levels of homelessness are four times that of the non-Indigenous population and Indigenous households are ten times more likely to live in overcrowded conditions (Australian Institute of Health and Welfare (AIHW) 2011). This disadvantage is not just in remote areas but is severe across the settlement hierarchy in Australia (Council of Australian Governments (COAG) 2010: xiv).

The problems faced by Indigenous people in accessing and sustaining secure, safe and affordable housing arise from a mix of historical, structural and cultural factors. Colonisation shattered traditional Indigenous culture, separating Indigenous people from their land and livelihood. This was followed by decades as a 'protected' people when they were denied all citizenship rights and controlled by Euro-Australian missionaries and administrators. Even after they were granted formal citizenship in the mid-1960s many were subject to white control through the welfare and criminal justice systems, including high levels of incarceration and the removal of children. These experiences have left a legacy of welfare dependence, low income, poor health, family violence, mental illness, substance use, and limited participation with the formal economy.

The impact of these factors on the ability of Indigenous individuals and families to access and sustain safe and appropriate housing is exacerbated by the crisis in affordable housing. The high cost of home ownership means this is rarely an option, with less than 40 per cent of Indigenous adults being home owners (Australian Bureau of Statistics (ABS) 2011). Access to the private rental market is also difficult because of high rental costs and discrimination. Housing discrimination occurs in both the private housing market and in social housing (Chapter 3; Stracey 2003; Roberts et al. 2006). Indigenous people living in

---

1   The term 'Euro-Australian' is used to refer to all non-Aboriginal people in Australia in order to signal the cultural, social, political and economic dominance of Anglo-Celtic and European values in the nation.

rental accommodation are the most likely group to be complained about, most often for reasons of property appearance, bad behaviour or high numbers of people at the property. The effect is a high level of dependence on social housing. In major cities Indigenous people are seven times more likely to rely on public housing than Euro-Australians, rising to 85 per cent in remote communities (see Table 5.1) (ABS 2011). This reliance on social housing means that government housing policies are especially influential in shaping Indigenous housing outcomes.

Table 5.1   Household tenure type, persons aged 15 years and over

	Indigenous				Non-Indigenous
	Major Cities	Regional	Remote	Total	Total
Owners (%)	38.6	33.3	10.6	29.4	72.3
Renters					
Public housing	23.0	23.0	24.0	23.3	3.2
ICHO/Community	3.1	8.0	43.8	15.3	
Private (%)	33.8	33.9	17.4	29.8	23.0
Total renters (%)	60.1	65.0	85.4	68.5	26.1

Source: Adapted from The Health and Welfare of Australia's Aboriginal and Torres Strait Islander Peoples, Oct 2010 Australian Bureau of Statistics, Cat. No. 4704.0, 2011 http://www.abs.gov.au/AUSSTATS/abs@.nsf/lookup/4704.0Chapter855Oct+2010.

Addressing the poor housing of Indigenous people has been policy focus of successive Australian governments since 2007. Under the *Closing the Gap* strategy, housing is one of five areas identified as essential to improving Indigenous health and well-being. The aim is to substantially reduce homelessness, crowding and poor housing conditions by the end of the second decade of the 21st century. However although the investment in improving Indigenous housing is substantial, the interventions associated with *Closing the Gap* are controversial because they mainstream formerly specialised Indigenous housing and are associated with the decline of State owned and managed Aboriginal housing and Indigenous community housing (Habibis 2013; Milligan et al. 2010). They are also occurring at a time of increasing welfare conditionality in which welfare benefits are tied to demands that recipients conform to a range of behavioural requirements through punitive strategies including probationary leases, acceptable behaviour contracts and provisions to refer tenants to Centrelink for income management if they fall behind in rental payments (Habibis et al. 2013).

These developments are problematic for Aboriginal populations because of the context of cultural difference in which they take place. There is extensive evidence about the contribution of cultural fit to Aboriginal housing exclusion. State housing is based on the Western model of the nuclear family that is distinct from Aboriginal household formations, kinship obligations and uses of external and internal living spaces (Long et al.

2007; Memmott et al. 2003). Principles of kin-based mutual reciprocity can compete with the requirements of tenancy agreements especially in relation to the management of visitors (Memmott et al. 2011). This poor alignment between the conditions attached to tenancies and Aboriginal cultural contexts is implicated in high rates of tenancy turnover and eviction as a result of crowding, property damage, problems of good order and rent arrears. The literature shows that these problematic outcomes arise because Aboriginal identity and culture are not simply add-ons that can be adapted and adjusted at will, but are engrained in lifestyles, habits and social connections (Birdsall-Jones et al. 2010; Habibis 2011; Milligan et al. 2010). This shapes and constrains Aboriginal understandings of what is possible, socially desirable or appropriate in their engagements with social housing providers and helps to explain why Aboriginal tenants may resist efforts to enforce behavioural change when policies are not aligned with their own norms and values.

Policy directions for the normalisation of Indigenous housing and increasing demands for conformity to white values and standards of behaviour run counter to the arguments of recognition theory which suggest that in multicultural societies such as Australia, meaningful social inclusion requires some acknowledgement by the state of the aspirations of cultural minorities to maintain aspects of their different cultural inheritance (Honneth 1996). The significance of culture in shaping how people engage in housing systems is captured in Habermas' (1987) concept of the lifeworld. This refers to the lived realities of individuals that are derived from socially acquired shared cultural systems of meaning and everyday understanding including values and lifestyles. These shape and constrain an individual or group's understanding of what is possible, socially desirable or correct in their engagements with social housing providers. This chapter uses these ideas to argue that while it is important to narrow the gap in health and well-being between Indigenous and non-Indigenous Australians, if policies are implemented in a way that does not recognise and respect Indigenous values and aspirations, they risk falling short of achieving their goals.

This argument is developed in this chapter through an outline of recognition theory followed by an analysis of the structural and cultural factors that explain the vulnerability of Indigenous people to poor housing outcomes and homelessness. This is followed by an outline of changes in Indigenous housing policy which have seen a decrease in specialised Indigenous housing services and evidence that in some remote locations of the Northern Territory, South Australia and Western Australia these policies have been met with varying degrees of accommodation and resistance, including population movement associated with homelessness. The chapter concludes by arguing that housing can be a progressive force in addressing Indigenous housing need so long as governments develop flexible policies for service delivery and a range of housing models that are adjusted to Indigenous lifeworlds and the aspirations of Indigenous people for some control over their service delivery environment.

Recognition Theory

Recognition theory provides a helpful framework for analysing the intersection between housing services and Indigenous people because it is concerned with the struggles for cohabitation that arise between different cultural groups. Bauman (2001) has argued 'recognition wars' are one of the characteristics of contemporary modernity as globalisation pushes different groups into closer contact. Each group struggles to assert its right to existence in a politics of identity which lacks a yardstick for measuring cultural worth. Conflicts over values, beliefs and preferences, as well as demands for self-determination and the right to live differently, are central themes (Honneth 1996). Claims for the right to be different run parallel to claims to distributive justice where the demand is for a more equitable distribution of material goods as the foundation for full citizenship (Fraser 2000).

The premise of recognition theory is that recognition and respect are fundamental human needs and are critical in three separate spheres where they take different forms. Within the family recognition concerns love, within the legal sphere it concerns respect and in co-operative relationships it concerns esteem (Honneth 1996). Relationships involving recognition are fundamentally moral ones involving exchanges between agents often positioned in unequal power relations. They occur in interpersonal relationships and at the level of social organisations and institutions where they are structured by the legislative framework of the state (Honneth 1996). In settler colonial societies struggles for recognition take place in the context of the hegemonic power of whiteness in which white cultural norms, values and behaviours serve as the invisible standard against which all other cultures are judged (Frankenberg 1993).

These conflicts over the right to be different have an important interpersonal dimension. Taylor (1994) points out that when the state denies claims to cultural difference, the impact is personally felt. Since cultural difference is tied to a sense of personal and collective identity the denial of claims may be deeply wounding. Taylor (1994: 25) writes:

> Our identity is partly shaped by recognition or its absence, often by the *mis*recognition of others, and so a person or group of people can suffer real damage ... if the people or society mirror back to them a confining, demeaning or contemptible picture of themselves.

This moral-psychological dimension of misrecognition possesses 'a *normative* core' that may motivate social discontent and resistance (Honneth 2003: 129). Habermas' theory of communicative action suggests social integration results from the development of mutual understanding, so the legitimacy of a social order requires the achievement of positive feelings of 'individual and cultural self-worth' (Honneth 2003: 245). If feelings of mutual respect are lacking they may give rise to a sense of injustice and 'moral feelings of humiliation' (Honneth 2003: 247). The literature on the social protests of the 'lower classes' shows that, although not always articulated as breaching moral principles, they always involve violated 'notions of justice' (Honneth 2007: 71). This is in keeping with Altman's (2010: 266) observation that Indigenous people are 'experts in state evasion', an insight confirmed by the complex history of compliance and resistance which has characterized Indigenous engagement with public housing (Habibis et al. 2013; Morgan 2006).

This approach helps to explain the ambiguous engagement of Indigenous people with mainstream housing systems when these operate in ways that prevent Indigenous populations from retaining their own cultural values and practices. Milligan et al. (2011: 63) observe, 'public housing tends to operate as an undifferentiated, tightly controlled housing service that is not responsive to individual needs or cultural differences', making

Indigenous individuals and families vulnerable to tenancy failure. The next section provides a profile of Indigenous housing, and reviews growth in the mainstreaming of Indigenous housing through the lens of recognition theory.

Crowding, Population Mobility and Homelessness

Indigenous people in Australia comprise 3 per cent or 669,900 people of the nation's total population (ABS 2013). The largest number live in New South Wales, but the highest proportion of any state or territory are in the Northern Territory, where one third of the population is Aboriginal (see Table 5.2).

Table 5.2   Australia's estimated Aboriginal and Torres Strait Islander population by state and territory (at 30 June 2011)

	NSW	Qld	Vic	Tas	NT	WA	SA	ACT
Number	208,476	188,954	47,333	24,165	68,850	88,270	37,408	6,160
Proportion of jurisdiction ATSI population (%)	2.9	4.2	0.9	4.7	29.8	3.8	2.3	1.7

Source: Australian Bureau of Statistics, Estimates of Aboriginal and Torres Strait Islander Australians, June 2011, Cat No. 3238.0.55.001. Available at http://www.abs.gov.au/ausstats/abs@.nsf/mf/3238.0.55.001.

Contrary to public perceptions (Stolper and Hammond 2010), most Indigenous people live in urban areas, but while only 3 per cent of the Euro-Australian population live in remote and very remote areas, 21 per cent of the Indigenous population live there (ABS 2011) (see Table 5.3). Of these, many are resident in small, kin-based communities with populations of less than 100.

Table 5.3   Estimated Resident ATSI Population by Remoteness Areas, 2011

	Aboriginal and Torres Strait Islander %	Non-Indigenous%	Total%
Remoteness Areas			
Major City Areas	34.8	71.3	70.2
Inner Regional	22.0	18.3	18.4
Outer Regional	21.8	8.7	9.1
Remote	7.7	1.2	1.4
Very Remote	13.7	0.5	0.9

Source: Australian Bureau of Statistics, Estimates of Aboriginal and Torres Strait Islander Australians, June 2011, Cat No. 3238.0.55.001. Available at http://www.abs.gov.au/ausstats/abs@.nsf/mf/3238.0.55.001.

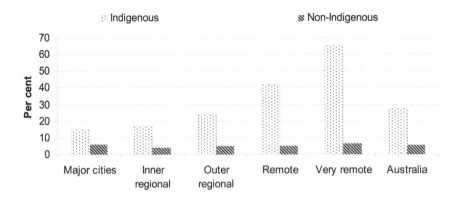

Figure 5.1 Proportion of people living in overcrowded housing, by remoteness area, 2006

Source: Productivity Commission 2009, *Overcoming Indigenous Disadvantage: Key Indicators 2009*, Australian Government, 9.8. Available at http://www.pc.gove.au/gsp/reports/indigenous/keyindicators2009.

Housing shortages, and differences in the way Indigenous people use household space, result in high levels of crowding, with rates almost five times that of Euro-Australian households. In remote locations, 50 per cent of houses are overcrowded, rising to 70 per cent in very remote areas (see Figure 5.1, Productivity Commission 2009). Crowding occurs when the level of household density is both involuntary and stressful to household members (Memmott et al. 2011) so it is important to distinguish between high levels of household density that are culturally sanctioned and those that arise from a lack of housing choice and cause homelessness, poor health, low school attendance, family and community violence and other behaviours that are detrimental to individual and community well-being (Productivity Commission 2009).

The shortage of affordable housing, and inadequate, inappropriate or poorly maintained housing is the most important cause of crowding, especially in remote locations. Large families and the value Indigenous people place on connection to kin are also contributing factors. Family relationships are embedded within a moral economy of cooperation and mutuality and give rise to a culture of reciprocity in which caring and supporting kin is a critical social obligation. Reciprocity is central to the kinship system and structures both private relationships and economic, social and political relations.

Indigenous relationships to place are also associated with high levels of residential mobility and this can lead to crowded households and the destabilisation of tenancies (Figure 5.1). Visits to kin are essential for social identity, the maintenance of important relationships and for social interaction. Short-term mobility is also associated with caring for country and historical attachments to particular locations as well as with the cultural expectations associated with particular demographic groups (Habibis 2013).

Seasonally related mobility is also a regular feature of many regions as a result of the wet season, cyclones and extremely hot weather, affecting parts of the Northern Territory, the Anangu Pitjantjatjara Yankunytjatjara Lands in South Australia, parts of central and southern Western Australia, including the Goldfields-Esperance region, inland areas of the Kimberley region, and far western regions of Queensland. These journeys often involve travel from inland areas to coastal ones, and coincide with school holidays.

Low income, discrimination and an absence of culturally appropriate and affordable short-term accommodation mean that for many Indigenous people accommodation options when travelling are likely to be limited and risky so population mobility is associated with homelessness. They can stay with relatives, or in public spaces with health, safety and criminalisation risks, or at one of the hostels operated under the Federal program, Aboriginal Hostels Limited. These are not always available, and may exclude some categories of people, for example, individuals on bail. Population mobility can also cause tenancy failure and homelessness because visitors may threaten the stability of households by leading to breaches in tenancy agreements through crowding, behaviours that result in neighbour complaints and through demand sharing that undermines household budgets and the capacity to maintain rental payments.

Australian Indigenous Housing Policy as a Recognition Field

In Australia, policies to address the poor housing outcomes of Indigenous people have shifted from an emphasis on self-determination through greater Indigenous control over housing policy and service delivery, to policies of mainstreaming in which there are fewer Indigenous specific services or programs run by Indigenous organisations. From the 1970s to the start of the 21st century, Indigenous housing services included a mix of public, semi-government, non-government and market providers with some provision for direct management and delivery of housing programs by Indigenous community organisations. Under the Community Housing and Infrastructure Program (CHIP) the Federal government provided funding to Indigenous community housing organisations (ICHOs) for provision of housing services to Indigenous communities via the Aboriginal and Torres Strait Islander Council (ATSIC). Indigenous specific funding was also provided to the States and Territories through the Aboriginal Rental Housing Program (ARHP) under the Commonwealth State Housing Agreement (CSHA). This resulted in a 'mishmash of roles and responsibilities resulting in multiple and often inconsistent policies and a plethora of programs that often functioned with little or no co-ordination within single jurisdictions or even local areas' (Milligan et al. 2010: 16). Under CHIP Indigenous people were supported to establish communities on their traditional lands and other locations where they had historical and cultural attachments. This homelands movement was accelerated from the mid-1970s following land rights legislation and changes to income support. The Community Development Employment Projects (CDEP) program provided paid community managed activities on Indigenous communities, enabling productive labour in locations distant from the mainstream economy.

In 2004 ATSIC was disbanded and responsibility for CHIP was transferred to the then Federal Department of Families and Housing, Community Services and Indigenous Affairs (FaHCSIA). A 2007 review of CHIP found the program was failing to provide adequate housing for Aboriginal people residing in remote communities and recommended its abolition and replacement with a remote Indigenous housing program managed by state housing authorities, with the aim of establishing housing management standards equivalent to those in public housing programs in comparable locations elsewhere (PWC 2007). In the ensuing years these recommendations were gradually implemented resulting in the gradual decline of the Indigenous community housing sector.

This process of mainstreaming Indigenous social housing was accelerated with the introduction of the Northern Territory Emergency Intervention (NTER) in 2007. The NTER was introduced in response to concerns about high levels of child abuse within remote Indigenous communities in the Northern Territory. The policies were controversial, not least because they were introduced without consultation with the affected communities and because most of the recommendations did not address the issue of child abuse. Although welcomed by some Indigenous leaders (Langton 2008; Price 2012), others saw the NTER as returning Indigenous Australia back to the days of assimilation (Dodson 2009; Coyne 2008:8).

The NTER combines a substantial investment by the Australian federal government into Northern Territory Aboriginal communities with a range of regulatory measures imposed on 73 prescribed areas of the Northern Territory designed to normalise and stabilise them. As well as restrictions on alcohol and pornography and welfare quarantining the delivery of housing to all Indigenous people in the Northern Territory, including those in remote communities, became the responsibility of the Territory government. By the end of 2008 this transfer of responsibility for housing became national policy through the National Partnership Agreements (NPAs) that followed the 2008 Council of Australian Governments. Today state housing authorities are responsible for Indigenous housing across all jurisdictions and in all locations (Habibis et al. 2014).

Under the NPAs the Australian government committed almost $5 billion over ten years for programs designed to improve housing infrastructure through a building and refurbishment program scheduled to deliver more than 4200 new houses and rebuilding or refurbishment of more than 4876 existing houses by the end of 2014 (COAG 2010). This program focuses mainly on remote Australia, especially the Northern Territory, Western Australia, Queensland and South Australia. The aim is to address issues of crowding, homelessness, poor housing conditions and severe housing shortages through the establishment of 'normalised service arrangements'. These are defined as service provision that is accountable and reflects 'a standard of service delivered to non-Indigenous people in communities of similar size and location'. Outputs include the 'resolution of land tenure on remote community-titled land in order to secure government and commercial investment, economic development opportunities and home ownership possibilities in economically sustainable communities' (COAG 2010: 4–5). Residents are expected to move to areas of employment, with performance indicators including the 'number of Indigenous people from remote communities housed in employment related accommodation in regional areas' (COAG 2010: 9). The Agreement makes no reference to the need for consultation with Indigenous populations or groups, nor is there any mention of principles of self-determination. State and Territory governments are also required to implement 'standardised tenancy management of all remote Indigenous housing that is consistent with public housing tenancy management' (COAG 2008: 29). This has therefore introduced a regulatory regime for Indigenous housing which is radically different from the way houses were formerly managed by ICHOs.

Mainstream models of social housing are predicated on an individualistic model of tenancy responsibility quite distinct from the ICHO arrangements which were located within the collective structure of kinship relations (Milligan et al. 2011). In remote settings, ICHOs are usually localised, kin-based, community organisations operating on a consensus basis. ICHOs are more responsive to individual circumstances, with assessment of housing claims involving a holistic accounting of need rather than the impersonal application of rules and regulations. Tenancy management decisions such as allocations, debt collection and housing maintenance are usually made through face-to-face consultations, often between individuals related by family or tribal ties with personal knowledge of tenants.

This is markedly different from the bureaucratic, hierarchical model of public housing applying centrally developed policies designed to ensure uniform treatment of tenants and with limited capacity for flexible implementation. As Milligan et al. (2011: 63) observe, 'public housing tends to operate as an undifferentiated, tightly controlled housing service that is not responsive to individual needs or cultural differences'. Decisions are often communicated impersonally by print or electronic media and personal contact limited, especially in remote settings.

Implicit within these policies is a construction of citizenship that includes a set of moral imperatives about the behaviour of 'the good citizen'. Because these values are predicated on white, European, liberal cultural values they sometimes sit uncomfortably and disproportionately alongside Indigenous cultural norms and behaviours exposing many Indigenous people to the regulatory and disciplining actions of the state. This white cultural knowledge frame is a barrier for many remote living Aboriginal people. Successive studies attest to language differences, and difficulties in meeting rental and home management obligations (SCATSIA 2001; Memmott 2004). For Aboriginal people kinship ties are a vital source of social capital with looking after family 'what we're all about'. (Indigenous informant cited in Birdsall-Jones et al. 2010: 52). Denying a relative's need for shelter, because it violates occupancy provisions, may come at the cost of valued social capital as relatives depend on one another for support in times of need.

The NPA reforms have accelerated the decline of the ICHO sector, due to the loss of dedicated national funding, especially in Queensland, Western Australia and the Northern Territory. If ICHOs wish to operate within the state housing system they must meet mainstream community housing funding, policy and regulatory conditions. There are many barriers to achieving this including their small size and limited financial and organisational capacity and complex legal and financial arrangements. Although there are some ICHOs that continue to provide housing, including a small number that have formed partnerships with state housing authorities, most IHCOs operating in remote locations have had little choice but to relinquish management of their housing to state housing authorities. In non-remote locations they are increasingly subject to mainstreaming. The exception is NSW where adapted policy, funding and regulation are in place (Milligan et al. 2010).

The shift towards mainstreaming has therefore been associated with concerns about whether the new arrangements are adequately adjusted to Indigenous cultural realities. According to Milligan et al. (2010: 49):

Appreciation of, and respect for ATSI identity and cultural values and understanding the implications of cultural norms and life styles for housing aspirations and the variety of needs and living patterns ... is the fundamental starting point for designing and delivering housing service responses.

Population Mobility, Recognition and Resistance

Recognition theory suggests that these radical changes to Indigenous housing delivery are likely to receive a mixed response from Indigenous peoples, and will include forms of resistance if they are imposed in ways that suggest disrespect or denial of important cultural values. One of the ways in which resistance can occur is through population mobility. Ethnographic analyses suggest that population mobility serves to resolve the tension between relatedness and autonomy that characterises some Indigenous communities. In her account of life in Yuendumu in the Northern Territory, Musharbash cites Kendon's observation of 'the continual need to maintain personal autonomy and equality in the face of generational hierarchy (Kendon 1988: 451 in Musharbash 2009: 146). Musharbash suggests departures from the family home operate as a culturally sanctioned way of resolving this conflict. Peterson similarly notes that 'adult men and women place great emphasis on their personal autonomy, rejecting attempts by others to control or direct them, often solving the problem by moving' (2004: 224). He argues constructions of 'the abrupt departures and absences of Indigenous workers from pastoral stations in the past' as 'the walkabout' are a mystification of Indigenous resistance to their employers' attempts to control them. Their mobility was a culturally rooted response to racism, establishing an arc of agency for a population subject to excessive social control (2004: 235).

This interpretation of population mobility helps to explain the population churn that followed the announcement of the NTER. In the months following this, media reports identified hot spots of population mobility with individuals and families moving from prescribed communities to town camps in cities including Alice Springs and Darwin to avoid the measures (Kearney 2007). Research by Holmes et al. (2007) and Taylor (2008) supported these accounts with respondents explaining that feelings of anxiety, discrimination and resistance were associated with the decision to move away. These accounts suggest population movement may result from 'horizons of experience' involving 'moral feelings of humiliation' associated with perceptions that 'legitimate expectations of recognition' have not been met (Honneth 2003: 246).

An analysis of population mobility in remote Indigenous communities undertaken in 2010 provides further evidence for this argument (Habibis et al. 2011). This study found that the National Partnerships were implicated in three forms of population mobility. One form was increased population stability. In Fitzroy Crossing, Nhulunbuy and Tenant Creek, many respondents spoke of their determination to remain on their lands and their refusal to move to larger communities. They saw remaining on country as fundamental to well-being and cultural survival partly because it was only in these locations that they were able to exercise traditional forms of authority over their family. A second form was involuntary mobility due to the defunding of small communities and housing shortages 'pushing' people from smaller communities into larger communities where the increase in population caused overcrowding and resulted in further departures. Tenants were also concerned at their capacity to conform to public housing tenancy requirements, especially higher rents, and feared this could lead to eviction. A third response was departure from the community. This was most prominent at Burringurrah where a cluster of factors, including the policy changes, had drastically diminished resident numbers. Between 1997 and 2003 the Western Australian Indigenous Community Environmental Health Needs Survey showed the usual population of Burringurrah was stable at around 150 usual residents. But in 2008, figures provided by the Burringurrah Management Committee showed that the population had dropped to 116 individuals (Habibis et al. 2011: 44). A field visit in July 2011 found the community almost deserted apart from service providers. The immediate cause of these departures was flooding in December 2010 and the closure of the community store but six months later residents had not returned. Respondents explained the declining population as due to changes to income support, employment and training programs, the construction of a police station and uncertainty as a result of financial insolvency in 2009.

These accounts suggest that population movement is working as a form of Indigenous agency in response to the way the state recognises and responds to Indigenous housing need. In one account, concerns that the state will withdraw support of housing infrastructure from some communities heightened population stability through a resolve to remain on communities even if people have to make their own shelter. In another, the closure of communities risks forced relocation and unstable housing arrangements. In a third account, increased state regulation and control is associated with departure from the community. All these forms of resistance carry with them a vulnerability to homelessness and inadequate forms of shelter that threaten efforts to improve Indigenous well-being.

Conclusion

This analysis highlights the risks associated with current trends towards mainstreaming and the white regulatory regimes that accompany this. An emphasis on recognition assumes that social cohesion and the achievement of policy goals requires some correspondence between the lifeworlds of citizens and the state's construction of the 'good citizen' and that achieving this requires careful negotiation, meaningful communication and the establishment of relationships of respect and trust. It suggests that the negotiation of rights and duties between citizens and the state involves relationships of exchange and reciprocity which must be recognised as legitimate by both sides of the dyad and that this is of crucial importance if the housing situation of Indigenous people is to be improved. Housing services need to develop policies which are adapted to the lifeworlds of their tenants and provide strategies which ensure that tenants understand and are able to meet their tenancy expectations. Tenants must also be willing to consider the legitimacy of the demands that accompany the benefits they receive including some willingness to change behaviours if these impact negatively on themselves, their families and neighbours.

Research suggests there is much to be gained from this approach (Flatau 2009; Memmott and Nash 2013). Housing policies should recognise the importance of social and kin ties and the deep obligations to house kin that remain strong for many Indigenous people in urban areas. This requires developing a shared approach to problem solving that starts with a recognition of local contexts and the importance of good communication between housing providers and tenants in order to build mutual trust and respect (Moran 2010). Indigenous housing design should incorporate the need to accommodate larger households and socio-spatial patterns of sleeping arrangements.

The efforts of some state governments in adapting public housing models of tenancy management to remote locations suggests that in some jurisdictions policies are moving in this direction but there remains much work to be done (Habibis et al. 2014). Examples include allocating larger homes and supporting individuals who often receive visitors to manage their guests and maintain their tenancy. Strengthening the capacity of local Indigenous organisations through identifying and supporting the positive and innovative aspects of their work and promoting governance structures and organisational values and arrangements that enhance community well-being is also important (Milligan et al. 2011; Tsley et al. 2012).

Bauman observes that 'recognition wars' trigger a 'protracted, convoluted and contorted process of getting to know each other, coming to terms with each other, striking a bargain, seeking and finding a modus vivendi or rather coexistendi' (Bauman 2001:138). The multi-racial context in which social housing services operates locates them at the forefront of these engagements. Despite the difficult conditions in which they operate they have potential to be a progressive force through the development of innovative practices to support Indigenous housing access and tenancy sustainment.

References

Altman, J. (2010) 'What future for remote Indigenous Australia?', in J. Altman and M. Hinkson (eds), *Culture Crisis: Anthropology and Politics in Aboriginal Australia*, Sydney: UNSW Press: 259–280.

Australian Bureau of Statistics (ABS) (2010) 'Indigenous disadvantage and selected measures of wellbeing' *Year Book Australia 2009–10* Cat. No. 1301.0. Available at http://www.abs.gov.au/AUSSTATS/abs@.nsf/Lookup/1301.0Feature+Article9012009–10.

—— (2011) *Estimates of Aboriginal and Torres Strait Islander Australians*, June 2011, Cat. No. 3238.0.55.001. Available at http://www.abs.gov.au/ausstats/abs@.nsf/mf/3238.0.55.001.

—— (2013) *Estimates of Aboriginal and Torres Strait Islander Australians*, June 2011 Cat. No. 3238.0.55.001. Available at http://www.abs.gov.au/ausstats/abs@.nsf/mf/3238.0.55.001.

Australian Institute of Health and Welfare (AIHW) (2011) *Housing and Homelessness Services: Access for Aboriginal and Torres Strait Islander people* Cat. No. HOU 237. Available at http://www.aihw.gov.au/publication-detail/?id=10737419006.

Bauman, Z. (2001) 'The great war of recognition', *Theory, Culture and Society* 18: 137–150.

Birdsall-Jones, C., Corunna, V., Turner, N., Smart, G. and Shaw, W. (2010) *Indigenous Homelessness*, AHURI Final Report No. 143, Australian Housing and Urban Research Institute, Melbourne.

Canada Mortgage and Housing Corporation (CMHC) (2005) *Focus on Aboriginal Housing. Canadian Housing Observer 2005*. CMHC, Ontario.

Council of Australian Governments (COAG) (2008) National Partnership Agreement on Remote Indigenous Housing. Available at http://www.coag.gov.au/intergov_agreements/federal_financial_relations/docs/national_partnership/national_partnership_on_remote_indigenous_housing.pdf.

—— (2010) *National Partnership Agreement on Remote Indigenous Housing – Variation*. Available at http://www.federalfinancialrelations.gov.au/content/national_partnershp_agreements/indigenous.aspx.

Coyne, D. (2008) 'Brothers helping brothers', *Koori Mail*, 16 July: 13.

Dodson, P. (2009) 'Intervention turned our backs on reconciliation', Sydney Morning Herald, 20 August 2009. Available at http://www.smh.com.au/opinion/contributors/intervention-turned-our-backs-on-reconciliation-20090819-eqhv.html.

Flatau, P., McGrath, N., Tually, S., Cooper, L., Morris, M., Adam, M. Marinova, D. and Beer, A. (2004) *Indigenous Access to Mainstream Public and Community Housing*, AHURI Positioning Paper No. 82, Australian Housing and Urban Research Institute.

Flatau, P., Coleman, A., Memmott, P., Baulderstone, J. and Slatter, M. (2009) *Sustaining at-Risk Indigenous Tenancies: A Review of Australian Policy Responses*, AHURI Final Report No. 138, Australian Housing and Urban Research Institute, Melbourne.

Frankenberg, R. (1993) *The Social Construction of Whiteness, White Women, Race Matters*, Minneapolis: Minnesota Press.

Fraser, N. (2000) 'Rethinking recognition', New Left Review, 3 May–June. Available at http://newleftreview.org/?page=article&view=2248.

Habermas, J. (1987) 'The theory of communicative action', (Vol. 2). *Lifeworld and System: A Critique of Functionalist Reason*, Cambridge: Polity Press.

Habibis, D., (2011) 'A framework for reimagining indigenous mobility and homelessness', Urban Policy and Research 4(4): 401–414. Available at http://www.tandfonline.com/doi/abs/10.1080/08111146.2011.613146.

—— (2013) 'Australian housing policy, misrecognition and indigenous population mobility', *Housing Studies* 28(5): 764–781.

Habibis, D., Birdsall-Jones, C., Dunbar, T., Scrimgeour, M. and Taylor, E. (2011) *Improving Housing Responses to Indigenous Patterns of Mobility*, AHURI Final Report No. 162, Australian Housing and Urban Research Institute, Melbourne.

Habibis, D., Phillips, R., Phibbs, P. and Verdouw, J. (2014) Improving Tenancy Management On Remote Indigenous Communities, AHURI Final Report No. 223, Australian Housing and Urban Research Institute, Melbourne. Available at http://www.ahuri.edu.au/publications/projects/p41023.

Holmes, C., Ahmat, S. Henry, A. Manhire, J., Mow, M., Shepherd, J. and Williams, G. (2007) *Preliminary Inquiry into the Recent Influx of Indigenous Visitors to Darwin from Remote Communities*, Larrakia Nation Aboriginal Corporation, Darwin.

Honneth, A. (1996) *The Struggle for Recognition: The Moral Grammar of Social Conflicts*, Cambridge, MA: MIT Press.

—— (2003) 'Redistribution as recognition: A response to Nancy Fraser', in N. Fraser and A. Honneth (eds), *Redistribution or Recognition?* New York: Verso, 110–197.

—— (2007) *Disrespect: The Normative Foundations of Critical Theory*, Cambridge: Polity Press.

Kearney, S. (2007) 'Policy to force urban drift crisis', *The Australian*, 26 October 2007. Available at http://search.ebscohost.com/login.aspx?direct=true&db=anh&AN=2007 102610 06396618&site=ehost-live.

Langton, M. (2008) *Trapped in the Aboriginal Reality Show*, ABC News: the Drum, 8 February 2008. Available at http://www.abc.net.au/news/2008-02-08/trapped-in-the-aboriginal-reality-show/1036918.

Long, S., Memmott, P. and Seelig, T. (2007), *An Audit and Review of Australian Indigenous Housing Research*, AHURI Final Report No. 102, Australian Housing and Urban Research Institute, Melbourne.

Memmott, P. (2004). 'Aboriginal housing: Has the state of the art improved?', *Architecture Australia*, January/February 2004. Available at http://www.architecturemedia.com/aa/aaissue.php?issueid=200401&article=7&typeon=1.

Memmott, P. and Nash, D. (2013) *No Wrong Door? Managing Indigenous Homelessness in Mt Isa*, Report by the Institute for Social Science Research, University of Queensland for the Department of Families, Housing, Community Services and Indigenous Affairs. Available at http://homelessnessclearinghouse.govspace.gov.au/whats-new-3/research-release-no-wrong-door-managing-indigenous-homelessness-in-mt-isa-2012-aust/.

Memmott, P., Birdsall-Jones, C., Go-Sam, C., Greenop, K. and Corunna, V. (2011) *Modelling Crowding in Aboriginal Australia*, AHURI Positioning Paper No. 141, Australian Housing and Urban Research Institute, Melbourne.

Memmott, P., Birdsall-Jones, C. and Greenop, K. (2013) *Australian Indigenous House Crowding*, AHURI Final Report No. 194, Australian Housing and Urban Research Institute, Melbourne.

Memmott, P., Long, S., Chambers, C. and Spring, F. (2003). *Categories of Indigenous 'Homeless' People and Good Practice Responses to their Needs*, AHURI Final Report No. 49, Australian Housing and Urban Research Institute, Melbourne.

Milligan, V., Phillips, R., Easthope, H. and Memmott, P. (2010) *Service Directions and Issues in Social Housing for Indigenous Households in Urban and Regional Areas*, AHURI Positioning Paper No. 130, Australian Housing and Urban Research Institute, Melbourne.

Milligan, V., Phillips, R., Easthope, H., Liu, E. and Memmott, P. (2011) *Urban Social Housing for Aboriginal People and Torres Strait Islanders: Respecting Culture and Adapting Services*, AHURI Final Report No. 172, Australian Housing and Urban Research Institute, Melbourne.

Moran, M., McQueen, K. and Szava, A. (2010) 'Perceptions of home ownership among indigenous home owners', *Urban Policy and Research* 28(3): 311–325.

Morgan, G. (2006) *Unsettled Places: Aboriginal People and Urbanization in New South Wales*, Kent Town: Wakefield Press.

Musharbash, Y. (2009) *Yuendumu Everyday: Contemporary Life in Remote Aboriginal Australia*, Australian Institute of Aboriginal and Torres Strait Islander Studies, Canberra.

Peterson, N. (2004) 'Myth of the "walkabout": movement in the Aboriginal domain', in J. Taylor and M. Bell (eds), *Population Mobility and Indigenous Peoples in Australasia and North America* London: Routledge, 223–238.

Price, B. (2012) Welcome to My World, ABC Radio National, Background Briefing 15 January 2012. Available at http://www.abc.net.au/radionational/programs/backgroundbriefing/bess-price-welcome-to-my-world/3725896.

Price Waterhouse Coopers (PWC) (2007) *Living in the Sunburnt Country: Indigenous Housing Findings of the Review of the Community Housing Infrastructure Program*, Price WaterHouseCoopers. Available at http://www.fahcsia.gov.au/sites/default/files/documents/05_2012/livingsunburntcountry.pdf.

Productivity Commission (2009) *Overcoming Indigenous Disadvantage: Key Indicators 2009*, Australian Government. Available at http://www.pc.gov.au/gsp/reports/indigenous/keyindicators2009.

Roberts, D., Fuller, D., Bradley, H., Hugo, G., Coffee, N. and Gollan, S. (2006) *The Emerging Housing Needs of Indigenous South Australians*, AHURI Final Report, Australian Housing and Urban Research Institute, Melbourne.

Standing Committee on Aboriginal and Torres Strait Islander Affairs (SCATSIA) (2001) *We Can Do It! The Needs of Urban Dwelling Aboriginal and Torres Strait Islander Peoples*, Report of the House of Representatives Standing Committee on Aboriginal and Torres Strait Islander Affairs, The Parliament of the Commonwealth of Australia, Canberra.

Stolper, D. and Hammond, R. (2010) *'Reconciliation Barometer'*, Reconciliation Australia. Available at http://www.reconciliation.org.au/getfile?id=1303&file=Australian+Reconciliation+Barometer+2010+-+full+report.pdf.

Stracey, M. (2003) 'Sustaining Indigenous tenants at risk of eviction: A Victorian homelessness strategy pilot', *Parity*, 16(9): 5–6.

Taylor, C. (1994) 'The politics of recognition', in A. Gutmann (ed.), *Multiculturalism: Examining the Politics of Recognition*, Princeton, NJ: Princeton University Press: 25–74.

Taylor, J. (2008) *Determinants of Development Success in the Native Nations of the United States*, Native Nations Institute for Leadership, Management and Policy and Harvard Project on American Indian Economic Development. Available at http://nni.arizona.edu/resources/inpp/determinants_of_development_success_english.pdf.

Tsley, K., McCalman, J., Bainbridge, R. and Brown, C. (2012) *Improving Indigenous Community Governance through Strengthening Indigenous and Government Organizational Capacity*, Australian Institute of Health and Welfare and Closing the Gap Clearinghouse. Available at http://www.aihw.gov.au/closingthegap/documents/resource_sheets/ctgc-rs10.pdf.

Chapter 6
Reshaping Housing Consumption and Production from the Bottom Up: Insights from Interpretivist Housing Research

Wendy Stone

Introduction

Worsening problems of housing affordability in Australia have driven a gap between the housing-related hopes and expectations of many Australian households, and their housing and home life realities. Research about the impact of housing affordability problems for households typically focuses on the extent and impact for households of consequent problems such as financial stress, housing security and precarity, locational choice and trade-off and the impact of such factors on various aspects of household wellbeing. An emerging but compelling body of research demonstrates adverse health, child development, educational, employment and happiness outcomes that are directly attributable to these housing-related problems (Mallett 2004; Phibbs and Thompson 2011; Yates and Milligan 2011).

The research presented in this chapter complements such studies, from a different perspective. In this chapter, the focus is on the various ways *some* households consciously renegotiate housing issues to 'solve' their own housing affordability problem at a household level. At the core of the approaches examined here, is a household-based questioning of 'usual' patterns of housing consumption and, in some cases, housing production, as households actively and deliberately 'narrate' their own housing pathways. Specifically, the chapter presents a case study exploring the housing and home practices of 25 Australian households that voluntarily reduced their earnings and expenditure in pursuit of life quality, to examine the nature of the household-housing-home relationship from 'the bottom up'.

These voluntary changes made by households are termed 'downshifting'[1] in this chapter. While downshifting in Australia is non-normative and undertaken by a minority of households, the extent of downshifting is far from trivial and provides insights into the ways problems of housing affordability are negotiated privately, by a diversity of Australian households. Measured conservatively, around a quarter of Australian adults aged 30–59 downshifted between 1993 and 2003 (Hamilton and Mail 2003), numbers that have since increased (Chhetri et al. 2009).

---

1 'Downshifting' can be variously called 'voluntary simplifying', 'living simply', or 'cultural creatives'. Such terms are largely dependent on country-specific terminology (Stone 2010).

Importantly, 'downshifting' is not necessarily equal to 'downsizing', a term used to describe a practice in which households relocate from larger or more expensive dwellings to more modestly sized or priced ones (Judd et al. 2014). The two terms can be related, such as when retirees whose incomes reduce *also* opt to live in smaller dwellings, but are not always related and are thus not interchangeable. As the findings below illustrate, downshifting can lead to a wide and sometimes creative range of housing outcomes including but not limited to those involving 'downsizing'.

While housing practices of this heterogeneous population of downshifters are of interest in their own right, the focus of the chapter is upon illustrating (i) the variable and potentially non-normative nature of *household-based* housing consumption and production in Australia and (ii) the ways usual categorisations of housing 'consumption' and 'production' can conflate in the lived experience of some Australian households, and their housing-home practices. Perhaps most significantly, the analysis also offers rare insight into the ways increasing numbers of Australian households affected by housing affordability problems may creatively adapt to current housing conditions to keep a roof overhead.

The Context: Housing Affordability and Individualised Possibility

On average, Australian house prices almost doubled between 1996 and 2006 relative to income, even controlling for inflation (Disney 2006). During the same period and the 10 years prior (1985–2004), income doubled while house prices increased fourfold (NATSEM 2008). Between this time and the present, prices have continued to increase. By international standards Australian housing is now among the least affordable in the western world (Cox and Pavletich 2014).

Numerous factors, including supply shortages, land prices, intergenerational discrepancies in wealth holdings and the small-scale nature of housing investment in Australia, affect housing purchase affordability (Burke and Hulse 2009). In turn, the lack of affordable options for home purchase for many households has a ripple effect across the whole housing system, as would-be home purchasers spend longer periods of time in affordable segments of other tenures (Yates and Milligan 2007).

Home ownership typifies Australia's love affair with real estate, yet is now out of reach of many people for significant periods of their adult lives (Stone et al. 2013). Social housing, now in decline, provides little relief, characterised by lengthy waiting lists, payment of market rent and a shift away from life tenancies (McNelis 2006). Problems of housing affordability affect all housing tenures (Rowley and Ong 2014), with 'housing stress'[2] most acutely felt in the private rental market and among purchaser owners (Hulse et al. 2012; Yates and Milligan 2007).

The relative lack of housing choice in Australia exacerbates the 'heat' in the housing system. Home ownership remains dominant because it affords the kind of ontological and financial security which other tenures, particularly private rental, currently fail to provide

---

2   Housing stress is measured using a 30% of income among bottom 40% of income distribution (30/40) rule.

(Hulse et al. 2011). Households living in either private or public rental almost always trade off perceived choice, security and control (Burke and Pinnegar 2007). And while low to moderate income home owners can be at risk of mortgage arrears, problems of insecurity and forced mobility are now common place in the Australian private rental market; a market characterised by light regulation relative to international standards (see Chapter 9).

The housing affordability crisis affects not only what Australians live in but also *how* they live. Working hours have increased in Australia in the last 30 years, particularly for women. The traditional 'dip' seen in women's working rates for those aged 25–44 years has lessened in recent years due to delayed or foregone child bearing and an increase in the number combining work and family (ABS 2013). Over a third of full-time working mothers would prefer part-time hours (Skinner and Pocock 2008: 9) and a decrease in preference for more working hours among men, arguably indicates a desire for better work-life balance (Heady and Warren 2008: 78).

Many Australian households now live with debt to income ratios far above those seen in previous times (Keen 2007), keeping average working patterns high. Rates of mortgage arrears and loan foreclosure are at an all-time national high (Keen 2007; Berry et al. 2009). Housing debt masks other consumer debt as it has become easier to withdraw credit against existing mortgages (Berry et al. 2009), while financial deregulation has enabled an increase in household debt among public and private renters (Burke and Ralston 2003).

However, financial deregulation and casualisation of large sectors of the Australian work force (which contribute to the housing problems described above) have presented opportunities as well as insecurity for *some* Australian households. A loosening of traditional norms and structures has opened the way for individuals to choose their own life course, managing risks and opportunities along the way – a set of circumstances termed 'individualisation'. The certainties and givens of previous eras have been dissolved and citizens are at once local and global, given the complexity of information, material and decisions to which they are exposed (Giddens 1991). The increased flexibility and individualisation of daily life associated with late modernity and 'risk society' (Beck 1992, 2000; Giddens 1991) arguably enables alternative lifestyle choices – such as those associated with voluntary reduction of income and expenditure in the pursuit of life quality – to be made.

The implication of individualisation for housing experience – particularly in the context of a pressured housing system – is that housing options and choices are open to questioning and individual narration, leading to potentially creative, non-normative and diversified approaches (even where 'choices' are significantly constrained) as well as the more well researched effects of housing stress and other housing-related problems associated with record low housing affordability. *En masse*, a highly varied range of housing experiences and patterns of consumption and production are emerging, particularly among households with the human, cultural and sometimes financial capital, to 'write their own housing stories'.

Researching 'New' Housing Problems

Increasing diversity in the ways households consume housing requires new approaches to the study of household consumption and production practices. The assumptions underpinning traditional housing consumption research methods, as well as the methods supporting them, are limited in their capacity to enable analysis of household motivations, strategies and experiences of housing and home.

Most commonly, patterns of housing consumption have been conceptualised in terms of 'housing careers' or 'housing histories' (Baum and Wulff 2003; Beer et al. 2006). 'Housing careers' are conceptualised in terms of a tenure ladder. Households begin at the lowest rung (leaving home, typically into private rental) and move upwardly throughout their lives to reach the top, home ownership. Founded firmly in a normative view, progressions from the parental home to rental to home purchase and outright ownership are positive, and other moves negative. 'Housing histories' provides an alternative framework (Forrest and Murie 1991), also based on tenure change however this time far more grounded in external factors. Structural, institutional conditions are seen as having substantial impact on the position of individuals and households within any given local housing system.

From differing perspectives, each approach enables analysis of key events and circumstances, in relation to housing change, however, each is limited in its capacity to inform upon increasingly diversified relationships between households, housing and home, including the non-normative ones reported on in this research. Most fundamentally, both the housing careers and histories approaches rely heavily on universal assumptions about households' motivations for housing and locational change. Each approach relies on housing tenure change and/or geographic mobility as a point of analysis, an emphasis which is unable to capture household nuances and housing-related changes that occur *in situ*. Furthermore, neither of these traditionally dominant approaches includes a focus on *home*. Differences in the motivations, experiences and ways of living *within* apparently similar housing circumstances (using measures such as tenure) are thus not accounted for.

Existing research has identified key factors involved in home meaning and the main avenues through which people make sense of their homes (Easthope 2004; Mallett 2004). These include: ontological security and family life, household routines and rituals and the time taken for the development of such routines (Dupuis and Thorns 1998). Home is also integrally related to 'place', a concept that can draw together the physical, social and emotional aspects of home with the physical and tenurial aspects of dwellings (Easthope 2004). Finally, factors contributing to ontological security stemming from housing will be country and historically context specific (Saunders and Williams 1988; Dupuis and Thorns 1998). The dominance of home ownership in Australia is thus likely to influence perceptions held by householders about their homes, among both those who are owners and those who are not.

Finally, much research about housing consumption focuses on conspicuous consumption at the expense of the majority of consumption, which is routine and based in ordinary household objects, systems and domestic routines (Gronow and Warde 2001; Shove 2003). Home based production, a corollary to consumption, is another form of regular or routine social action which 'makes' a home and at the same time contribute to an environmentally sustainable way of life (Chevalier 2005; Trainer 1995).

In response to the limitations of traditional housing research approaches, there has been a recent and energetic re-analysis of traditional housing 'problems', as well as the pursuit of 'new' types of problems associated with late modernity. Notably, Clapham (2002, 2005) proposed a 'housing pathways' approach which draws both 'housing' *and* 'home' together within a single approach. Housing pathways can be understood as 'patterns of interaction (practices) concerning house and home, over time and space' (Clapham 2002: 63). They are continually changing sets of relationships and interactions, which it experiences over time in its consumption of housing (Clapham 2002: 64).

Subjectivity is emphasised in the housing pathways approach as a means of overcoming the application of universal assumptions about housing preferences. As Clapham describes, 'in order to understand the fulfillment that housing provides, it is necessary to employ a framework that places the subjective nature of the meanings held by households at the centre of the analysis' (Clapham 2005: 17). Hence, one of the most important implications is the recognition that there may be extensive variation in the experience of housing, despite households occupying objectively similar positions in the housing market.

The housing pathways approach draws upon the well-established traditions of 'housing careers' and associated concepts discussed above, yet makes a significant departure from these by positioning at its centre a household's subjective assessment of its housing circumstances. The approach also borrows heavily from the work of Giddens including concepts such as risk, life planning, time and space, lifestyle, identity and power. In doing so, traditional approaches are expanded to potentially enable a far deeper understanding of, among other things, the relationships between the meaning of housing and lifestyle choices in late modernity.

When aligned with an interpretivist perspective, Clapham's articulation of the housing pathways approach is highly relevant for the analysis of 21st-century household-based housing and home perspectives, including for the present study. Often referred to as 'grounded' research (Glaser and Strauss 1967), an interpretivist housing research approach, positions at its centre the meanings held by *households* about their housing and homes. Household perspectives and meanings, and their own interpretation of their housing and home experiences, are explored. The assumption underlying the illustrative case study in this chapter, presented next, is that perspectives and meanings held about downshifting shape the housing experiences of downshifter households and are in turn shaped by them.

'Alternative' Housing Pathways: An Illustration

By definition, downshifters lie outside of normative values and behaviours associated with wealth accumulation and usual patterns of work and spend, are a group for whom normative assumptions about housing motivations and experience may not apply, and which can illustrate the potential of a household-based approach.

The sample of 25 downshifter households upon which this research is based is diverse, including those who are well and poorly resourced financially, those who are more or less attached to labour market, those living in metropolitan as well as regional Australia and differing in the types of homes in which they reside. Despite this diversity all have chosen to reduce their income and/or expenditure to pursue a better quality of life. Most are well-educated, a number consider themselves 'broke but not poor'.

Downshifter Characteristics		
Conventional ←——————————→		**Alternative**
Highly attached; usual hours; slight reduction; high priority	*Work*	Highly reduced or ceased; flexible; low priority
Reduced but similar to general population	*Consumption*	Re-use, trade, recycle; minimise consumption
Identify as similar to mainstream population	*Identity*	Distinguish self from mainstream population
Few trade-offs made to downshift	*Trade-offs*	Many or extensive trade-offs made
Non-green or moderately green awareness	*Environmentalism*	Environmental concerns integral to daily practices
Do not engage in self-provisioning or household production	*Self-provisioning*	Engage in self-provisioning and household production

Figure 6.1 Downshifters' characteristics, attitudes and engagement with income/expenditure

Source: Stone 2010.

Respondents were classified as being either 'conventional' or 'alternative' in their degree of downshifting, taking account of: work practices and priorities around labour market engagement; consumption practices; identity and sense of self with regard to being similar or different to the mainstream population; trade-offs made to pursue a downshifting lifestyle; extent of environmentalism; and extent of self-provisioning and household production (Figure 6.1).

In-depth interviews were undertaken with all households. Key themes included downshifting, housing and home, place, mobility/stability, family life, risk, priorities, and life planning. Additional topics felt to be significant by respondent households were also discussed, including home-based production and community, and basic demographic information was collected. Importantly, *all* households in this study perceived a clear relationship between housing affordability and lifestyle choice.

> I think that housing is dominating the way that we are living, housing prices. It is going to change families fundamentally for quite a while because anyone who tries to enter the market in the last two years from now on is facing an enormous mortgage and therefore an enormous lifestyle change. People talk about flexibility but you can't have flexibility if you have that sort of a debt. I just look at how it shapes everyone's lives and I think this is a really big thing, and think, I wonder who's buying all these houses? And how? [female, early 30s, partnered, one pre-school aged child, resident of intentional community, rural]

Downshifting the 'Great Australian Dream'

A usual tenure-based classification shows that, of the households in this study, four were outright home owners (no mortgage), 11 were purchaser owners (with mortgage/debt), seven were private renters, three were in 'other' housing circumstances and none lived in public rental housing. On the basis of this, it can be assumed that some have greater levels of control and security (legal and perceived) than others, since home ownership is generally associated with higher levels of security and rights to change one's housing than non-ownership tenures in Australia.

However, a typology based solely upon tenure tells us little more than this: it is a partial story only. Based on households' perspectives and experiences an alternative typology emerges that comprises tenure as well other factors important to downshifter experience, notably security and control – *across* housing tenures. The typology differentiates between the circumstances of households within the same housing tenure, illustrates how 'other' housing tenures relate to levels of housing security and control typically associated with ownership, and includes some of the transitional stages between tenures (Figure 6.2).

'Self-provisioners' are owner builders who, to varying degrees, played a large part in the design and construction of their homes. In this study all were 'alternative', with strong environmentally-informed values and reduced attachment to the labour market, and were households with low and medium financial resources. In all but one case, owner builder households lived in non-metropolitan areas, enabling building to occur according to household budgets (often very low) and timelines (often lengthy due to low budgets).

Owner building provided an alternative to the high upfront cost and relative lack of design choice offered within the mainstream housing market, enabling the input of individuality, environmentally sound building principles, cost effective measures and a great degree of control over which aspects of housing would be/not be afforded within any given budget – requiring a great deal of reflection on housing, home and lifestyle.

> We designed it. We had some great designs with towers and all sorts of things but the financial budget was a constraint … But I do love it and enjoy it and I can see what doesn't

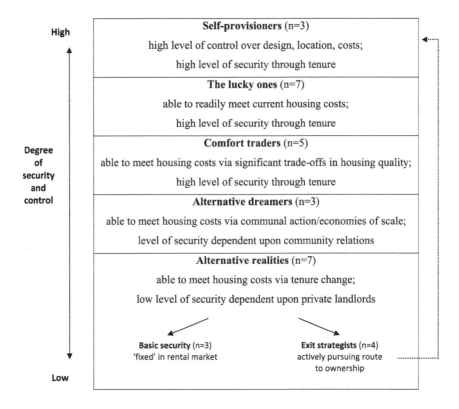

Figure 6.2 Typology of downshifters' housing circumstances
Source: Stone 2010.

work and what does work and I love architecture and I'm always designing houses. ... And I like, I just love being practical, I suppose, and questioning. [female, early 30s, partnered, one pre-school aged child, owner builder, rural]

To enable owner building, highly deliberate and conscious financial strategies were employed, including 'drip feeding' and modest borrowing, including informal loans, another. Hence, in at least some cases, substantial compromises to life options were made.

It's taken us eight years to build, just because of the time and the stop-start and the money flow. That's what was stressful ... it was so grinding, and the poverty was so grim. [female, late 30s, partnered, one pre-school aged child, owner builder, rural]

Once completed, houses provided a great deal of satisfaction and security to the owner builders, including financial security. In some cases building could be achieved mortgage-free (no ongoing debt) or with limited borrowing.

That asset gives you that feeling of security. I would not say that assets aren't important. I'm not a hippy where 'Oh, assets aren't important'. They are important. We will all grow old.

> What's going to happen to us? And just having one big primary asset, I think it does matter. [female, late 30s, partnered, one pre-school aged child, owner builder, rural]

'The lucky ones' are also homeowners, enjoying a high degree of housing control and security. Due to household resources and histories, ownership was achieved without the kind of personal costs experienced by some owner builder households, above, nor the trade-offs experienced by other owners, explored below. All households in this group were more conventional than alternative, had high or medium levels of financial resources (including housing equity), and most lived in metropolitan areas.

Circumstances enabling home purchase included strong and fixed attachment to the labour market (even though this had reduced through downshifting), household wealth and, in some cases, historical factors such as good timing. For most, stability related to security resulted in the capacity to afford home ownership comfortably and had become part of a financial strategy enabling downshifting to occur, with many households purchasing their homes many years earlier.

> We were so lucky, we were soooo lucky ... house prices have doubled and we bought before that, just before. [female, late 30s, partnered, three school-aged children, purchaser owner, rural]

As well, decisions to limit housing expenditure in ways consistent with downshifting values by, for example, renovating and improving homes slowly over time, rather than purchasing immediate renovation, repair or upgrades, feature in conscious housing strategies. For 'the lucky ones', the perceived benefits of home ownership relating to emotional and financial security strongly underlie the housing choices they have made and their ongoing housing strategies.

> I suppose for the security and, yeah, just that sense of actually having something you're building on. I sometimes don't know about the choice we made in terms of the actual house we bought but I think we did the right thing to buy a house. [male, mid-30s, partnered, two young children, purchaser owner, metropolitan]

'Comfort traders' included both outright and purchaser owners and all can be considered more alternative than conventional, having significantly different views and relationships to work and consumption patterns than associated with mainstream society. Most lived in non-metropolitan areas and the category included households with a mix of low and medium levels of financial resources.

Households in this group emphasised the sense of security – physical, emotional and financial – that comes from owning or purchasing their homes and it is the perceived benefits of home ownership which drive their choices and strategies. For many comfort traders, the apparent security that home ownership affords acted to offset relative insecurity in other life spheres, notably reduced earnings and wealth holdings related to downshifting.

> We've got the oldest house on the street. [laughing] It's what we could afford ... We're just trying to work out how the heck we can do it up. We don't have a lot of savings to

do anything with. I don't quite know how, we haven't got a solution yet. [male, mid-30s, partnered, five school-aged children, purchaser owner, metropolitan]

Limited resources mean home ownership was achieved with significant trade-offs to housing quality and comfort, sometimes creatively. Strategies included debt minimisation/avoidance, and relocation to affordable housing markets (away from metropolitan centres). However, even factoring in potential savings gained through relocation, many downshifter households living in rural areas clearly compromised quality and/or housing size in order to pursue their downshifting priorities.

> The realities of living in it are not ideal in the sense that it's not clean, there's cracks in the floor, there's wind that whistles up through the cracks, there's spiders getting in all the cracks and putting cobwebs up all over the place. It often feels dirty and untidy just by being old. It's a barn ... You know, all of these things drive you insane, and they don't until you live in it. They look charming to the outsider. [female, late 30s, partnered, six school-aged children, purchaser owner, rural]

In contrast with all of the home purchasers and owners described above are two groups of non-home owners in this typology, described as 'alternative dreamers' and 'alternative realities'.

'Alternative dreamers' are households that achieve high levels of housing security, by living in homes supported by community or multi-family relationships. Clearly, one of the most significant benefits of living in any kind of communal housing arrangement in which costs of land, buildings and household infrastructure can be shared is the reduced expense. This was particularly so where regular costs are able to be 'paid' in a variety of ways (including communal work). Additional advantages such as in-built company, support with domestic tasks including child care, and a lifestyle which places reduced pressure on couple and nuclear family units, were also evident.

Living communally in various types of arrangements afforded some households a great deal of flexibility regarding how they live, due to reduced housing costs and enhanced community relationships. In all cases, a high level of emotional security was experienced despite foregone benefits associated with private ownership such as capital gains and individualised control.

> So I really feel like this is very much a secure home. ... For me, the economics is all about stability. But because I have a community that I know is one that will care for us and look after us I don't have that worry about not having a house because I have a home. [female, early 30s, partnered, one pre-school aged child, residents of intentional community, rural]

Most downshifters interviewed in this research who neither owned their homes outright or with a mortgage were renting in the private rental sector, in 'alternative realities'. Two distinct types of private renters were evident: those whose living circumstances are relatively fixed and who are 'comfortable' with what one respondent described as 'the basic level of security'; and those who were actively pursuing exit strategies from private rental, towards their goal of home ownership.

Among those who were 'fixed' were single parent headed households who had previously been home purchasers. In these cases, private rental facilitated the decisions to downshift in order to spend more time with children. The security of home ownership was contrasted with the perceived insecurity and uncertainty of renting privately. Due to their choices about paid work and family time, these parents believed they were likely to continue to rent their homes privately in the medium to long term, at least.

> Being a single dad with two young babies, it was a bit of a shock. So I wanted all responsibilities away so I could totally put my effort into me and the kids. It's only now that everything's settled and life's gone on and they're getting older that I'm thinking 'Oh, geez, I wish I had a house'. [male, late 30s, unpartnered, two school-aged children, renter, rural]

'Exit strategists', in contrast, were either actively pursuing exit plans at the time of interview or were planning future exit strategies, all of which involved the end goal of home ownership. All owned or were purchasing land they intended to build upon in the near future; many were actively engaged in the design phase of building their homes; and in all cases, exit strategists were alternative, with low or medium levels of financial resources.

The views expressed by exit strategists reflected those of other renters, showing awareness of the flexibility afforded by private rental as well as its potential insecurity. However, the housing preferences of 'exit strategists' more closely matched those of self-provisioners (who emphasised control, cost minimisation and environmental sustainability). Consistent with all households that owned or were purchasing their homes, financial security was one of the principal perceived benefits of ownership in addition to a sense of control, stability and emotional or ontological security.

Lifestyle Choice and the 'Making of Home'

Analysis of the ways downshifter households 'make home' serves to further illustrate a diversity of practices and experiences despite a commonality of underlying downshifter values. First, results support the findings of existing research which emphasise the importance of family life for the making of a strong sense of home (Dupuis and Thorns 1998). The increased amount and fluidity of time in the lives of downshifter families on a daily basis acted to emphasise their home lives, as more time was spent at home, including for domestic and work related activities. Consistent with existing research, it was also found that home-family relationships were strengthened over time as well as through large volumes of regular, daily time.

Two additional significant influences on the making of home among downshifter families were evident: community life and the environment. Community life was a priority for many households interviewed and typically, local lives become central hubs of interaction and activity, related again to the increased amount of time spent at or near home. Some housing circumstances and home arrangements (notably communal ones) facilitate vibrant community interactions within downshifter families' homes, blurring boundaries between family and community spaces.

Environmental concerns were centrally important in the home lives of downshifter families in several ways, including the places they choose to live in, the material fabrics of their homes, as well as their consumption (and production) practices within and about home. These relationships were most pronounced among those who were more alternative than conventional, yet were evident among all downshifters interviewed to some degree.

A final theme to emerge with downshifter households about their home lives concern production – a home-based activity that can draw together the family, community and environmental priorities of downshifters. The most extensive illustration of this was the production of dwellings themselves, described above in terms of self-provisioning, however a majority of households also engaged in other productive practices as part of routine, domestic life, often incorporating community involvement and environmentally-based motivations.

Most common was the production of food. A number of households had small vegetable gardens or orchards and engaged in small-scale animal husbandry. 'Doing home' as family time occurred as a result of the increased amounts of time spent at home by downshifters, where aspects of the running of homes become inclusive, family based activities. Multiple forms of production were most prevalent when downshifting formed part of an integrated, holistic approach to living and was strongly aligned to environmental principles. Not surprisingly, some of the households engaged in the most extensive home based production lived in community cooperatives in which home based work was integral to the operation of the community.

Interpretivist Insights into Downshifting, Housing and Home

Overall, findings indicated the housing experiences of downshifter households vary significantly, affected by financial resources, world values and priorities. Additionally, *common* factors across housing circumstance types include: a preference for high levels of security and control over housing – most often manifesting in a preference for home ownership (also achieved via other housing routes); reflexivity regarding the relationship between housing choices and other life spheres; conscious implementation of housing strategies to reduce debt and enhance financial manoeuvrability; and a strong emphasis on prioritising lifestyle ('making do' in order to achieve priorities).

The control and security that support the capacity of downshifter households to enjoy lifestyle priorities in their home lives and practices are most strongly supported by certain types of housing arrangements. Previous literature has focused upon home ownership, almost exclusively, as relating to housing related control. These findings are supported here, however control and security are also found in other housing circumstance types, notably, arrangements based in personal, community relationships, as well as market-based arrangements including private rental where stability, and hence strong relationships between downshifter households and homes over time, are supported. Clearly, objectively similar housing circumstances can be experienced – and understood – as highly nuanced and heterogeneous when the perspectives, strategies and experiences of downshifter households are explored.

Conclusion

The research presented in this chapter forms part of an emerging body of work in which the relationships between households, housing and homes, from the grounded perspective of households, form the focus of analysis. A theme developed throughout this chapter is that in the 'late modern' 21st-century era, understanding the increasingly diverse practices associated with housing and home in Australia, requires 'new' housing research approaches. Consistent with Kemeny (2004), insights which supplement housing research methods charting broad housing trends and their relationships to other life spheres *with* interpretivist, grounded analyses based on household perspectives and practices are required.

This need arises from the dual conditions of (i) increased individualisation and diversity associated with the risks and opportunities represented by late modernity and (ii) the crisis of housing affordability which currently overshadows housing and life opportunities in Australia and elsewhere. Combined, these two factors challenge households to explore adaptive, creative responses to crises of housing affordability and access – both voluntarily, as in the illustrative research example presented here, and involuntarily, to keep a roof overhead. As shown in this chapter, interpretivist methodologies, in this case applied within a housing pathways approach (Clapham 2002), enable normative and non-normative relationships between household values, circumstances, housing experience and home-based practices to be understood.

Importantly, the approach enables consumption and production processes to be analysed from the perspective of households. While households often form the focus of housing research, remarkably little attention is paid to the role households themselves play as active agents in processes of housing production or housing consumption. Housing *production* research typically focuses on the regulatory and economic dynamics of supply, and stakeholders such as regulators, financiers and house builders (see Ball 2012). Where households are included, their role tends to be residualised to that of end-users, whose purchase preferences may shape the nature of housing commodities being produced. And, while households are central to housing *consumption* research, their inclusion has traditionally been via approaches firmly rooted in normative assumptions around preferences and behaviours, most notably economic maximisation and 'rational' market behaviour.

Taking a bottom-up approach to investigate the ways households consciously negotiate their housing pathways can – in some cases at least – challenge traditional boundaries relied upon in housing policy and research – including those of production and consumption. Ranging from the self-provisioning of housing itself via owner building to the production of home-grown food, the research illustrates that a household-based research perspective can unearth practices associated with households as 'productive consumers' in the everyday experience of housing and home.

As households adapt their housing expectations and behaviours to 21st-century housing system constraints, the ways in which practices associated with a 'blurring' of traditional boundaries between housing production and housing consumption, as well as other 'taken for granted' aspects of housing such as tenure (see Hulse 2008), are likely to become more varied and relationships between households, households' housing strategies and practices related to housing and home, more individualised and diverse.

Finally, while the research presented here focused deliberately on non-normative housing and home practices, its findings have broader significance. Linking household decisions about employment, earnings and housing costs draws attention to the extent to which these are treated *separately* within public policy, despite compelling research indicating integral connections between these life domains (Pocock et al. 2007). The escalating cost of housing across the Australian housing system has significance for work life balance and work practices and policy to support this. Analysis of the experience of downshifting demonstrates how centrally important housing and home are to achieving a balance between life and work. Yet, with some few exceptions (for example, HREOC 2007), housing costs and the experience of home are as yet rarely acknowledged within the work-life policy arena.

As Australian households continue to adapt to constraints in their housing options and opportunities related to the problem of lack of affordable housing, responses such as those illustrated here that challenge typical patterns of housing consumption and production are likely to become more evident, as households react to the 'true costs' of housing.

> When you start to actually work out what the cost of having those things might be to your relationship, to your family, to your children, in that you would have to go out to earn more ... then the costs are too great. And while it would be nice to have all those things, living with a little bit less you can have the things that are important. Family. Happy children. In the scheme of things, we're fine. [female, late 30s, partnered, six school aged-children, purchaser owner, rural]

References

ABS (2013) *Australian Social Trends*, Cat. no. 4102.0, Canberra: Australian Bureau of Statistics.

Ball, M. (2012) 'Housing building and housing supply', in Clapham, D., Clarke, W. and Gibb, K. (eds) *The SAGE Handbook of Housing Studies*, London: Sage.

Baum, S. and Wulff, M. (2003) *Housing Aspirations of Australian Households*, Final Report, Australian Housing and Urban Research Institute, Melbourne.

Beck, U. (1992) *Risk Society: Towards a New Modernity*, London: Sage.

—— (2000) *The Brave New World of Work*, Cambridge: Cambridge University Press.

Beer, A., Faulkner, D. and Gabriel, M. (2006) *21st Century Housing Careers and Australia's Housing Future*, Positioning Paper and Literature Review, Australian Housing and Urban Research Institute, Melbourne.

Berry, M., Dalton, T. and Nelson, A. (2009) *Mortgage Default in Australia: Nature, causes and social and economic impacts*, Positioning Paper No. 114, Australian Housing and Urban Research Institute, Melbourne.

Burke, T. and Pinnegar, S. (2007) *Experiencing the Housing Affordability Problem: Blocked aspirations, trade-offs and financial hardships*, National Research Venture 3, Research Report No. 9, Australian Housing and Urban Research Institute, Melbourne.

Burke, T. and Ralston, L. (2003) *Analysis of Expenditure Patterns and Levels of Household Indebtedness of Public and Private Rental Households, 1975–99*, Australian Housing and Urban Research Institute, Melbourne.

Chevalier, S. (2005) 'Value, social identity and household consumption practices: A Bulgarian case study', *Human Relations, Authority and Justice* (e-journal).

Chhetri, P., Stimson R.J. and Western J. (2009) 'Understanding the downshifting phenomenon: A case of South East Queensland, Australia', *Australian Journal of Social Issues* 44(4): 345–362.

Clapham. D. (2002) 'Housing pathways: A post modern analytical framework', *Housing, Theory and Society* 19(2): 57–68.

—— (2005) *The Meaning of Housing: A Pathways Approach*, Bristol: Policy Press.

Cox, W. and Pavletich, H. (2014) *10th Annual Demographia International Housing Affordability Survey: 2014*, Belleville, IL: Demographia.

Dupuis, A. and Thorns, D.C. (1998) 'Home, home ownership and the search for ontological security', *Sociological Review* 46(1): 24–48.

Easthope, H. (2004) 'A place called home', *Housing, Theory and Society* 21(3): 128–138.

Forrest, R. and Murie, A. (1991) 'Housing markets, labour markets and housing histories', in J. Allen and C. Hamnett (eds), *Housing and Labour Markets: Building the Connections*, London: Unwin Hyman, pp. 63–93.

Giddens, A. (1991) *Modernity and Self-Identity: Self and Society in the Late Modern Age*, Cambridge: Polity.

Glaser, B.G. and Strauss, A.L. (1967) *The Discovery of Grounded Theory*, Chicago, IL: Aldine.

Hamilton, C. and Mail, E. (2003) *Downshifting in Australia: A Sea-change in the Pursuit of Happiness*, Discussion Paper 50, The Australia Institute, Canberra.

Heady, B. and Warren, D. (2008) *Families, Incomes and Jobs, Volume 3: A statistical report on Waves 1 to 5 of the HILDA Survey*, Melbourne Institute of Applied Economic and Social Research, University of Melbourne, Melbourne.

Hulse, K. (2008) 'Shaky foundations: moving beyond "housing tenure"', *Housing, Theory and Society* 25(3): 202–219.

Hulse, K., Burke, T., Ralston, L and Stone, W. (2012) *The Australian Private Rental Sector: Changes and Challenges*, Positioning Paper, Australian Housing and Urban Research Institute, Melbourne.

Hulse, K., Milligan, V. and Easthope, H. (2011) *Secure Occupancy in Rental Housing: Conceptual Foundations and Comparative Perspectives*, Final Report, Australian Housing and Urban Research Institute, Melbourne.

HREOC (2007) *It's About Time: Women, Men, Work and Family*, Final Paper, Human Rights and Equal Opportunity Commission, Sydney.

Judd, B., Liu, E., Easthope, H., Davy, L. and Bridge, C. (2014) *Downsizing amongst Older Australians*, AHURI Final Report No.214. Melbourne: Australian Housing and Urban Research Institute.

Keen, S. (2007) *Deeper in Debt: Australia's Addiction to Borrowed Money*, Occasional Paper No. 3, Centre for Policy Development, Sydney.

Kemeny, J. (2004) 'Extending constructionist social problems to the study of housing problems', in Jacobs, K., Kemeny, J. and Manzi, T. (eds), *Social Constructionism in Housing Research*, Aldershot: Ashgate, pp. 49–70.

Mallett, S. (2004) 'Understanding home: A critical review of the literature', *Sociological Review* 52(1): 62–89.

McNelis, S. (2006) *Rental Systems in Australia and Overseas*, Final Report, Australian Housing and Urban Research Institute, Melbourne.

NATSEM (2008) *Wherever I Lay My Debt, That's My Home: Trends in Housing Affordability and Housing Stress, 1995–95 to 2005–06*, AMP-NATSEM Income and Wealth Report, Issue 19, National Centre for Social and Economic Modelling, Sydney.

Phibbs, P. and Thompson, S. (2011) *The Health Impacts of Housing: Toward a Policy-Relevant Research Agenda*, Final Report, Australian Housing and Urban Research Institute, Melbourne.

Pocock, B., Williams, P. and Skinner, N. (2007) *The Australian Work and Life Index (AWALI): Concepts, Methodology and Rationale*, Discussion Paper No. 1/07, Centre for Work + Life, University of South Australia, Adelaide.

Rowley, S. and Ong, R. (2012) *Housing Affordability, Housing Stress and Household Wellbeing in Australia*, Final Report, Australian Housing and Urban Research Institute, Melbourne.

Saunders, P. and Williams, P. (1988) 'The constitution of the home: Towards a research agenda', *Housing Studies* 3(2): 81–93.

Shove, E. (2003) *Comfort, Cleanliness and Convenience: The Social Organization of Normality*, Oxford: Berg.

Skinner, N. and Pocock, B. (2008) *Work, Life and Workplace Culture: The Australian Work and Life Index 2008*, Centre for Work + Life, University of South Australia, Adelaide.

Stone, W. (2010 unpublished PhD thesis) 'Downshifter Families' Housing and Homes: An Exploration of Lifestyle Choice and Housing Experience', Swinburne University of Technology, Melbourne.

Stone, W., Burke, T., Hulse, K. and Ralston, L. (2013) *Long-term Private Rental in a Changing Australian Private Rental Sector*, Final Report, Melbourne: Australian Housing and Urban Research Institute, Melbourne.

Trainer, T. (1995) *The Conserver Society: Alternatives for sustainability*, London: Zed.

Yates, J. and Milligan, V. (2007) *Housing Affordability: A 21st Century Problem*, Final Report, Australian Housing and Urban Research Institute, Melbourne.

Chapter 7
Boomer Housing Preferences: Active Adult Lifestyle Communities versus Aging in Place

Caryl Bosman

Introduction

Population aging is a feature of many developed countries due to higher life expectancy and a collapse in birth rates following the post-war baby boom (Fishman 2010). The vanguard generation of this demographic shift are the 'baby boomers' – people born between 1946 and 1965 in the so-called post–World War II baby boom. In Australia baby boomers make up a significant proportion of the population and the effects of the aging of this cohort are increasingly the focus of housing scholarship. Between 1993–2013 the proportion of Australia's population over 65-years increased from 2.8 per cent to 14.4 per cent (Australian Bureau of Statistics (ABS) 2013). Furthermore, the over 65-years cohort is projected to increase to 25 per cent of the population by 2056 (ABS 2013). The aging population presents a number of challenges in Australia: a reduction in the workforce; an increase in welfare/pension dependence; a change in consumer and lifestyle patterns; and most significantly for this book, the provision of housing.

One important facet of the intersection between the ageing of the baby boomer generation in Australia and the housing industry is the type of housing that this cohort will seek to live in as they age. This chapter will investigate two such build form options: 1) the master planned, age segregated, Active Adult Lifestyle Community (AALC) and 2) aging in place. Specifically, the chapter will examine the reasons why some baby boomers opt to buy into age-restricted communities, specifically AALCs, while others decide to age in place. Key indicators of baby boomer housing choice used in this study are affordability, sense of community, safety and security and staying physically active. Drawing on these key indicators, the aim of this study was to understand some of the benefits and disadvantages of aging in place and living in an AALC. This analysis provides an insight into some of the key housing attributes that can be drawn upon to inform housing choices and innovation in the housing industry, and to address the diverse housing needs and requirements of an aging population (Boldy et al. 2009).

Active Adult Lifestyle Communities (AALCs) and Aging in Place: A Review

While previous research suggests that the majority of baby boomers show a preference to age in place, others indicate their intention to move to a location that more directly facilitates their lifestyle aspirations (Beer et al. 2009; KPMG 2009; Smith 2009; Judd et al. 2014; Myers and Ryu 2008; Harding and Kelly 2007). This section will outline some of the differences between AALCs and aging in place.

AALCs: What are They?

AALCs began to emerge in Australia, New Zealand and United States in the early 2000s (Bosman 2012; Grant 2006; Fishman 2010). AALCs are age segregated master planned developments that are designed specifically for active adults between the ages of 55–74 (Bosman 2012; Suchman 2001). They are usually niche market developments, targeted toward the financially secure, healthy and active baby boomer cohorts or WOOAPies (well off older active persons). According to Grant (2006: 103) AALCs 'provide an alternative perspective on the notion of aging in place ... [and] are intended to be dynamic environments, advocating independent living and a good quality of life'. Moving into an AALC for some baby boomers is about 'making a transition to a new life ... bypassing and resisting the negative expectations and stereotypes of what growing older is supposedly about' (Grant 2006: 102).

While AALCs offer their residents a suitable model for their lifestyle life-stage it is only an option available to those who have the financial security to buy into this type of housing. Those within this cohort are not financially homogeneous and these baby boomers have diverse financial positions. For many Australian baby boomers affordable and appropriate housing has become a real concern (Kendig et al. 2013). This concern is not unique to Australian baby boomers, many of which will not have more than the equity in their house and the government funded age pension. Baby boomers who have a sufficient self-funded income have the opportunity to choose their place and type of house to suit their preferred lifestyle and for some an AALC fulfils these criteria.

One reason that AALCs are becoming popular in both America and Australia is that they offer their residents the opportunity to reside within a 'collaborative of individuals who are connected via their pursuit of a common lifestyle' (Buys et al. 2007: 288). Most literature confirms that social bonds are more commonly created between people of similar age, income, values, background and experiences (Rosenblatt et al. 2009; Panelli and Welch 2005). In AALCs resident age restrictions are enforced by property Title Deed and covenants and children are prohibited from residing in the community for any length of time. There are no investors or renters in AALCs resulting in a narrow socio-economic and demographic composition that McHugh and Larson-Keagy (2005) describe as 'birds of a feather'.

Concerns about safety and security often increase as people age. Walters and Bartlett (2009) found that many people in their study who were about to retire, or had already retired, wanted to move from their current suburban environments to a master planned community (MPC). The primary motivation for the move was based on the understanding that the majority of MPC residents owned their own home, i.e. no rental properties. Home ownership has a strong correlation with the lack of housing risks associated with aging in place; principally fear of isolation, crime and risks attached to property (as opposed to home) ownership.

Walters and Bartlett (2009) found that strong social relationships were of great importance for physical and mental wellbeing as people changed their lifestyle in retirement. It is often the appeal of remaining independent and active that attracts many baby boomers to move into an AALC. It is also this appeal that makes these developments attractive to government agencies and developers. Active and independent (and therefore healthy) residents can lead to economic savings and other indirect benefits. Suchman (2001: 21) argues that 'active adults impose less of a burden on most public services than do residents of other types of developments'. This is because residents of AALCs are (required to be) healthy and most formally public services are offered privately within the confines of the gates. Friendships also become more important as many residents do not expect support, nor want to be a liability on family members. In fact, in Walters and Bartlett' (2009) study, many of the aging baby boomers have no expectations that their children would or should provide support for them as they age. This trend contradicts convention because, 'for many years the traditional support network in old age has been the family, particularly the spouse and children' (Winter 2000).

Aging in Place: A Preferred Option?

Drawing on Olsberg and Winter (2005) aging in place relates to the neighbourhood and familiarity with place rather than the actual dwelling. Successful aging in place requires sustaining participation in the home and community throughout the course of older adulthood. The perceived benefits and disadvantages of aging in place are numerous. Benefits include opportunities to retain connections to long-term neighbours and friends within communities. In addition there are no covenants to be observed, governing visitors among other things, as there are in AALCs. However the demographic profile of many suburban areas in Queensland shows a high degree of 'churn', and this is particularly the case for the study region of the Gold Coast (Dredge and Jamal 2013). The concept of neighbourhood 'churn' refers to changes in the demographics of a longstanding and relatively stable neighbourhood as some older residents die and others move into alternative types of accommodation. This change can contribute to the social isolation of residents who remain to age in place, as new residents move into the area with different interests, life stages and attitudes. Significantly, community facilities are often targeted to the dominant demographic of the neighbourhood resulting in potentially reduced physical and social opportunities for those that age in a changing place.

Personal mobility can become a barrier to social engagement, active aging and independence. Likewise, neighbourhoods that are perceived as not being conducive to walking and where there is a lack of public transport may also lead to social isolation, ill health and dependence (Pearson et al. 2012; Siebert 2007). Research conducted by Bowling (2009) determined that the physical characteristics of a neighbourhood could contribute to the sense of safety and security of older Australians. The physical characteristics of the

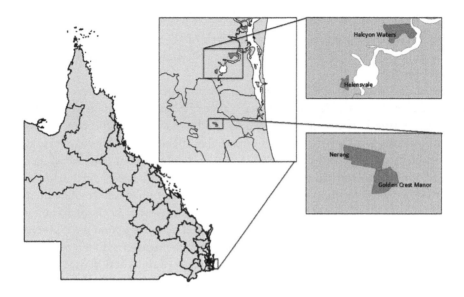

Figure 7.1 Location map of the case study sites: Halcyon Waters, Helensvale, Golden Crest Manors and Nerang, Gold Coast City Region, Queensland.

house may also be a cause of risk and expense. As a house ages it often requires costly maintenance and as residents of the house age retrofitting is frequently required to ensure safety and usability of the spaces (Judd et al. 2014).

Methods and Case Study Background

This chapter draws on data gathered through two comparative case studies. In each case study area there was one AALC and one suburban zone (four in total). The case study locations were selected from the Gold Coast City region, in the South East of the State of Queensland, Australia (see Figure 7.1). The Gold Coast has a long established reputation as a retirement hotspot (Ogilvie 2010) and has seen a variation in retirement housing tenure and type since 2000. The Gold Coast is a regional, largely suburban, city of approximately half a million people. It is one of the fastest growing areas in Australia. By 2021 almost one third of the city's population will be over 55. This will have a significant impact on the provision of facilities and amenities for aging residents in many suburbs. The aging profile of the Gold Coast means that services for the aged will increasingly be needed: lifestyle life-stage housing, medical facilities, home care support and an increase in reliable and accessible public transport.

The two case studies selected from the Gold Coast City region were:

1. *Case Study Site 1*: Halcyon Waters, an AALC and a suburban area in Helensvale and
2. *Case Study Site 2*: Golden Crest Manors, an AALC and a suburban area in Nerang.

Both AALC zones were developed after 2005 and both suburban zones date back to the early 1980s. Using data drawn from the Australian Bureau of Statistics 2011 Census of Population and Housing, the two AALC sites were chosen for their difference in locational and socio-economic characteristics and the suburban sites were chosen because they are representative of the type of development in that specific suburban area (see Table 7.1).

Table 7.1 Statistical comparison of the two case study sites (four zones) highlighting key socio-economic characteristics of the different areas.

	Case Study Site 1		Case Study Site 2	
	Halcyon Waters SA1 3125322	Helensvale SA1 3125232	Golden Crest Manors SA1 3124718	Nerang SA1 3124818
Median age	65	38	72	32
Households with Children	NA	58%	NA	59.3%
Lone persons	20.2%	22.9%	39.9%	12.8%
Median household weekly income	$830	$1154	$601	$1249
Low income households	27.6%	18.2%	45.2%	18.6%
Unemployment	NA	6.7%	NA	11.4%
2+cars/household	43.9%	56.1%	17%	65.1%
Dominant dwelling	separate house	separate house	separate house	separate house
Dominant tenure	fully owned	being purchased	fully owned	being purchased
Renting	NA	23.7%	NA	23.3%

Source: ABS 2011.

Case Study Site 1 – Helensvale and Hope Island-Halcyon Waters

Planning for the suburb of Helensvale began in the mid-1970s in response to strong population and economic growth in what is now the Gold Coast City. The area was predominantly sugar cane plantation prior to its suburban transformation. The suburb was designed to incorporate substantial open space in the form of a centrally located golf course and a series of interconnected linear parks that provided most houses with access to open space. By 1991 the suburb had both a primary and high school and a shopping centre (University of Queensland 2013). Hope Island was also a sugar cane plantation with the majority of the land being floodplain for the adjacent Coomera River. After significant dredging and engineering works, the first residential development emerged in the mid-1980s. Development on Hope Island is explicitly exclusive, being at the high end of the property market and consisting in the main of gated residential estates. Halcyon Waters (2005–2013) is one such master planned lifestyle residential resort, planned and designed specifically for the over 50 active cohorts (i.e. baby boomers). Halcyon Waters, built on about 14 hectares, is situated within 100 acres of protected wetland.

Case Study Site 2 – Nerang and Golden Crest Manors

Residential development in Nerang is not typically exclusive. The township was surveyed in 1865 and by 1876 it was a small rural settlement and a railhead for local produce and timber. During the population and economic booms of the region in the 1970s and 80s the town grew and piecemeal residential subdivisions replaced pastoral landscapes. The Nerang case study zone, like Helensvale, was strategically planned. Planning and development of Golden Crest Manors in Nerang began around the same time as Halcyon Waters. Golden Crest Manors is located in Nerang, which is one of the earliest townships in the Gold Coast region (see Figure 7.1 above). Golden Crest Manors, sited on 27 hectares, is on a rise overlooking light industry and bulk retail outlets.

Both AALC developments offer detached 2–3 bedrooms, mostly single storied houses on 250–350 square metre blocks. The Helensvale suburban zone primarily consists of project houses with facebrick veneer and on-ground slab construction, and a few architecturally designed houses, on 800–1000 square metre allotments. The Nerang zone is characterised by lightweight prefabricated houses, mostly pole construction about two metres off the ground, on approximately 800 square metre allotments.

Interview participants from the four areas were selected based on age cohort (born between 1946–1965) and housing tenure and type (i.e. those residing within the case study zones, in detached houses, and home owners). A total of 13 individuals, five who are aging in place in a suburban setting and eight living in AALCs, were interviewed. Participants' gender was balanced and interviews took place in their homes. The familiar environment enabled participants to feel comfortable, which increased rapport, in turn increasing more informed and relevant discussion. Interviews were semi-structured and questions were open ended. Questions were designed to solicit information about some of the key drivers for housing choice for these baby boomers: this included affordability, sense of community, safety and security and staying physically active. Questions directed to AALC residents were focused on whether this housing typology met their physical, social and financial expectations. Questions directed at baby boomers aging in place sought to establish if the suburban setting was appropriate for their life-stage and lifestyle.

Limitations to data collection emerged during the course of procuring participants for interviews. It was difficult to gain access to the residents of AALCs because all initial contact was made via onsite management, who were reluctant to approach residents. To overcome this, a snowballing method was employed. Initial access to residents was achieved via a friend that had personal connections within one of the AALCs; this provided someone who could vouch for the research and assist in the recruitment of initial participants. Data limitations include a potential bias as many of the interviewees were from the same social network. Nonetheless, the benefits of procuring contacts in an otherwise inaccessible environment are balanced by this limitation (Streeton et al. 2004).

There is also an important caveat to make here. It would be incorrect to think that all baby boomers are alike and have the same capacity to be active consumers (see Chapter 9).

Baby boomers are as diverse as any other cohort and many will not fit the characteristics outlined in this chapter. The findings from this study should not be taken as representative of the heterogeneous generation known as baby boomers. Notwithstanding this caveat, a set of key baby boomer characteristics is commonly cited in academic, marketing and real estate literature and the term baby boomers, therefore, holds some contextual weight for an analysis of AALCs. The term 'retirement' also needs to be clarified. The official retirement age for many Australian baby boomers is 65 and this is mooted to increase to 70 as of 2035. The current accepted definition of retirement is generally related to a life-stage characterised by leaving the work-force and being eligible for government pensions and a range of fiscal incentives. Many baby boomers are in the process of remodelling this life-stage (KPMG 2009) and are predicted to go through several stages of stepping back before finally leaving the work force. These years are often referred to as the 'lifestyle phase' characterised by part time work and focused on lifestyle amenity. In this chapter I use the term 'lifestyle life-stage' to emphasis this life-stage (denoting baby boomers aged 65–68 in 2014).

The case study analysis is structured around the four key indicators of baby boomer housing choice outlined above: 1) affordability, 2) sense of community, 3) safety and security and 4) staying physically active. Where significant differences occur across the two case studies the specific zone is named, otherwise the following summary reflects both case study sites (all four zones). As already highlighted, there is an identified need for greater housing choice and innovation in the housing industry to address the aging population phenomena (Judd et al. 2014). This analysis provides an insight into one set of the key housing attributes that can be drawn upon to inform new housing choices and innovation in the housing industry.

Understanding the Lived Experience: AALCs and Aging in Place

Affordability

Affordability is a key component of housing choice for many Australian home owning baby boomers given many will only have the equity in their house and the government funded age pension (non-home-owning baby boomers face a set of different challenges). The term housing affordability is typically used to relate housing costs to household incomes. The term affordable or social housing typically refers to a form of housing tenure. A lack of funds (or housing equity) to access desired housing could result in baby boomers having little choice about the location where they live. As a consequence of this, some people may find themselves living in areas with poor access to public transport, community services and support networks.

The study did not determine the affordability or social housing status of households within the two case studies. All houses were generally of good quality and the urban form was well maintained. The major differences between the AALCs and the suburban zones were the age of the development and the extent of, and budget allocated to maintenance. Both AALCs were recent developments and were immaculately maintained by the Body Corporate. In addition, residents were obliged to comply with a suite of stringent covenants. These covenants contribute to the degree of homogeneity in the urban form. The suburban zones reflect a much more diverse and less regulated landscape partly because the development is older and alterations, additions and landscaping reflect personal, rather than Body Corporate, endeavours.

Another significant point of difference between the AALCs and the suburban zones is the cost of purchasing a house. An AALC home (which does not include the land) costs significantly more than a home in the neighbouring suburban area. For example, homes in the Halcyon Waters AALC development were advertised as selling for between AU$445–850K plus expenses, while a Helensvale property (which included both house and land) were generally advertised for around AU$350,000. The ABS data in Table 7.1, above, also shows the median household weekly income for residents living in Golden Crest Manors estate to be AU$601 and in Halcyon Waters AU$830. While both of these are lower than in the adjoining suburban zones (AU$1154 in Helensvale and AU$1249 in Nerang) the dominant tenure of the AALCs was 'fully owned' and the suburban zones are 'being purchased'. Affordability in respect to living in an AALC is therefore in relation to paying Body Corporate fees and other related expenses rather than in purchasing a home. Moving into an AALC however does require sufficient equity to purchase a home, which limits who can and who cannot move into these communities.

Sense of Community

In both the suburban zones the only communal areas and social infrastructure are green open spaces and a Returned and Services League (RSL) club with an associated bowling green in the Nerang area. By contrast, residents in AALC developments were provided with a range of informal and formal communal areas including: a clubhouse, barbeque areas, herb gardens and sporting facilities. Most of this social infrastructure is located to create an active mixed-use hub that provides a focal point for residents. This hub is conveniently located and accessible by foot for all residents. In addition, public art and design features encourage a sense of place within these developments. Because the communal green areas in the Helensvale and Nerang zones are informal and low maintenance there is no provision for specific place making design features. These green spaces are however interconnected with adjoining green spaces within the wider area thereby promoting physical and social integration of the zone. The communal areas and social infrastructure within both the AALCs are only available to residents, as these developments are gated and privatised. In this respect the urban form of the AALCs reinscribe socio-economic divisions. Also because they are AALCs, the degree of social mix within the development is limited: all residents are of similar age and abilities and housing tenure is all owner occupied.

However, while the AALCs were designed specifically to facilitate some forms of 'community' these developments were also seen as restricting other forms of 'community'. For instance, Sue said she decided to age in place because she regularly had family members over to visit and stay overnight; this would prove difficult in an AALC. John also chose to age in place because:

> ... people of the same age usually talk about similar subjects, I think it would be boring not to have a mix of people living around you.

Yet, for those who had moved into an AALC it was this social homogeneity that all interviewees valued. As Peter explains:

> ... you drive around, not with hoons running up and down the street, all the people are like-minded. A place like this you develop a lot of good friendships and then you get a very close nucleus of friends that you really love to go out with.

Likewise, Pam liked the fact that people were of a similar age and she resented the fact that in recent years the age profile was diversifying. She reflected:

> Nobody was old here that we saw ... but now they're starting to let in a lot of older people. It wasn't supposed to be [like that]. ... they can't look after themselves. And none of us moved in here to be looking after old people.

A sense of community is strongly correlated to social health and wellbeing of individuals, and this is particularly the case as people get older. As people age, changes in their circumstances – such as reduction in income, reduced mobility, illness, widowhood, moving house or taking on informal caring responsibilities – can increase the risk of social isolation (Australian Institute of Health and Welfare 2013), which relates closely to depression, low morale, and poor health. Conversely, social participation and connections are important sources of support for older people and contribute to good health and wellbeing throughout life (World Health Organization 2007). Results of a study by Cornwell and Waite (2009) indicated that social disconnectedness and perceived isolation are independently associated with lower levels of self-rated physical health. It is these concerns and anticipated outcomes that are frequently associated with ageing in place. This is largely due to the lack of infrastructure and accessible amenities and facilities appropriate to the needs and requirements of individuals as they age (Smith 2009; Walters 2005). In addition, as capital and voting power shift to newer and/or more conducive development areas that are 'age friendly' (such as AALCs) some suburban areas may become even more physically and socially isolated for many baby boomers as they age.

Safety and Security

Safety can be used to refer to two different concepts: one refers to the actual crime rate and another refers to an individual's perception of safety (Wilson-Doenges 2000). Feeling unsafe and fear of crime have negative impacts on individuals' quality of life. People restrict their activities because of feeling unsafe (Taylor 1988; McIntyre 1967). Wood et al. (2008) found that the level of upkeep of a neighbourhood environment positively impacts on feelings of safety and social interaction between neighbours.

Perceptions of and the provision for safety and security was key to many interviewees choosing to move into an AALC from a suburban environment. Perceptions of safety in the AALC case study zones emerge from living in a community where everyone was known, where only residents had access to facilities and where there was monitored and restricted access and egress to the development. The planning and design of the urban form also contributed to perceptions of safety. Public spaces were designed to exclude places of possible concealment and to maximise opportunities for surveillance. The street layout in both AALCs was simple and logical and way finding was easy. Spaces were specifically designed for intended uses including night time use. Perceptions of and the provision for safety and security in the suburban case study zones were very different. Landscaping of the public areas was designed to minimise places of possible concealment however surveillance from adjoining houses was limited. In both suburban zones the street pattern in combination with the topography did not make for easy way finding and there was little consideration of appropriate night time usage of the public green spaces.

All AALC interviewees rated safety and security as their primary reason for moving into the development. For example, Peter and his wife wanted to travel and they wanted to be sure their belongings were secure while they were away. Peter also identified safety and security as a feature of their enjoyment of the development when they were there:

> We love the idea of going through gates that lock behind us. So you feel very safe here, the ladies feel very safe in here and don't mind walking around at night or anything like that. Its biggest attraction for older people is going to be the security. For sure, it's got to be the attraction. As soon as you turn on TV, 'I don't want to live out there'. Whereas here, you don't think of that, you think you're quite safe.

The threat of crime was also identified as a disadvantage by those who were aging in place. As Arnie, a suburban-zone resident, identified,

> … like you see on the telly now, where every day multiple stabbings and robberies and that sort of stuff.

A personal sense of safety and security is heightened as people age and become less agile. The perception of crime or public nuisance problems within a person's neighbourhood are an important indicator of how they feel about their own safety and wellbeing. Tenure also plays a big role in the perception of security in Australian cities, where 'renters are regarded as potential perpetrators of anti-social behaviour, and are seen as likely to "lower the tone" of the community' (Walter and Bartlett 2009: 232).

Staying Physically Active

The physical planning of all four zones encourages some level of physical activity. All four zones included public open space that potentially meets the needs of residents. These open spaces were, however, limited to a narrow range of activities specific to the demographic characteristics of the area: the mean age of AALC residents were 68, while it was 35 for residents in the suburban zones. Also, almost 60 per cent of suburban zone households had children and there were no children residing in the AALCs. Notably, land use in Helensvale and Nerang is not specifically designed to encourage walking as the topography is steep and the zones are suburban and car dependant. Land use within both AALCs however is specifically designed to encourage physical activity with the location of recreational facilities and letterboxes planned to encourage walking. John explains:

> There are two hazards of Halcyon that I recognised early in the piece. One is you develop RSI of the right elbow from waving to people and if you want to get your mail from the mail box down the front in a hurry you've got to drive your car because if you try to walk it will take you an hour.

The planning of the AALCs is designed specifically to meet the needs of active baby boomers. Partly because the development is gated and partly because the lifestyle and planning emphasis is on the active years of the baby boomer cohorts, the urban form may not be suitable for those AALC baby boomers who wish to age in place, particularly if they require specialised care. In the suburban areas some house designs can be adapted to meet the needs of people who wish to age in place however the topography and density of the suburb and the reliance on private vehicular transport suggest the opportunities for physical and social activities will be limited.

Most houses in the suburban zones are within 400–500m of a bus stop and have pedestrian access to open green space. Neither of the AALC case study areas was on a public transport route. However all foot and cycle paths within the estates were interconnected and destinational. Importantly, AALC streetscapes are designed to be attractive, interesting and welcoming to pedestrians and they are universally accessible. This is not the case in the suburban zones where the 'carscape' is predominant, not all roads have footpaths and pedestrian areas are not all universally accessible. In these two zones the street pattern comprises cul-de-sacs and loop roads and the majority of everyday facilities (shopping centre, community centre, etc.) are within a 1.5 km radius of the zone. These facilities are accessible for cyclists and fit and healthy pedestrians. The development to the north and east of Golden Crest Manors comprises light industry and fast food outlets and a hardware retailer. These amenities are not easily accessible by foot because the topography is steep and the roads are not conducive to either cycle or pedestrian travel. At Halcyon a medical precinct and age care facility are planned for adjoining greenfield sites and there is a small shopping complex within 1.5 km, accessible by motor vehicle.

Conclusion

Baby boomers, both in Australia and internationally, are often characterised as a generation with higher expectations than interwar generations and a desire to stay involved with working life (KPMG 2009). It has been argued that baby-boomers have radically redefined each life stage as they have entered and moved through them (Hamilton and Hamilton 2006). Therefore, it is perhaps not surprising that home owning baby boomers involved in this study are in the process of remodelling what retirement means, a stage of life characterised by part time work and focused on lifestyle amenity. Housing is key to this stage. As such there is an identified need for increased choice in housing to accommodate the needs and desires of many baby boomers. The key indicators of housing choice (affordability, sense of community, safety and security and staying physically active) discussed in this chapter have both national and international relevance and in particular with regard to aging populations.

This study focused on the build form and AALCs emerged as the preferred housing option for some baby boomers according to the stated indicators. AALC developments were specifically designed to encourage a sense of community, safety and security and physical activity albeit within the gated perimeter of the development. Both AALCs include manicured open space and recreational facilities that encourage a broad range of activity choices. These facilities were arranged to be accessible to all residents without the need to drive to any of them. To encourage this physical exertion, street networks throughout the development are connected, pedestrian friendly and green and leafy. A major draw for some AALC residents is the provision of a clubhouse, which also acts as a venue for events and activities and where they can socialise with other residents. However, because these developments were *active* adult communities all infrastructure and resources for encouraging healthy aging were geared towards the 50–75 cohorts. This, of course, excludes those sorts of activities appropriate for children and the non-active adults. The downside to this 'advantageous' housing option is the cost related to the purchase of the house and Body Corporate fees, an exclusive and largely homogenous social structure, a reliance on residents being able to drive a motor vehicle and a lack of public transport. Nonetheless, AALCs were providing access to resources which appealed to their baby boomer residents, the oldest of whom were, as of 2014, in their 60s.

While the suburban areas offered some recreational opportunities, these were not as appropriate for all sections of the population; suburban street networks were not all connected and were not designed to encourage pedestrian travel. Impediments to the continuing engagement of older adults in these zones include discontinuous or broken footpaths, poor or no public transport and a lack of adequate lighting. Importantly, the suburban zones were designed primarily for vehicle travel and family living and intervention in these sites was difficult.

These case study findings are not unique; rather they reinforce the trends and evidence from international studies. Based on this analysis, some of the key housing attributes that can be drawn upon to inform new housing choices and innovation in the housing industry, and to address the housing needs and requirements of the aging population include:

- The design and delivery of an affordable product (relative to income from any source) that allows easy, universally accessible, pleasant and safe pedestrian access to core amenities and facilities such as communal outdoor and in-door spaces, as well as commercial and retail outlets.
- A product that gives security of tenure and appeals to baby boomers from a range of backgrounds and socio-economic brackets.
- A product that is well maintained and depicts a high level of appropriate design features (including crime prevention through environmental design, way finding and night time uses).
- A product that allows different levels of physical activity and caters for different circumstances and abilities.

To meet the challenge of housing a rapidly increasing lifestyle life-stage baby boomer population, the housing industry will need to deliver affordable housing that also responds to and encourages a sense of community, safety and security and staying physically active. This housing should not just be suitable for the younger baby boomer cohorts, the housing products need to remain appropriate and relevant as they age. To quote the Australian demographer Bernard Salt (2010) 'there's nothing that should concern a government (at any level) more than a bored baby boomer in the burbs'.

References

Australian Bureau of Statistics (2013) *Where and How do Australia's Older People Live?*
Australian Institute of Health and Welfare, (2013) *Australia's Welfare 2013*. Available at: www.aihw.gov.au/WorkArea/DownloadAsset.aspx?id=60129544075 (accessed May 2013).
Beer, A., Faulkner, D., Baker, E., Tually, S., Raftery, P. and Cutler, C. (2009) *Our Homes, Our Communities: The Aspirations and Expectations of Older People in South Australia*, Report for ECH Inc, May 2009. Adelaide: Flinders University.
Boldy, D., Grenade, L., Lewin, G., Karol, E. and Burton, E. (2011) 'Older peoples' decisions regarding ageing in place: A Western Australian case study', *Australasian Journal on Ageing* 30(3): 136–142.
Bosman, C. (2012) 'Gerotopia: Risky housing for an ageing population', *Housing, Theory & Society* 29(2): 157–171.
Bowling, A. (2009) 'Perceptions of active ageing in Britain: Divergences between minority and whole population samples', *Age and Ageing* 38(6): 703–710.
Buys, L., Miller, K. and Bailey, C. (2007) 'Smart housing and social sustainability: Learning from the residents of Queensland's research house', *Australian Journal of Emerging Technologies and Society* 3(1): 43–57.
Cornwell, E.Y., and Waite, L.J. (2009). 'Social disconnectedness, perceived isolation, and health among older adults', *Journal of Health and Social Behaviour* 50(1): 31–48.
Dredge, D. and Jamal, T. (2013) 'Mobilities on the Gold Coast, Australia: Implications for destination governance and sustainable tourism', *Journal of Sustainable Tourism*, DOI:10.1080/09669582.2013.776064.
Fishman, T. (2010) *Shock of the Gray*. New York: Scribner.
Grant, B. (2006) 'Retirement villages: An alternative form of housing on an ageing landscape', *Social Policy Journal of New Zealand* 27: 100–113.
Hamilton, M. and Hamilton, C. (2006) *Baby Boomers and Retirement Dreams, Fears and Anxieties*, Discussion Paper Number 89, The Australian Institute. Available at: http://www.tai.org.au/documents/dp_fulltext/DP89.pdf
Harding, A. and Kelly, S. (2007) *Baby Boomers Doing It for Themselves*, Issue 16, March. AMP. NATSEM Income and Wealth Reports.
.id the population experts (2013) '*Atlas.Id: Social Atlas*'. Available at: http://atlas.id.com.au/gold-coast (accessed on May 2014).
Judd, B., Liu, E., Easthope, H., Davy, L. and Bridge, C. (2014) *Downsizing amongst older Australians*. Melbourne: Australian Housing and Urban Research Institute.

Kendig, H., Wells, Y., O'Loughlin, K. and Heese, K. (2013) 'Australian baby boomers face retirement during the global financial crisis', *Journal of Aging & Social Policy* 25(3): 264–280.

KPMG (Bernard Salt and Sally Mikkelsen) (2009) 'Monash baby boomer study', *Property and Demographic Advisory*. Available at: http://www.kpmg.com/AU/en/IssuesAndInsights/ArticlesPublications/Pages/Monash-Baby-Boomer-Study.aspx (accessed May 2013).

McHugh, K. and Larson-Keagy, E. (2005) 'These white walls: The dialectic of retirement communities', *Journal of Aging Studies* 19(2): 241–256.

McIntyre, J. 1967. 'Public attitudes toward crime and law enforcement', *The Annals of the American Academy of Political and Social Science*, 374(1): 34–46.

Myers, D. and Ryu, S.H. (2008) 'Aging baby boomers and the generational housing bubble: Foresight and mitigation of an epic transition', *Journal of the American Planning Association* 74(1): 17–33.

Ogilvie, F. (2010) *Boomers To Be Demanding But Inventive Retirees*. Available at: http://wwwabc.netau/pm/content/2010/s3016926.html (accessed May 2012).

Olsberg, D. and Winters, M. (2005) *Ageing in Place: Intergenerational and Intra-familial Housing Transfers and Shifts in Later Life*. Melbourne: Australian Housing and Urban Research Institute.

Panelli, R. and Welch, R. (2005) 'Why community? Reading difference and singularity with community', *Environment and Planning A* 37(9): 1589–1611.

Pearson, E., Windsor, T., Crisp, D., Butterworth, P. and Anstey, K. (2012) *Neighbourhood Characteristic's: Shaping the Wellbeing of Older Australians*, NSPAC Research Monograph, No. 2, National Seniors Productive Ageing Centre, Canberra. Available at: http://www.productiveageing.com.au/site/grants_nspac (accessed Feb 2014).

Rosenblatt, T., Cheshire, L. and Lawrence, G. (2009) 'Social interaction and sense of community in a master planned community', *Housing, Theory and Society* 26(2): 122–142.

Salt, B. (2010) 'Cashing in on baby boomer plans', *The Australian*, (Business/Property), 11 February. Available at: http://www.theaustralian.com.au/business/property/cashing-in-on-baby-boomer-plans/story-e6frg9gx-1225828942095 (accessed Feb 2014).

Siebert, C. (2007) 'Aging in place and occupational therapy', *Gerontology* 30(4): 2–4.

Smith, A. (2009) *Ageing in Urban Neighbourhoods: Place Attraction and Social Exclusion*. Bristol: Policy Press.

Streeton, R., Cooke, M., and Campbell, J. (2004) 'Researching the researchers: Using a snowballing technique', *Nurse Researcher* 12(1): 35–46.

Suchman, D. (2001) *Developing Active Adult Retirement Communities*. Washington D.C.: Urban Land Institute.

Taylor, R.B. (1988) *Human Territorial Functioning: An Empirical, Evolutionary Perspective on Individual and Small Group Territorial Cognitions, Behaviors, and Consequences*. Cambridge: Cambridge University Press.

University of Queensland. (2013) *Helensvale*. Centre for the Government of Queensland. Available at: http://queenslandplaces.com.au/helensvale (accessed Feb 2014).

Walters, P. (2005) 'Growing old on the suburban fringe: Master planned communities and planning for diversity', *State of Australian Cities Conference*, 30 November–02 December, Griffith University, Brisbane.

Walters, P. and Bartlett, H. (2009) 'Growing old in a new estate: Establishing new social networks in retirement', *Ageing & Society* 29: 217–236.

Wilson-Doenges, G. (2000) 'An exploration of sense of community and fear of crime in gated communities', *Environment and Behaviour* 32(5): 597–611.

Winter, I. (2000) *Towards a Theorised Understanding of Family Life and Social Capital.* Melbourne: Australian Institute of Family Studies.

Wood, L., Shannon, T., Bulsara, M., Pikora, T., McCormack, G., and Giles-Corti, B. (2008) 'The anatomy of the safe and social suburb: An exploratory study of the built environment, social capital and residents' perceptions of safety', *Health & Place* 14(1): 15–31.

World Health Organisation (2007) *Checklist of Essential Features of Age-Friendly Cities,* Geneva: WHO.

Chapter 8
Policy Implications for Governing Australia's Apartment Communities: Tenants, Committees of Management and Strata Managers

Erika Altmann

Introduction

Over the second half the 20th century Australia emerged as a home owning nation with much of that home ownership occurring within a suburban setting dominated by free title land holdings (see Chapters 9 and 10). However, as Randolph (2006: 474) notes, since the turn of the 21st century this freehold 'suburban option [has become] increasingly curtailed'. Australians are increasingly 'expected to spend substantial proportions of their lives in a form of housing that hitherto has only been a minority choice'. One such form is 'strata titled' housing. Australian Bureau of Statistics (2011) data reveals that in Australia one in four people live or own strata titled property in its various forms (units, flats, apartments, gated and master planned communities or commercial property). The growing dominance of 'strata titled' living is attributed in part to the increased prevalence of 'urban consolidation' agendas in the contemporary planning of Australia's cities and regions (Easthope and Randolph 2008) which results in higher density living.

Australia has much to contribute to research on high-density living. While there is debate as to where and how strata titled properties first originated,[1] the introduction of the strata title mechanism into Australia in the early 1960s means that there is a 50-year period of accumulated experience with this property type. Easthope and Randolph (2008: 244) note that Australian strata title property legislation has formed a basis for jurisdictional reform in countries such as Canada, New Zealand, South Africa, Singapore, Indonesia, Brunei and Malaysia. The take up of Australia's legislative framework by so many countries combined with urban consolidation policies and frameworks makes strata titled housing a significant area of housing research for Australian and international audiences.

---

1   McKenzie (1996) traces this back to a corrupted version of Ebenezer Howard's Garden City in Nebraska, USA while Webster and Le Goix (2005) note that Paris was a mid-19th century centre for similar types of property. Bagaeen and Uduku (2010) suggested that this form of shared living is significantly older.

Accompanying increased numbers of strata titled dwellings in Australia has been a shift in a range of rental sub-markets. Increasingly, Australians rent units and apartments rather than single dwellings. Governance issues increasingly coalesce around tenants and strata-titled building complexes. While there is an increasing body of academic research in this area, it has primarily been from the perspectives of the developer-buyer, owner-occupier or social housing tenant, and/or from the landlord. The view of the committee of management, or the strata manager has not previously been considered. This chapter explores this gap through presentation of findings from a qualitative research project that investigates the interaction between tenants, owner committees of management and strata managers of apartment developments in Melbourne, Australia. The research investigates tenancy and landlord issues that committees of management address as part of their usual business. First, the market changes that lead to greater numbers of tenants living in buildings with this type of governance mechanism is highlighted. Then the governance mechanism attached to this form of building complex is explained. Next, the research method is outlined. Finally, the thematic results are discussed and their impact on policy explored. Without identifying and exploring this lacuna, there can be no holistic understanding of how high-density living will play out within Australian society or how governments might introduce policies and legislation that would assist in closing the gap.

Tenurial Change in Australia

Within Australia, there are reasons why this gap has developed. Like other western nation-states, Australia has developed a culture of home ownership over the second half of the 21st century (Chapters 9 and 10). Australians have responded to a growing crisis in home ownership affordability in part by deferring home purchase in favour of renting for longer periods, switching into cheaper accommodation (such as apartments and townhouses) and moving to more affordable locations (Burke, Stone and Ralston 2014). There has been a significant research focus on the expansion of the private rental market since 2001 (Wulff et al. 2011). Over this period Australia's social rental market has contracted to just below 5 per cent of the total Australian housing stock while there has been a corresponding expansion in the private rental market. At the same time, the days of 'government as developer' building broad acre, low income housing has largely ceased. The historical, regulatory role of 'government as developer' on house and land purchase prices no longer exists. Australia's housing tenure system is market dominated (Yates and Bradbury 2010) whether owned or rented, public or private. Hence, there is an increased focus on housing affordability in the home ownership and rental areas. Rental is no longer seen as a transitional step to home ownership, but a long term tenure necessity as housing markets respond to increased population, short term employment contracts and housing product differentiation pressures. For policy makers, renting is seen as a responsive, flexible and affordable means of housing in a more mobile society. Within the Victorian context, apartments make up an increasing volume of rental stock. In particular, the inner city Melbourne apartment market is an investor driven market dominated by short and long term rental properties leaving few owner-occupiers *in situ*.

That tenants form a significant proportion of the apartment population is widely acknowledged (Kearns 2000; Mee 2007). However, it is a diverse population (Wulff et al. 2011). Randolph and Tice (2013) detailed different sub-markets within the Melbourne and Sydney apartment sector. At the lower end of the market they found there was a severe shortage of affordable properties. Randolph and Tice (2013) also pointed to differences in the Melbourne and Sydney apartment sector at the lower end of the market. They assert that Sydney's market is characterised by economic 'battlers' whereas the Melbourne market is characterised by a student population and young, upwardly mobile, single people. Economic 'battlers', young people, those employed or more educated, partnered and English speaking are more likely to seek rental accommodation within the private sector (Burke et al. 2005). Families with children and older households were less likely to be living in inner-city apartments and flats (Fincher and Gooder 2007; Whizman and Mizrachi 2012). Overwhelmingly, the inner city Melbourne apartment market is an investor driven market dominated by rental properties and young people.

Within the Victorian context, strata titled properties make up an increasing volume of rental stock. A marked shift in how this preoccupation manifests is the increasingly dominant role of the 'investor' in Australian property markets. For example, in 2010, the Owner Corporation of Victoria (OCV) reported that 95 per cent of strata titled properties in Victoria were sold to investors. The flip-side of this increasing prevalence of investors is an increasing prevalence of tenants in units and apartments, and their increasing interaction with these fourth tier governance mechanisms.

Strata Title Governance

A strata titled property development comprises at least two real property 'lots' plus communally owned property. On registration of the scheme, a separate organisation is created to manage and enforce the rules belonging to that organisation, known as an 'owner corporation'.[2] Strata titled properties involve a complex mix of governing systems. In the context of strata titled properties, Easthope and Randolph (2009, 247) define governance as the 'structure, processes and practices that determine how decisions are made in a system and what actions are taken within that system'. Important to strata governance is the role of the 'committee of management'. Within strata titled properties, all lot owners make up the 'owner corporation' and have shared rights over the common property. Some owners are elected to the 'committee of management'. The committee of management acts as the elected governing board for the organisation. In this way, ownership of strata titled properties, such as apartments, becomes both individual and collective in nature. The

---

2 There is a significant amount of variety in the legislation and legislative terminology nationally and internationally. Both Everton-More et al. (2004) and Johnston and Reid (2013) provide comparative analysis of jurisdictional terminology used to describe the strata title mechanism within Australia. However since the focus of this research is on the Melbourne apartment sector, terms relevant in that jurisdiction are used. The term 'owner corporation' is used instead of 'body corporate', 'HOA', 'CID' or 'condominium'.

decision-making power sits largely with committee of management, though all owners share voting rights along with the ability to nominate for a position on the committee. Increasingly, contract strata managers are appointed to assist in the administrative duties undertaken by owner corporations. Strata managers perform administrative, secretarial, and financial functions on behalf of the owner corporation (Lei and Van Der Merwe 2009).

Research on the strata-titled phenomenon has ranged from understanding management issues (Budgen 2005; Pouder and Clark 2009; Warnken and Guiding 2009), socio-cultural issues such as diversity, segregation and security (Brunn 2006; Low 2006; Kern 2007; Webster and Le Goix 2005), economic issues including housing stock planning, price and renewal, life cycle costs and strata scheme termination (Easthope and Randolph 2009; Johnston and Reid 2013; Warnken and Guilding 2009;) and environmental issues (Altmann 2013; Randolph 2006; Troy 2002). Issues of governance where addressed concentrate on owner's experience, building and strata manager's or developer's influence (Bajracharya and Khan 2010, Goodman and Douglas 2010; Randolph 2006). Few give serious attention to the tenants that live within these complexes, or their interaction with the governance systems in place. Where mentioned, it is more as passing glance that acknowledges presence but not the impact of governance structure, processes and practices. Everton-Moore et al. (2006) consider that changes to strata title legislation are attempts to mitigate conflict of interest among diverse stakeholder groups, though again tenants, their needs and their relationship with the committee of management are not discussed. Though Guilding et al. (2005) present a comprehensive list of more than 25 stakeholder groups, the committee of management, tenants or investor landlords do not make the list. This gap is surprising since as early as 1999, Blakely and Snyder (1999) noted that in the American context, strata titled property was more likely to be tenanted than owner occupied.

Problems Facing the Governance Relationship between Tenants and Committees of Management

A number of factors contribute to making the governance relationship between tenants and committees of management particularly difficult. The tiered ownership system that encompasses both individual and collective ownership is one difficultly. The associated rights, responsibilities and restrictions have the potential to obfuscate owners and tenants within this type of complex. Strata managers add further distance to this relationship. The owner-tenant relationship is also complicated by product differentiation created by developers and real estate markets. These include age exclusive villages, lifestyle villages, e-centric communities or nested developments.[3] How many owners and 'lots' within a strata titled building complex also makes a difference. For example, Hulse et al. (2011: 65) notes that where a single investor owns a block of flats or apartments, then tenancies are more stable. This may account for the higher rates of tenant stability in some European countries where the strata title mechanism is relatively recent.

---

3 'Nesting' is a tiered strata title structure. It occurs when several smaller owner corporation are governed by a larger, overarching one (Townshend 2006) and may entail designated mixed-use property within the one strata scheme.

Second, the governance relationship between tenants and committees of management is made more problematic by a disconnect between tenant legislation and strata title legislation. As Kemp (1987) explains, bundles of duties and rights are embedded in tenancy legislation for both owners and landlords. Easthope (2014) contextualises these duties and rights within an Australian context but fails to place them within the context of a rental sector that increasingly interacts with strata title legislation and accompanying committees of management. In Victoria, tenants' needs are to some extent acknowledged within current strata legislation. For example, Section 163 of the *Owner Corporation Act 2006* allows the occupier (including tenants) of an apartment to seek adjudication of complains by the Victorian Civil and Administrative Tribunal (VCAT). However under tenancy legislation, there is no reciprocation for the owner corporation seeking to remedy a tenant issue such as the negation of 'quiet enjoyment' by a tenant within the complex. Tenancy contracts and legislation deal with the owner/estate agent/tenant relationship. Yet a tenant, whether short or long term, will use property common to all owners for a variety of purposes (think lift, lobby, car parking, garden spaces or air conditioning) any one of which may be damaged by a tenant. There is no clear remedy for the owner corporation other than as a civil complainant. This is because the tenant signed their contract for a specific property or apartment with a specific landlord, not the owner corporation. Nor does the contract cover access to communal property.

Last, the governance of strata titled properties is further complicated by a number of centrally located apartments becoming short-term lets or unregulated tourist accommodation. These apartments are often missed or miscalculated in housing stock counts. This is because planners have approved these apartments as long-term residential accommodation, however, once in the hands of letting agents, they become short-term lets or tourist accommodation. This is despite short term lets falling within a different planning scheme designation. Investigating this experience, Guilding and others (Guilding 2003; Warnken and Guilding 2008, Warnken et al. 2003) have written extensively in this area. However, the experiences they describe are Queensland based and an indication of the mature tourism industry along the Gold and Sunshine coasts of Australia. The use of residential building managers is a feature of that market not seen in other jurisdictions to the same extent. The ability of the residential building manager to influence letting and sub-letting practices within a particular building is therefore not a significant feature of other jurisdictions (including Victoria).

A key gap in the current discussion on strata title governance is the placement of owner corporations (represented through committees of management) relative to the increasing number of long and short-term tenanted properties within the strata titled apartment sector.

Case Study and Methodology

The data for this analysis is drawn from a larger study on medium and high-density housing in Melbourne, Australia. As part of this research a series of qualitative interviews with strata managers and committee of management Chairs was conducted. The research reported here draws on a subset of 13 interviews where participants responded with tenancy related issues. All of the interviewees, including the committee Chairs came from a business or professional background.

Notwithstanding the limitations associated with drawing conclusions from small sample sizes, this dataset draws attention to emergent issues in the governance of strata title properties in Australia. The issues raised in these interviews are relevant to an increasingly dense living environment characterised by high numbers of renters and investor landlords. The data collected is both *rich* and *thick*. The interviews expose the detailed lived experiences of strata title governance in a way that larger studies are unable to. The data provides much needed insight into individual behaviour, societal attitudes and to some extent legislative attitudes as it applies to the strata environment. Owner corporations are set up to provide stewardship of collectively owned property. The structure, processes and procedures provide an insight into how that governance operates in a rental environment.

A thematic approach was used for analysis of the data. All participants were interviewed in relation to their knowledge and experience of governance within apartment complexes in Melbourne's CBD. The apartments had either been built within the past decade or had undergone substantial redevelopment within that time frame. Of the 13 interviews, five were able to provide insight on apartment buildings containing in excess of 100 lots in tower configuration and were part of larger building precincts that incorporated Townshend's (2006) concept of nesting. Three of these owner corporations collected in excess of $1 million in annual levies and were therefore required to have five-year rolling maintenance plans. The other eight interviews brought to the project knowledge and experience of governance within small apartment complexes. In this study, apartment complexes had high rates of rental properties which ranged between 50 per cent and 75 per cent. The research highlights the views of committee Chairs and Strata managers on tenancy issues. It explores a gap in understanding the complexity of governing within apartment rental markets.

Findings

This section is divided into a number of broad themes that deal with the impact of structural arrangements, processes and procedures relating to strata title governance generally rather than the actual issues raised according to tenancy type. The first is the various types of tenants that a strata title property will attract. Additional themes relate to process and procedural governance issues.

Tenants Leasing Strata Lots – Managing Behaviour

The interviews confirmed the use of apartments as unregulated tourist accommodation. Their growth in numbers is seen as problematic and difficult to regulate.

> We have issues of parties. We have issues with bucks' nights, hens' nights, grog being left out, bottles being left out in the hallways and other common property areas. They don't know

where the recycling rooms are. They park wherever they feel like it. They're pretty loud and unruly, and unfortunately cause damage to the building as well when they are drunk. (Chair K)

Committee Chairs commented on their inability to effect change through the implementation of by-laws that prohibited short-term letting from their buildings. Structurally they were unable to implement change:

The problem is by stealth they've [short-term rentals] grown ... – the vote has to be 70 per cent to change any owners' corporation rules. We would really struggle, because we probably have more than 30 per cent of the building now in serviced apartments. (Chair K)

What the committee was doing was making a new by-law to get rid of all short-term leasing from the building. ... Before we knew it, there were 30 partitions against the new by-law. (Chair N)

In hotels and the regulated serviced apartment industry, there are appropriate securities in place to deal with the issues outlined by Chair K. In Queensland, strata titled properties used in this way usually employ residential building managers to live within the building complex and are available to unruly behaviour if necessary. Such managers were missing from the Melbourne apartment sector. Even where concierge services were provided within the apartment buildings, disruption caused by short-term tenants did not appear to be dealt with by them. To the Chairs, the investor profit motive and the disturbance caused by the high rate of overnight rentals meant that preferred long-term renters were displaced.

I didn't even realise just to what extent it was (profitable). $320 a night for a three-bedder. A night!! ... It is not possible for long-term renters to compete with that. (Chair K)

This short-term commercial activity has the potential to displace preferred long-term tenants from the building. Committees of management and strata managers see long-term, stable residential tenancies as advantageous, since it is easier to induct them into processes and procedures within the building. However there were exceptions noted. Social housing tenants for example, were deemed to be unstable and as problematic as short-term lets due to noise and violence issues:

The previous Chair had difficulty with the violence when it erupted. Her response was to pack up her husband, go and rent somewhere else and put a tenant in here and leave them to deal with it. (Chair L)

It's almost impossible to get government landlords to act. They are the most disinterested owners. It took me two years and an appeal to the Minister to get a meeting to discuss the issues we have with their [social housing] tenants. (Chair L)

Indeed Burke (2004) noted that within suburban settings, a noisy minority of social housing tenants could hold whole streets or suburbs to ransom with antisocial behaviour.

Within apartment complexes, where there is an additional layer of governance albeit by a volunteer-run committee of management, how much more difficult it is to mediate issues of violence, unruly behaviour, or basic adherence to by-laws. Though Habibis et al. (2007) suggests that additional support be given to public housing tenants with complex needs and demanding behaviour lest they spiral into homelessness, the difficulties of managing such tenancies for an owner corporation is lost despite several decades of infill apartment purchase by housing authorities. In any case, within this passage, the key problem identified by the committee Chair was the unwillingness of government departments, as owners, to acknowledge that such problems existed, let alone work towards a solution with the owner corporation. There were no processes in place to cover this situation.

Then to, there were structural and procedural issues within mixed-use buildings. The commercial activities of cafés, takeaway food outlets and restaurants in particular created governance difficulties for committees of management. Noise and additional waste disposal were significant problems, as were café patrons wandering through private gardens and lift lobbies. In one interview, part of the common property had been included in a restaurant lease without the agreement of the owner corporation, making enforcement of by-laws especially problematic while protracted legal proceedings took place.

Procedural Challenges of Governing Strata Title Properties

Strata managers in particular noted that they took care to advise new owners and tenants about the by-laws that were in operation within a building complex.

> If I know that a property or tenancy has changed hands I ask the chairman to knock on the door, introduce themselves and hand over a copy of the by-laws to the new occupants. It nips trouble in the bud so to speak. (Strata manager G)

It is difficult for the committee of management and strata managers to argue for the enforcement of by-laws where occupants remain unaware of them. Even where no specific by-laws are in force, the model by-laws take effect. This means that no existing strata complex is without by-laws of some sort. The requirement within Victoria is for all prospective purchasers to receive information about the owner corporation prior to purchase. However, the by-laws still came as a shock to some:

> I had no idea these things existed [at the time of purchase]. (Chair L)

The situation for long-term tenants is different. Long-term tenants are not required to be given a copy of the by-laws for inspection prior to signing their lease. They may, however, be presented with them after the lease is signed. Thus the tenant may not know what living conditions they will need to meet until after the lease is signed. While many real estate agents may provide a set of by-laws to the incoming tenant, it was noted that they were not always the ones relevant to the building complex.

> So she [the tenant] showed me a copy and it was the wrong ones. Our company have a standard set of by-laws that are different to the model ones which are the ones she had. Ours are much more explicit and we ask all owner corporation to adopt them [when they sign with us]. (Strata manager D)

Strata managers are persuasive in influencing the structure, processes and procedures within apartment buildings. However the preferred structure is not always implemented due to process or procedural breakdown. This breakdown is best demonstrated through maintenance issues.

Tenant Involvement in Maintenance

Owner corporations are tasked with maintaining the common property as part of the legislative requirements. The owner corporations in this study had periodic maintenance contracts and strata managers in place. Yet there was no clear process in place to allow tenants to report maintenance problems identified within the common property. Moreover, there was confusion as to where the responsibility for actioning maintenance issues lay. Issues may arise between what the tenant believes needs to be maintained and what has been approved by the various stakeholders involved:

> If someone [the tenant] rings us we need to know what the situation is but we have found in past experiences that tenants have rung up wanting some works to be done which haven't been approved by the committee, owner or the agent. (Strata manager D)

However, if a maintenance issue exists within the common property, the landlord and estate agent have no right of veto except within the owner corporation structure. The landlord and estate agent have jurisdiction only for the leased apartment. Problems occur when systems such as air-conditioning, water reticulation and plumbing are deemed to be part of the tenant landlord responsibility when these reticulation systems usually remain part of the common property and under the control of the committee of management. There is no reference to the owner corporation in the above extract. A process failure occurs when tenants have to contend with a convoluted route in getting maintenance problems attended to within the common property. This places both the tenant and the owner corporation in a position of powerlessness relative to property maintenance. The owner corporation cannot undertake maintenance if it is not advised of the need for maintenance by a series of other stakeholders (tenants, landlord, estate agents or the strata manager). Though the tenant has the right to take action through VCAT, as Wulff et al. (2009) notes, it is more probable that the tenant will seek alternate accommodation:

> I lost a tenant. A good tenant. The window was leaking and I wanted it fixed. So I arranged with the estate agent to get someone in to fix it and the next thing all work had stopped because the strata manager said it was common property and there was no budget for it. … She [the tenant] moved. (Chair N)

The above passage highlights the difficulty of actioning items. While the structure is in place to facilitate maintaining common property, there is a lack of process and procedure that assist in positive outcomes. It may take significant amounts of time for the landlord to get agreement from the owner corporation for unscheduled maintenance to be completed. Other owners may not wish to share the cost and veto the repair unless it impacts directly on them. Meanwhile their property deteriorates and the tenant may seek alternative accommodation. The danger here is that where there is a process failure, buildings will spiral into a dilapidated state. Because so many high-density buildings are relatively new, it is sometimes difficult to imagine their decline. However the building that Chair N spoke about was less than ten years old, and already experiencing a number of significant maintenance issues. In addition to this, there is an uneven allocation of cost to owners for damage, wear and tear. This is because levy proportions are set and linked to each apartment at the development stage of the property rather than being based on actual usage or tenancy type. Post-development, no additional surcharge can be recouped by the committee of management to cover the additional cleaning and maintenance, wear and tear of common areas attributable to long-stay, short-stay or commercial tenants and associated maintenance issues. Alternately, owners may have been unaware of upcoming maintenance needs of the common property when they purchased their apartment, and therefore have failed to adequately budget for their share of the cost. One suggested way of addressing this and other procedural issues was presented by Strata manager D:

> I actually read an interesting article recently where it said that each property should have two voting rights. One for the owner and one for the tenant and if they are just unoccupied then the owner gets two voting rights because you see a lot of tenants that love their property and they do more to it than what the actual investor does. (Strata manager D)

For private rental housing within strata developments, tenant participation in governance is not considered a necessity at present and is unlikely to become so. One of the reasons for this is the current push for termination clauses to be included within current legislation. Investor owners are more likely to make a decision to sell or demolish and rebuild based on financial considerations. Increasing maintenance costs and high annual levy payments are more likely to be weighed against sale price, rebuilding costs or higher rental for new properties. These considerations do not, or will adversely impact tenants were they to be allowed to vote on this issue. For this reason it is likely that tenants will remain a sidelined stakeholder group without a voice within their residential communities despite the adverse effect on tenant security and housing availability that termination legislation may cause (Altmann 2011).

Tenants and Issues of Occupational Health and Safety

Finally, there is the issue of occupational health and safety (OHS). The following committee Chair raises a lack of knowledge by tenants as an OHS issue. The situation is discussed in the context of sub-letting and overcrowding (there were ten international students living within a two bedroom apartment), however her comments are relevant to leased apartments generally:

> They are always subletting and moving out and someone else moving in. And so no-one ever sees the documentation and no one knows where the stop cock for your room or apartment is. They don't know that. Where do you assemble if there is an alarm? Which fire alarm do you take notice of? No-one knows! (Chair E)

There are serious issues identified here. The owner-investor, strata manager and committee of management all have a role to play in informing people of the evacuation points and plans for their buildings. In case of a fire, who is responsible for evacuation? How do the police, fire fighters or the committee of management know how many people live within each apartment when there is no obligation for landlords to tell the owner corporation, or tenants sublease without the landlord's knowledge. How do emergency services people gain access an electronically gated apartment building in an emergency situation? Failure to address these issues may have serious insurance consequences for the owner corporation, as well as the injured. In a single dwelling, not knowing where a stop tap is located may have serious flooding consequences for that dwelling. In an apartment complex, damage to common areas and other apartments may be the result, creating significant repair and insurance difficulties. In case of illness requiring medical assistance or a domestic violence issue, police and ambulance officers may need to negotiate a variety of electronic swipe card access issues to access the door of the apartment. The time taken to do this, may mean the difference between life or death for the injured person, whether owner, tenant or visitor. In Australia, such issues have not yet been put to the test. Until this occurs, liability will remain a hidden risk for many owner corporations.

Discussion

Committees of management are presented with a variety of governance issues that relate to short and long-term tenants, social and commercial tenancies, and the economic activity of landlord owners. In these interviews, the proportion of rental properties within the complexes was significantly higher than for all residential rentals (up to 75 per cent against 30 per cent of the total population). Unregulated short-term letting within medium- and high-density apartments located within central business districts accounted for approximately one third of the apartments. These apartments were designated as residential housing units within planning schemes. The failure to regulate short-term letting combined with the high nightly tariffs has the potential to severely impact on the availability and price of housing within Melbourne's CBD. Counts of available residential housing by planning authorities potentially overestimate the amount of available housing through their failure to adequately regulate and assess the number of residential apartments lost to unregulated tourist accommodation. For owner corporations there are structures in place that may potentially limit the number of short-term lets within their buildings. However the likelihood of getting investor owners to vote for such by-laws is unlikely. Investor owners living elsewhere are not subjected to the noisy rituals of drunken revellers within the building or difficulties associated with other types of commercial lets. Committees of management have no ability to ban individuals from accessing their rental accommodation via the common areas. The additional clean-up costs are rarely attributable to the landlord, short-term tenants or leasing agents as there is no process in place to facilitate this. There is no simple contractual remedy to this situation. Unlike the tourist-based state of Queensland, live-in building managers are rarely employed. There is little likelihood of them being economically effective based on the existing rates of short-term lets, since the building managers in Queensland take a management fee for overseeing each short- or long-term tenancy.

The situation is unlikely to be a concern to policy makers at state and federal level. For the two higher tiers of government there are the advantages in terms of economic growth that tourist short-stays bring. Though issues of noise in short-term lets is being addressed, in several states (Stacks/ The Law Company 1 May 2013), court cases appear to rely on zoning requirements in third tier, local government planning schemes to gain wins. However, within apartment buildings the zoning of short and long-term lets often co-exist with commercial tenancies. The issue of noise (particularly party noise and violence) is therefore more difficult to address. There are fewer owner occupiers in place to object. Because of the higher rental yield attached to short-term letting, short-stay apartments are more likely to be positively geared within the taxation system rather than taking financial resources through negative gearing. Thus they provide income to treasury coffers. On the other hand, long-term tenancies have become synonymous with negatively geared properties in which rental yields are as low as 2–3 per cent in capital cities and no longer keeping pace with inflation.

Committee Chairs see the unsettled nature of the building complexes whether through commercial leases, tourist lets, private or social housing as a disincentive for long-term tenants on standard residential contracts to stay. To what extent the unregulated short-term leases impact on long-term residential lease renewal is unknown. Getting maintenance repairs to the common property undertaken in a timely manner was raised as an issue that impacted on keeping long-term tenants in place. Tenants were more likely to move rather than wait for the convoluted approvals processes to result in repairs. The distinction between repairs actionable by the landlord or real estate agent and those that require owner corporation approval is not straight forward since each apartment complex may have a different allocation of responsibility defined within their title documents. While the inclusion of maintenance plans and sinking funds have been included within the overarching legislation for some time, in Victoria they are only applied where more than $1,000,000 in levies are collected per annum. In these interviews having available funds to cover repairs identified by tenants and landlords was still problematic for committees of management who are the responsible actioning party. Moreover, within this research, sinking funds and maintenance plans were not in place even where there was a requirement for them to exist.

It has been proposed that owner corporation voting rights are also allocated to tenants as one way to overcome some of the process problems involved in getting owners (including landlords) to act in the collective interest to the benefit of long-term tenants. However, this is unlikely to occur due to the effect it may have on owner finances. This is particularly true in states where termination legislation is being considered such as New South Wales. Termination legislation will allow owners to vote to end the owner corporation scheme and allow the building to be demolished after buyout by building developers (Sherry 2006). It will make way for new developments that may better meet the changing needs of society. However, the possible effects of termination legislation on tenants are little understood (Easthope et al. 2013).

A lack of processes to ensure the safety of residents was raised in relation to building evacuation procedures. However this lack of procedures can also be extended to where ambulance, police and other emergency service personnel need to access individual apartments within electronically gated apartment building without dedicated concierge services. None of the Chairs or strata managers appeared to have an appropriate remedy.

Conclusion

A compact, walkable city in which home, work, shopping and entertainment are easily reachable is supported through current planning policies. Governments approve medium- and high-density apartment complexes, in part because of their supposed ability to mitigate the current housing shortage and bring workers closer to employment opportunities within the city centre. In this chapter I have outlined a range of tenancy related issues addressed by committees of management as part of their legislated duties. The high rate of investor-owned, inner-city apartments is a reversal of the overall rental figures available for Australia indicating the formation of a rental sub-market. The use of rental agents puts distance between the landlord and committee of management making it difficult for the renter and committee of management to interact effectively. Rental properties within strata titled complexes place renters within a complex organisation with little probity and in which the propensity to engage in self-interested behaviour rather than collective action occurs. It is an organisation in which renters have no direct voice and may be powerless to effect change. It is also one in which committees of management find it difficult to undertake their legislated duties of governing the common property, creating policy implications for government given the increasing overall numbers of apartments, and the range of tenants. Governance of strata titled complexes is made difficult not only by the range of stakeholder groups and their competing interests, but by the disconnect between various impacting pieces of legislation.

For governments to overcome these issues first tenants need to be provided with a greater voice, particularly in relation to maintenance and behavioural control issues and second, owner corporation need be more closely linked to the tenant leasing processes and have some redress within tenant contracts. A larger research project is required to probe these issues further, one in which the voices of the tenant is also heard.

By international standards, Australian tenants have little legislative protection afforded to them. Australia's early adoption and export of strata title legislation to other nations, makes what happens to tenants living within strata title schemes relevant to international audiences. By signalling the challenges faced by Australia in relation to tenancy issues in this area, other nations are able to develop pre-emptive actions that assist tenants.

References

Altmann, E. (2011) 'Strata title legislation and the implications for homelessness', *Parity: Responding to homelessness in Tasmania – putting the pieces together*, Nov 2011: 45–46.

—— (2013) 'Apartments, co-ownership and sustainability: Implementation barriers for retrofitting the built environment', *Journal of Environmental Policy and Planning*, *ifirst* at http://www.tandfonline.com/doi/full/10.1080/1523908X.2013.858593 accessed 25 November 2013.

Australian Bureau of Statistics (ABS) (2011) 'Census collector training 2011', *Census of Population and Housing Training*, Canberra: Commonwealth of Australia.

Bagaeen, S. and Uduku, O. (2010). *Gated Communities*. London: Earthscan.

Bajracharya, B. and Khan, S. (2010) 'Evolving governance model for community building: collaborative partnerships in master planned communities', *Urban Policy and Research* 28: 471–485.

Blakely, E. and Snyder, M. (1999) *Fortress America*, Washington DC: The Brookings Institution.

Brunn, S. (2006) 'Gated minds and gated lives as worlds of exclusion and fear', *Geojournal* 66: 5–26.

Budgen, G. (2005) 'Strata and community titles in Australia – Issues and current challenges', *Strata and Community Title in Australia for the 21st Century Conference*, Griffith University, Brisbane.

Burke, T. (2004) *Governance and Social Housing: Can Good Governance Be Bad Practice?* Swinburne University of Technology, Institute for Social Research.

Burke, T., Neske, C. and Ralston, L. (2005) *Entering Rental Housing*, Project 50142, Australian Housing and Urban Research Institute, Melbourne.

Burke, T., Stone, W. and Ralston, L. (2014) *Generational Change in Home Purchase Opportunity in Australia*, AHURI Final Report No.232. Melbourne: Australian Housing and Urban Research Institute. Available from: http://www.ahuri.edu.au/publications/projects/51002 accessed 2 December 2014.

Easthope, H. (2014) 'Making a rental property home', *Housing Studies*, DOI: 10.1080/02673037.2013.873115 accessed 19 January 2014.

Easthope, H. and Randolph, B. (2008) 'Governing the compact city: Challenges of Apartment Living in Sydney, Australia', *Housing Studies* 24(2): 243–259.

Easthope, H., Hudson, S. and Randolph, B. (2013) 'Urban renewal and strata scheme termination: Balancing communal management and individual property rights', *Environment and Planning A: International Journal of Urban and Regional Research* 45(6): 1421–1435.

Easthope, H., Tice, A. and Randolph, B. (2009) *The Desirable Apartment Life? The Demand for Higher Density Housing in Sydney and Melbourne*, Working Paper 5. City Futures Research Centre, University of New South Wales, Sydney.

Everton-Moore, K., Ardill, A., Guilding, C. and Warnken, J. (2006) 'The law of strata title in Australia: A jurisdictional stocktake', *Australian Property Law Journal* 13: 1–35.

Fincher, R. and Gooder, H. (2007) 'At home with diversity in medium density housing', *Housing Theory and Society* 24: 166–182.

Goodman, R. and Douglas, K. (2010) 'Life in a master planned estate – Community and lifestyle or conflict and liability?' *Urban Policy and Research* 28: 451–469.

Guilding C. (2003) 'Hotel owner/operator structures: Implications for capital budgeting process', *Management Accounting Research* 14(3): 179–199.

Guilding, C., Warnken, J., Ardill, A. and Fredline, L. (2005) 'An agency theory perspective on the owner / manager relationship in tourism-based condominiums', *Tourism Management* 26: 409–420.

Habibis, D., Atkinson, R., Dunbar, T., Goss, D., Easthope, H. and Maginn, P. (2007) *A Sustaining Tenancies Approach to Managing Demanding Behaviour in Public Housing: A Good Practice Guide, Affordable Housing, Urban Renewal and Planning: Emerging Practice in Queensland*, South Australia and New South Wales, AHURI Report 103, Melbourne.

Hulse, K., Milligan, V. and Easthope, H. (2011) *Secure Occupancy in Rental Housing: Conceptual Foundations and Comparative Perspectives*, Australian Housing and Urban research Institute Final Report No 170, Melbourne.

Johnston, N.R. and Reid, S. (2013) 'Multi-Owned Developments: a life cycle review of a developing research area', *Property Management* 31(5): 366–388.

Kearns, A., Hiscock, R., Ellaway, A. and Macintyre, S. (2000) 'Beyond four walls. The psycho-social benefits of home: evidence from West Central Scotland', *Housing Studies* 15(3): 387–410.

Kemeny J., (1983) *The Great Australian Nightmare: A Critique of the Home-ownership Ideology*, Melbourne: Georgian House.

Kemp, P. (1987) 'Some aspects of housing consumption in late nineteenth century England and Wales', *Housing Studies* 1: 3–16.

Kern, L. (2007) 'Reshaping the boundaries of public and private life: Gender, condominium development, and the neoliberalization of urban living', *Urban Geography* 28(7): 657–681.

Lei, C. and Van Der Merwe, C. 2009. Reflections on the role of the managing agent in South Africa and Chinese sectional title (condominium) legislation. *Journal of South African Legislation* 22: 22–38.

Low, S. (2006) 'Unlocking the gated community: Moral minimalism and social (dis)order in gated communities in the United States and Mexico', in G. Glasze, C. Webster and K. Frantz (eds) *Private Cities: Global and Local Perspectives*, London: Routledge.

McKenzie, E. (1996) *Privatopia: Home Owner Associations and the Rise of Residential Private Governments*, New Haven, CT: Yale University Press.

Mee, K. (2007) '"I ain't been to heaven yet? Living here, this is heaven to me": Public housing and the making of home in inner Newcastle', *Housing, Theory and Society* 24: 207–228.

Pouder, R. and Clarke, J. (2009) 'Formulating strategic direction for a gated residential community', *Property Management* 27: 216–227.

Randolph, B. (2006) 'Delivering the compact city in Australia: Current trends and future implications', *Urban Policy and Research* 24(4): 473–490.

Randolph, B. and Tice, A. (2013) 'Who lives in higher density housing? A study of spatially discontinuous housing sub-markets in Sydney and Melbourne', *Urban Studies*, DOI: 10.1177/0043098013477701, accessed 6 January 2014.

Sherry, C. (2006) 'Termination of strata schemes in New South Wales – proposals for reform', *Australian Property Law Journal* 13(3): 227–239.

Stacks/The Law Company (2013) 'Court case threatens holiday home renting', 1 May 2013, http://thelawcompany.com.au/court-case-threatens-holiday-home-renting/.

Townshend, I.J. (2006) 'From public neighbourhoods to multi-tier private neighbourhoods: The evolving ecology of neighbourhood privatisation in Calgary', *GeoJournal* 66: 103–120.

Troy, P. (2002) 'Change or turbulence', *City* 6(1): 7–24.

Warnken, J. and Guilding, C. (2008) 'Multi-ownership of tourism accommodation complexes: A critique of types relative merits, and challenges arising', *Tourism Management* 30: 704–714.

Warnken, J. and Guilding, C. (2009) 'Multi-ownership of tourism accommodation complexes: A critique of types, relative merits, and challenges arising', *Tourism Management* 30: 704–714.

Warnken J., Russel, R. and Faulkner, B. (2003) 'Condominium developments in maturing destinations: Potentials and problems of long-term sustainability', *Tourism Management* 24: 155–168.

Webster, C. and Le Goix, R. (2005) 'Planning by Commonhold', *Economic Affairs* 25(4): 19–23.

Wulff, M., Dharmalingam, A., Reynolds, M. and Yates, J. (2009) *Australia's Private Rental Market: Changes (2001–2006) in the Supply of, and Demand for, Low Rent Dwellings*, AHURI Positioning Paper No. 122, Melbourne, Australian Housing and Urban Research Institute.

Wulff, M., Reynolds, M., Darmalingam, A., Hulse, K. and Yates, J. (2011) *Australia's Private Rental Market: The Supply of, and Demand for, Affordable Dwellings*, AHURI Final Report No.168. Melbourne: Australian Housing and Urban Research Institute.

Yates, J. and Bradbury, B. (2010) 'Home ownership as a (crumbling) fourth pillar of social insurance in Australia', Special Issue: Home ownership and asset-based welfare *Journal of Housing and the Built Environment* 25(2): 193–211.

PART 2
Policies

Chapter 9
Private Rental Housing in Australia: Political Inertia and Market Change

Kath Hulse and Terry Burke

Introduction

The private rental sector is a growing and increasingly important part of the Australian housing system. Almost one in four Australian households lives in private rented housing and their lives are affected by the cost and quality of this accommodation; its location relative to transport, jobs, services and facilities; the type of service offered in areas such as property maintenance; and their capacity to make a home in rented housing. Many Australians own properties which they rent out. Colloquially known as 'rental investors', they are concerned with the value of their asset, the rental yield, and having good tenants who pay the rent and look after the property. Many Australians thus have a vital interest in the way the private rental sector operates and it is perhaps not surprising that tension between the interests of those who live in, and those who own, properties in the private rental sector lies at the heart of some of the most heated debates about housing in 21st-century Australia.

In this chapter we argue that many of the institutional settings, policies, practices and cultural norms regarding private renting have not kept pace with market trends, being based on a view that the sector provides a flexible and relatively short term option for younger people who will move on to become home owners. This view has *de facto* supported the interests of rental investors who value flexibility in the face of increased economic volatility and the capacity to buy and sell property at short notice to capture capital gain rather than those of renters who may value stability, good housing management, and the capacity to make a home.

We first review some theoretical perspectives on the private rental sector before discussing some of the key Australian literature which has informed understanding of the sector. The chapter then discusses three hotly contested debates about the private rental sector in Australia: can the sector provide sustainable housing for lower income households; does current tax treatment of rental investment increase supply or drive up housing prices and rents; and is current regulation of residential tenancies appropriate to the contemporary private rental sector?

Theoretical Perspectives on the Private Rental Sector

Two key perspectives have shaped understanding of the private rental sector internationally: one based on historical power relations and one on economic factors.

Historical Power Relations and Rental Market Structuring

A key contribution has been Kemeny's (1995) causal explanation of the distinction between the unitary/integrated rental systems of some European countries such as Germany and Austria and the dual rental systems in a small group of Anglophone countries including Australia. Unitary/integrated rental systems provide support for social (cost) renting such that over time this sector matures financially and can compete with private rental, exerting a downward pressure on rents generally (Kemeny 1995: 56). In contrast, dual rental systems have relatively large and lightly regulated private rental sectors which are shielded from competition from small but highly regulated social rental sectors, enabling the for-profit sector to thrive with little moderation of rent levels. The causal explanation is said to lie in historical power relations such that unitary/rental systems are the result of the tradition of compromise and coalition-building which characterise some of the European countries whereas the dual rental systems are found in the Anglophone countries which have political systems dominated by two party adversarial political systems, broadly representing the interests of capital and labour (Kemeny 1995: 65–71).

This type of explanation is influenced by, extends and in part rebuts broader developments in the political economy of welfare. In particular, it engages with the contention that Anglophone countries have liberal welfare regimes which are underpinned by dualism in power relations such that states encourage markets and provide small, strictly regulated and often stigmatised welfare for those with high needs (Esping-Andersen 1990: 26–27). Importantly, these dualist power relations become embedded in 'welfare regimes' and even where there is disjuncture between existing institutional arrangements and emerging risk profiles affecting family and labour markets in a post-industrial society, the response of a welfare regime will be 'path dependent' (Esping-Andersen 1999: 172).

Theoretical perspectives based on historical power relations thus suggest that institutional settings once established are difficult to change, although this has to be established empirically in different countries. They are useful in drawing attention to the factors which shaped current institutional settings as well as underlying patterns in power relations which create policy inertia. This type of theoretical explanation, however, appears less adequate in explaining some of the dynamism apparent in housing systems which is reflected in the private rental sector.

Housing Market Dynamics

There is a parallel strand in the literature, whereby changes in the private rental sector are explained by housing market dynamics. Such explanations see changing market circumstances as the major drivers of the private rental system both on the demand and supply side. Increased rental demand can be understood as a function of changing consumer preferences such as the desire of many young people to enjoy an inner city café culture and to be flexible around labour market choices but also of constraint in that many households who desire ownership can no longer afford it or who face uncertainty of income which makes it difficult to take on repayment of a mortgage over a long period, and private rental is a reluctant second best. The growth in small scale rental investment in many countries has been the major change on the supply side even in countries which, unlike Australia, have had a history of institutional investment in rental housing and a designated private rental stock (Hulse and Milligan 2014). Growth in supply has reflected both domestic demand and in some cases additional demand from overseas investors seeking financial security, the latter heightened in the post Global Financial Crisis environment.

A broader perspective on 'the housing economy' as a multi-disciplinary project has drawn attention to risk (Smith et al. 2010: 9–14), and arguably provides a link between economic analyses and the welfare regime approaches discussed above. In housing as in other areas of economy and society, the dominance of neo-liberal ideas has emphasised deregulation, privatisation and individualism, captured in terms such as 'the risk society' (Beck 1992). In the process, some of the risks in housing have moved from governments to those involved in the rental system, both owners and private renters. In this vein, analysis of the housing economy has tackled questions of the market effects of government policy settings with regard to supply of private rental in the context of the broader housing system.

A key area of debate has centred on whether government regulation 'distorts' markets because it deters investors due to limited or uncertain returns (e.g. Ball 2010) or whether the effects of such regulation varies according to historical and institutional context (e.g. Oxley 2010; Whitehead et al. 2013). A further area of debate has been the market effects of government subsidies to private rental households. Such subsidies can be seen (at least indirectly) as addressing income risks due not only to life event such sickness, disability, old age and lone parenthood but also those associated with changes in the labour market and welfare systems (Kemp 2007: 269).

Australian Studies of Private Rental

The Australian literature on the private rental sector has drawn on, and contributed to, these theoretical perspectives. There have been a handful of comprehensive reviews (Paris 1984; Maher et al. 1997; Hulse et al. 2012) which have detailed the historical development of institutional settings for the sector. For the most part, however, research has adopted an economic or public policy perspective. A series of four studies has estimated the supply of low-rent dwellings affordable, and available, to lower income households (Wulff et al. 2001, Yates and Wulff 2005; Wulff et al. 2011; Hulse et al. 2014) along with other studies such as analysis of vacancy rates (Wood et al. 2006) which provide insights into market trends. Research into rental investors has indicated the prevalence of small investors with one or two properties who want a 'safe' investment (Yates 1996; Beer 1999; Berry 2000; Seelig et al. 2009; Wood and Ong 2013). There has been a small body of research into financial assistance for private renters (Wulff 2000; Hulse 2007; Jacobs et al. 2007; Randolph and Holloway 2007).

It is notable that there has been limited research on the physical, legal and socio-cultural aspects of private rental in Australia. Some exceptions to this have been research into environmental sustainability of private rental accommodation (Gabriel et al. 2010) and the legal relationships between owners and tenants (Hulse and Pawson 2010; Hulse et al. 2011). In short, and reflecting the international literature, the focus in the Australian literature has been on the private rental sector in politico-economic terms rather than socio-cultural and legal perspectives.

The Australian Private Rental Sector: Three Critical Debates

Private rental in the Australian context refers to households who pay rent to private landlords or real estate agents who manage rental properties on behalf of landlords. There has been a slow but steady increase in private rental since the early 1980s such that by 2011 almost one in four households (or 1.8m households) lived in private rental housing in Australia (Hulse et al. 2014), significantly higher than the one in six households who rent privately in some other advanced economies (Crook and Kemp 2014: 10). A third of private renters have been renting for 10 or more years although not necessarily in the same property (up from 27 per cent in 1996) and families with children now comprise 40 per cent of all private renter households in 2011 (Stone et al. 2013: 29, 11). Although the sector accommodates a broad range of households such as students, recent migrants and higher income professionals (Hulse 2014), it has an increasingly important role in housing lower income households. These private renters have the most severe affordability problems of any housing tenure, with around 30 per cent experiencing housing stress (Yates and Milligan 2007, Burke et al. 2011).

At the same time, investment in residential property has become increasingly popular with about 1.8 million taxpayers declaring that they had rental income (about 14 per cent of all individual taxpayers) in 2011–2012 (ATO 2013). Many of these taxpayers (1.2m of them) claim a loss on their rental property which results in reduced income tax ('negative gearing'), which is of most benefit to those on the highest tax rates, generating heated debates about tax advantages for rental investors.

The relationships between owner/investors and tenants occur within a broader institutional framework in which governments have an important role in determining tax settings for rental investment and subsidies to tenants as well as regulation of the contractual relationships between owners/investors and tenants. There are, however, also a number of other key players and intermediaries, often neglected in contemporaneous research, such as real estate agents, specialist property managers, financial institutions, insurance companies, developers, self-managed superannuation funds, property trusts and industry organisations and lobby groups, each of which has its own set of interests.

In this section we provide three case studies of contemporary debates about the private rental sector which illustrates the tension between the politics of inertia due to mobilisation of vested interests and the ongoing dynamics of housing market change: Rent Assistance, negative gearing tax concessions and regulation of residential tenancies.

The Rent Assistance Debate

In the decades from World War II to the early 1980s, many lower income people were able to buy their own home with the assistance of discounted/controlled interest rates for home mortgages, provision of low interest home loans; sales of public housing to sitting tenants, development of 'affordable' home ownership lots by state land developers and cash grants to first home buyers (Berry 1999). Working households of modest means and pensioners were able to access public rental housing, the main features of which were controlled rents and security of tenure, often accompanied with an option to purchase at a favourable price.

In the mid-1980s these policy settings were changed as federal Labor governments (1983–1996) began to deregulate the economy. Changes included the deregulation of housing finance accompanied by removal of some of the more explicit measures to assist lower income buyers into home ownership. Governments continued to provide tax advantages for those who were already owners through exclusion from capital gains tax (Berry 1999: 116). Starting in the 1980s and accelerating in the 1990s, governments began to allocate public rental housing to those with the most urgent and chronic housing needs rather than working households of modest means (Hayward 1996, Troy 2012).

Labor federal governments turned increasingly to Rent Assistance (RA) as the policy instrument to assist people on pensions and welfare benefits to afford private rental housing. RA had started life as a small flat-rate supplement to the single aged and invalid pensions in the late 1950s but over time was extended incrementally to cover other pensioners and beneficiaries, with payments based on household type and size. By the late 1980s, further incremental changes extended the payment to families with dependent children in receipt of family payments and changes were made to the payment formula to target households paying higher rents as part of a strategy to reduce poverty, particularly among families with children. Subsequent changes were relatively minor adjustments, most designed to contain expenditures, such as introduction of a lower 'sharers' rate' in the early 1990s.

There have been a number of failed attempts to reform RA. In the mid-1990s, the federal Labor government proposed that it be responsible for a new unified system of 'housing assistance payments' to all low-income renters (public and private) in which RA for private tenants would be 'substantially increased' and there would be protection for public housing tenants. These reforms attracted substantial criticisms from supporters of public housing and were unable to get agreement from the states and territories, subsequently stalling after a change of federal government. Coalition federal governments (1996–2007) indicated some disquiet about the mounting cost of the payment to the government and instigated reviews of RA but little change to policy settings resulted.

More recently, there were three further attempts to address 'the problem' of RA under the federal Labor Government (2007–2013). The proposal to pay housing assistance payments to the states for their public housing tenants as well as payments to private tenants was revived in the context of negotiations for a new National Affordable Housing Agreement in 2008. The Harmer Pension Review proposed to restructure RA to further target those paying higher rents as well as 'addressing inequities that have arisen with the sharers rate of Rent Assistance' (Harmer 2009: 94). The Henry Tax Review recommended that rates of RA should be substantially increased and linked to movement in market rents and that public housing rent concessions should be replaced by Rent Assistance and a new form of assistance for high-needs tenants, to improve equity and work incentives (Henry et al. 2009: 66).

None of these suggestions for major reform were adopted, indicating policy inertia for almost 25 years, during which time more lower income households than ever became dependent on the private rental market. By June 2013, 1.27m 'income units'[1] on pensions/

---

1 Data on RA are only supplies based on 'income unit' which is an administrative category referring to the recipient of an income support or family payment and any dependent children. It is not the same as a household.

benefits and family payments were in receipt of RA with annual expenditure of $3.63 billion, far in excess of that spent on public rental housing and other forms of social housing (FaHCSIA 2013: 48–9). It has been clear since the work of the National Housing Strategy in the early 1990s that lower income households in receipt of statutory incomes form the majority of those who are in rental stress in the private rental sector notwithstanding receipt of RA (National Housing Strategy 1991: 43) and that this remained the case in the 2000s (Yates and Milligan 2007). As rents have increased due to high demand particularly in large cities, regular indexing of RA payments has become increasingly ineffective in enabling lower income households to rent affordable housing (Colic-Peisker et al. 2010). There is clear evidence over many years that RA, whilst it provides additional money to some low income households, does not make housing affordable for many recipients and there is little evidence on whether and how they are able to sustain their tenancies. There is, however, clear evidence that RA has not stimulated an increase in the supply of lower rent housing (Hulse et al. 2014).

The development of RA as the major means of assisting low income households with their housing resulted from a series of incremental policy decisions rather than a 'big picture' change in policy. It has resulted in a hybrid system in which the major means of housing assistance for low income households is embedded in the nation's income support system, which itself is subject to ongoing scrutiny and change under the rubric of 'welfare reform'. Reliance on private rental accorded with neo-liberal ideas which became increasingly dominant in federal policy: markets were viewed as the most efficient means of allocating resources with governments having a reduced role in providing a safety net for some 'at risk' either directly (public housing) or increasingly indirectly (funding other social housing providers). Attempts to reform policy settings foundered on polarisation of views, including muted support from the 'housing lobby' for strategies to assist low income households to rent privately. This history provides support for politico-historical theories which suggest that institutional settings once established are difficult to change despite significant changes in the private rental market and the Australian housing system more generally over the last 25 years.

The 'Negative Gearing' Debate

We next turn to another key issue in relation to private rental, the so-called 'negative gearing' debate, much discussed in public and media discourse, on which opinion is highly polarized. Negative gearing is a tax rule that allows all investors to write off the costs of borrowing to acquire an asset, as well as other holding costs, against their total income for the purposes of calculation of their individual income tax. Until the 1980s, it was a relatively little known and used tax provision in respect of investment in private rented property and was largely invisible to the degree that that the first major study of private rental in Australia (Paris 1984) made no mention of it.

In the mid-1980s, the federal Labor government became concerned about future tax losses from negative gearing for what they saw as producing little housing benefit (O'Donnell 2005: 4) and in 1986 brought in legislation to quarantine deductions such that they could not be used to reduce tax on other sources of income. Successful lobbying by real estate interests in the context of impending elections at the federal level and in New South Wales mean that the federal government reversed the decision in 1987 even though it remains far from clear that quarantining deductions had the effect of reducing investment beyond what could be expected in a normal business cycle (Hayward and Burke 1988; Badcock and Browett 1991). Perversely the effect of the reversal of the real estate industry-led campaign was to make many more potential rental investors aware of the tax provision and subsequently, and in the context of broader financial deregulation, an industry of brokers, marketers, property advisors and other intermediaries emerged using negative gearing as the 'hook' to attract investors into the residential property sector. It is a widely used tax provision used by 1.2m taxpayers and has become one of the major sources of forgone tax revenue of the Commonwealth government (estimated at around $5 billion per annum (ATO 2013: Table 15) and appears to be a major driver of rental investment along with a 50 per cent concession on capital gains tax on sale of rental properties introduced by the Coalition federal government in 2000.

The arguments in favour of continued negative gearing are articulated by organisations representing property owners and real estate interests. They include that it is meeting increased demand for private rental due to high levels of migration and demographic change and that it will increase rental supply thus assisting in moderating rents. Another form of argument is the counter factual i.e. the 'disaster' that would occur if negative gearing was abolished including withdrawal of investors leading to a large loss of rental stock, resulting in increased rents and homelessness, as well as a potential fall in all dwelling sales prices (Bushby 2013, Goodwin 2014, Yardney 2012).

The arguments against negative gearing are made by a range of policy commentators with some support from housing research. They point out that most investment goes into existing properties and not new construction accentuating demand pressures and house prices inflation (Hulse et al. 2012). In turn the higher house prices and competitive advantage over owner purchases (who cannot claim interest costs as a tax deduction) is displacing first home buyers from the market and slowly converting an ownership society into a rental society (see Eslake 2013, Gittens 2003, Van Onsolen 2014 and Kelly 2013 for arguments against). A further consideration raised internationally is investors driven by investment outcomes such as capital gain and rental yields potentially makes the housing market more unstable than if driven by households who just want a dwelling to live in (Logan and Molotch 1987).

Neither side of the debate has been able to offer convincingly detailed evidence in support of their arguments, although it is important to note that those who advocate changes to negative gearing to produce more efficient outcomes in the rental market appear to be less conflicted by self-interest than most of the pro negative gearing supporters. However, the effect is that although many recognise the inefficiencies of negative gearing and its potential deleterious effect on the housing market, reform has become virtually a politically 'taboo' topic.

Perhaps the most important aspect of the negative gearing debate has been the political effect of a proliferation of small investors, the so called 'mum and dad' investors, who are the major participants in the market (Berry 2000). Widespread use of negative gearing, along with other factors, has created a whole class of people concerned with property rights at the expense of tenants' rights. This is of concern in view of market changes in the sector noted earlier including an increasing group of long term private renters and the increase in low income families with children living in the sector. This new political reality, political fear of the reaction of household residential investors, also affects the capacity of governments to undertake residential tenancy reform to accommodate the changing role of the private rental sector as we discuss next.

The Residential Tenancies Reform Debate

In Australia's federal system of government, whilst the federal government has a key role in housing policy, the six states and two territories are responsible for regulation of residential tenancies. Despite incontrovertible evidence of the strong association between private rental and living in poverty over the past 40 years, there have only been three occasions when federal governments have made explicit connections between housing policy and this type of regulation. Examining each of these in turn reveals that legislative reform to improve tenant protection is always hotly contested as it runs counter to strongly held assumptions about property rights.

On the first occasion in 1975, in work for the Commission of Inquiry into Poverty, Professor Sackville in a damning report excoriated landlord and tenant legislation as based on feudal property relations and recommended wide-ranging reform with an emphasis on the protection of tenants (Bradbrook 1975). This was part of a series of strategies to address the strong association found by the Commission between living in poverty and renting privately. The report led to most (but not all) jurisdictions enacting comprehensive legislation on residential tenancies separately form commercial and other tenancies from the late 1970s (Bradbrook 2003).

On the second occasion, in 1994, the Labor federal government commissioned a comprehensive review of legislative provisions for residential tenancies across Australia as a follow up to the National Housing Strategy of the early 1990s. This resulted in a framework for minimum standards covering key issues including: forms of agreements; bonds and condition reports; rent setting and review; anti-discrimination; access provisions and resident privacy; termination, eviction and dispute resolution; and special provisions for non-self-contained housing forms, such as shared housing, boarding houses and caravan parks (Kennedy et al. 1995). The proposed standards were designed to achieve consistency across jurisdictions, to be in keeping with modern principles for regulating landlord and tenant relationships, and to balance the conflicting interests of landlords and tenants. The incoming Coalition federal government (1996–2007), however, took a different approach to national housing policy, focusing on reform to public rental housing rather than the private rental sector. However, in the late 1990s, the jurisdictions that had not previously introduced comprehensive residential tenancies legislation did so (Tasmania 1997; ACT 1997 and NT 1999) and there were continuing incremental changes in other jurisdictions (Blunden and Martin 2004).

The third occasion followed the release by the Labor federal Government of a White Paper on homelessness (Australian Government 2008) when the government funded a review of tenancy laws as one aspect of preventing and mitigating homelessness. The review explicitly recognised difficulties in accessing rental housing in current market conditions as a cause of homelessness and as a barrier to ending homelessness and made a number of recommendations for improvement to tenancy law that were specifically focused on mitigating homelessness and tenancy protection (National Shelter 2010). At the time of the review, four jurisdictions had just completed or were in the final stages of major reviews of tenancies legislation: (Queensland, Western Australia, NSW and Tasmania) which to varying degrees acknowledged the connection between their housing policies and changes to residential tenancies legislation.

A further trend in more recent state and territory legislative reform in Australia is a gradual extension of regulation to households living in 'non-standard' form of rental housing, in particular, boarding/rooming houses and residential/caravan parks, although not in all jurisdictions and generally these tenants have fewer rights. Some types of non-standard rental arrangements are still not generally covered by residential tenancies legislation, although they may be covered by other legislation types, including various forms of occupancy of aged care units on a rental basis, other types of supported accommodation, tertiary student accommodation, holiday rentals, rent-buy arrangements, and head-lease arrangements. As the private rental sector becomes more diverse, it is likely that further issues will arise in respect of these types of tenancy arrangements.

Recent comparative research into regulation of tenancies across diverse developed countries have indicated that, despite ongoing reviews and reforms, current provisions in Australian states and territories give tenants fewer protections than in many other developed countries (Crook and Kemp 2014). Key examples are shorter initial tenancy periods (6–12 months); provision for more frequent rent increases; no system of moderation of rent increases during tenancy; and permitted termination without specific grounds (along with Scotland) (Hulse and Milligan 2014: Table 2). Some of the jurisdictions with greater tenant protections also had large private rental sectors, most notably Germany, indicating that legislation that provides greater tenant protection is not incompatible with a large and functioning private rental sector. However, this finding should be understood in the context of different historical factors and legal systems.

The difficulties of implementing reform to residential tenancies legislation over many years indicate not only the relatively weak position of successive federal governments in obtaining agreement from the states/territories who in Australia's federal system are responsible for such legislation but also the failure to take a coordinated view of the private rental sector encompassing such legislation and policies to assist private tenants. At a state/territory level, residential tenancies reform is largely the responsibility of departments of consumer affairs or fair trading which are distinct from departments with responsibilities for housing market analysis, housing policy development, and development of programs for lower income and vulnerable households. It also appears that property interests are better organised than private tenants who have only a weak level of organisation. Opportunities for broader discussion of key issues and consideration of potential innovations are quite limited.

The only issue to get some traction nationally in the 2000s has been electronic tenancy databases which have been increasingly used in the private rental sector over the last 20 years. They are run by private operators and provide information on the tenancy history of households, including debts from prior tenancies and other issues (Short et al. 2003: ii) and are not generally covered by state/territory residential tenancies legislation. After almost a decade of discussion, in December 2010 the Ministerial Council on Consumer Affairs formally adopted a set of model provisions for regulation which had then to be incorporated into state-specific legislation. Interestingly there is no data base on poorly performing landlords/agents.

Changes to residential tenancies legislation has proved a lengthy process because of an underlying principle of the need to provide 'balance' between changes that give perceived benefits to tenants and those that benefit landlords and property managers. This implies that current legislation is 'balanced', a view disputed by some (National Shelter 2010). Whilst the recent reviews are broader in scope than previously, and do consider the rental market context, the primary focus remains regulation of the rights and responsibilities of parties to tenancy agreements and provision of means of resolving disputes between them. It is also notable that while there is awareness of reform in other jurisdictions, there is little consideration of equivalent legislation and regulation of residential tenancies internationally.

Although there have clearly been advances, changes have been hotly contested and proved difficult to implement and, when compared with other developed countries, the Australian legislation has weaker provisions for tenant protection. The questions which have never been fully resolved are whether legislation is adequate for a sector which houses many low income tenants often for lengthy periods and whether the legislation gives sufficient weight to the sector as a place to live rather than a place to invest.

The three case studies illustrate considerable policy inertia and that settings for the private rental sector, once established are difficult to change. They also illustrate the hotly contested nature of these debates, the various sets of interest which are involved including owners/investors and private tenants and a range of intermediary organisations. It is important to note that there are other issues associated with the private rental sector which require policy consideration and further research. These include the increasing concentration of lower cost rental on the urban fringe, problems of housing quality and environmental sustainability, and the challenges of accessibility including discrimination against particular groups of vulnerable households.

Conclusion

The Australian private rental sector has changed from its historical role as a transitional sector for households moving into home ownership or social housing to become a long-term sector for a significant number of households. It has also become a major investment sector for Australian households. These changes can be explained partly in economic terms. Demand for private rental appears to be increasing in Australia and internationally for a raft of reasons. These include social changes which make the private rental sector more attractive, such as longer periods in education, delays in partnering and having children and greater labour mobility including between countries. There are also a range of 'push' factors in that it is becoming more difficult for households to access other options due to persistently high housing prices relative to wages/salaries and a general trend to retrenchment of social housing. It also appears that there is a greater demand for investment in residential property to boost asset holdings, involving not only domestic demand but also some international investment.

These market changes highlight a paradox in institutional and policy settings. On the one hand, the private rental sector is a place to live for an increasing number of householders who require some stability in their housing circumstances so that they and their children have the same opportunities as the rest of the community. On the other hand, it is seen increasingly as an investment opportunity, such that the sector is more unstable and less likely to provide good housing outcomes. There are emerging risk profiles both for tenants and for those investing in the private rental sector stemming from a variety of factors for which there was greater protection in the past. Risks for tenants include the rise of precarious work and a decline in wage regulation as well greater conditionality around welfare benefits. Risks for rental investors are typically seen as changes in asset values (for different property types in different locations) and rental yields, but there are a variety of other risks including tenant demand, the financial capacity of tenants to sustain rental payments, damage to properties and, as the Global Financial Crisis illustrated, the imbedding of housing investment into an unstable global financial system.

In the face of these changes, many of the policy settings for the private rental sector have changed relatively little. RA continues to provide financial support to low income private tenants but appears increasingly ineffective in providing affordable and sustainable housing for low income households, despite their increasing dependence on this sector. Negative gearing for rental investors arguably contributes to the surge of investor activity which contributes to higher property prices which make buying a house unaffordable for even those on quite moderate incomes and putting an upward pressure on rents to obtain reasonable yields. Changing residential tenancies legislation have proved to be a highly contested and slow process and, despite improvement, current state and territory based legislation appears to fall short in terms of tenant protections relative to other developed countries. There is considerable evidence to suggest that politico-historical explanations of institutional path dependency and policy inertia have been important in the Australian context. Over the longer term, it appears that property rights have had greater priority than citizens' requirements for housing. The challenge for the future is to develop a modern rental sector that provides a better place to live as well as a place to invest in.

References

Australian Department of Families, Housing, Community Services and Indigenous Affairs (FaHCSIA) (2013) *2012–13 Annual Report*, Australian Government, Canberra.

Australian Government (2008) *The Road Home: A National Approach to Reducing Homelessness*, White Paper, Australian Government, Canberra.

Australian Taxation Office (ATO) (2013) *Taxation Statistics 2011–12*, Australian Government, Canberra.

Badcock, B. and Browett, M. (1991) 'The responsiveness of the private rental sector in Australia to changes in Commonwealth taxation policy', *Housing Studies* 6(3): 182–192.

Ball, M. (2010) *The UK Private Rented Sector as a Source of Affordable Accommodation*, York: Joseph Rowntree Foundation.

Beck, U. (1992) *Risk Society: Towards a New Modernity*, London: Sage.

Beer, A. (1999) 'Housing investment and the private rental sector in Australia', *Urban Studies* 36 (2): 255–269.

Berry, M. (1999) 'Unravelling the "Australian Housing Solution": The post-war years', *Housing, Theory and Society* 16(3): 106–123.

Berry, M. (2000) 'Investment in rental housing in Australia: Small landlords and institutional investors', *Housing Studies* 15(5): 661–681.

Blunden, H. and Martin, C. (2004) *Leaking Roofs: Australian Tenancy Law*, Tenants Union of NSW, Sydney.

Bradbrook, A. (1975) *Law and Poverty in Australia*, Commission of Inquiry into Poverty: Second Main Report, Australian Government Publishing Service, Canberra.

—— (2003) 'Rented housing law: Past, present and future', *Flinders Journal of Law Reform* 7(1): 1–14.

Burke, T., Stone, M. and Ralston, L., (2011) *The Residual Income Method: A New Lens on Housing Affordability and Market Behaviour*, Final Report No 176, AHURI, Melbourne

Bushby, N. (2013) 'Negative gearing must not be meddled with', *REIA NEWS* Issue 29 November.

Colic-Peisker, V., Ong, R. and McMurray, C. (2010) *Falling Behind: The Growing Gap between Rent and Rent Assistance 1995–2009*, RMIT University, Melbourne.

Crook, T. and Kemp, P.A. (2014) 'Introduction', in T. Crook and P.A. Kemp, (eds), *Private Rental Housing: Comparative Perspectives*, Cheltenham: Edward Elgar.

Eslake, S. (2013) *Housing Policy in Australia: Fifty years of Failure* Submission to the Senate Economics References Committee Inquiry into Affordable Housing, submission no 2, http://www.aph.gov.au/Parliamentary_Business/Committees/Senate/Economics/Affordable_housing_2013/Submissions (accessed 19 March 2014).

Esping-Andersen, G. (1990) *The Three Worlds of Welfare Capitalism*, Cambridge: Polity.

—— (1999) *Social Foundations of Postindustrial Economies*, Oxford: Oxford University Press.

Gabriel, M., Watson, P., Ong, R., Wood, G. and Wulff, M. (2010) *The Environmental Sustainability of Australia's Private Rental Housing Stock*, Final Report no. 159, AHURI, Melbourne.

Gittens, R. (2003) 'Pollies tell fibs about negative gearing', *Sydney Morning Herald*, August.

Goodwin, S. (2014) 'Negative gearing fills a crucial gap in housing', *The Australian Financial Review*, Jan 21.

Harmer, J. (2009) *Pension Review Report*, Department of Families, Housing, Community Services and Indigenous Affairs, Canberra, http://www.dss.gov.au/sites/default/files/documents/05_2012/pensionreviewreport.pdf (accessed 3 February 2014).

Hayward, D. (1996) The reluctant landlords? A history of public housing in Australia, *Urban Policy and Research* 14(1): 5–35.

Hayward, D. and Burke, T. (1988) 'Justifying the unjustifiable', *Australian Society* 7(8): 16–18.

Henry, K., Harmer, J., Piggott, J., Ridout, H. and Smith, G. (2009) *Australia's Future Tax System: Report to the Treasurer*, Commonwealth of Australia, December, http://www.taxreview.treasury.gov.au/content/downloads/final_report_part_1/00_AFTS_final_report_consolidated.pdf (accessed 20 March 2014).

Hulse, K. (2007) 'Housing allowances and the restructuring of the Australian welfare state', in P.A. Kemp (ed.), *Housing Allowances in Comparative Context*, Bristol: Policy Press.

—— (2014) 'Australia', in T. Crook and P.A. Kemp (eds), *Private Rental Housing, Comparative Perspectives*, Cheltenham: Edward Elgar.

Hulse, K. and Milligan, V. (2014) Secure occupancy: A new framework for analysing security in rental housing, *Housing Studies* 29(5): 638–656.

Hulse, K. and Pawson, H. (2010) Worlds apart? Lower-income households and private renting in Australia and the UK, *International Journal of Housing Policy* 10(4): 399–419.

Hulse, K., Milligan, V. and Easthope, H. (2011) *Secure Occupancy in Rental Housing: Conceptual Foundations and Comparative Perspectives*, Final Report no. 170, AHURI, Melbourne.

Hulse, K., Reynolds, M. and Yates, J. (2014) *Changes in the Supply of Affordable Housing in the Private Rental Sector for Lower Income Households*, Final Report, AHURI, Melbourne (forthcoming).

Hulse, K., Burke, T., Ralston, L. and Stone, W. (2012) *The Australian Private Rental Sector: Changes and Challenges*, Positioning Paper No. 149, AHURI, Melbourne.

Jacobs, K., Natalier, K., Berry, M., Seelig, T. and Slater, M. (2007) 'Band-aid or panacea? The role of private rental support programs in addressing access problems in the Australian housing market', *Housing Studies* 22(6): 901–919.

Kelly, J-F. (2013) *Renovating Housing Policy*, Melbourne: Grattan Institute.

Kemeny, J. (1995) *From Public Housing to the Social Market*, Abingdon: Routledge.

Kemp, P.A. (2007) 'Housing allowances in the advanced welfare states', in P.A. Kemp (ed.), *Housing Allowances in Comparative Perspective*, Bristol: The Policy Press.

Kennedy, R., See, P. and Sutherland, P. (1995) *Minimum Legislative Standards for Residential Tenancies in Australia*, Department of Housing and Regional Development, Canberra.

Logan, J. and Molotch, H. (1987) *Urban Fortunes: The Political Economy of Place*, Los Angeles: University of California Press.

Maher, C., Wulff, M., Yates, J., Beer, A., Karmel, R., Stimson, R., Wood, G., Department of Social Security and National Shelter (1997) *Australia's Private Rental Housing Market: Policies and Processes*, Working Paper no. 9, AHURI, Melbourne.

National Housing Strategy (1991) *The Supply Side of the Rental Market*, Background Paper no. 2, Department of Health, Housing and Community Services, Canberra.

National Shelter (2010) *A Better Lease on Life: Improving Australian Tenancy Law*, Canberra: National Shelter.

O'Donnell, J. (2005) 'Quarantining interest deductions for negatively geared rental property investments', *eJournal of Tax Research* 3(1).

Oxley, M., Lishman, R. Brown, T., Haffner, M. and Hoekstra, J. (2010) *Promoting Investment in Private Rented Housing Supply, International Policy Comparisons*, Department for Communities and Local Government, London https://www.dora.dmu.ac.uk/bitstream/handle/2086/7535/CLG%20PRS.pdf?sequence=1 (accessed 20 February 2014).

Paris, C. (1984) *Affordable and Available Housing: The Role of the Private Rental Sector*, Canberra: Australian Institute of Urban Studies.

Randolph, B. and Holloway, D. (2007) *Commonwealth Rent Assistance and the Spatial Concentration of Low Income Households in Metropolitan Australia*, Final Report no. 101, AHURI, Melbourne.

Seelig, T., Thompson, A., Burke, T., Pinnegar, S., McNelis, S. and Morris, A. (2009) *Understanding What Motivates Households to Become and Remain Investors in the Private Rental Market*, Final Report no. 130, AHURI, Melbourne.

Short, P., Minnery, J., Mead, E., Adkins, B., Peake, A., Fedrick, D. and O'Flaherty, M. (2003) *Tenancy Databases: Risk Minimisation and Outcomes*, Final Report no. 31, AHURI, Melbourne.

Smith, S., Searle, B. and Powells, G. (2010) 'Introduction', ch. 1 in S. Smith and B. Searle (eds), *The Blackwell Companion to the Economics of Housing, The Housing Wealth of Nations*, Chichester: Wiley-Blackwell.

Stone, W., Burke, T., Hulse, K. and Ralston, L. (2013) *Long-term Private Rental in a Changing Australian Private Rental Sector*, Final Report No 209, AHURI, Melbourne.

Troy, P. (2012) *Accommodating Australians*, Australia: The Federation Press.

Van Onsolen, L. (2014) *Busting the negative Gearing Myth* http://www.macrobusiness.com.au/2014/01/busting-the-big-negative-gearing-lie/ (accessed 20 February 2014).

Whitehead, C.M.E., Monk, S., Scanlon, K., Makkanen, S. and Tang, C. (2012) *The Private Rented Sector in the New Century – A Comparative Approach*, Cambridge: Cambridge Centre for Housing and Planning Research.

Wood, G. and Ong, R. (2013) 'When and why do landlords retain property investments?', *Urban Studies* 50(16): 3243–3261.

Wood, G., Yates, J. and Reynolds, M. (2006) 'Vacancy rates and low rent housing: A panel data analysis', *Journal of Housing and the Built Environment* 21(4): 441–58.

Wulff, M. (2000) *The 1998 National Survey of Rent Assistance Recipients: A Report on Key Findings*, Department of Family and Community Services, Canberra.

Wulff, M., Reynolds, M., Dharmalingam, A., Hulse, K. and Yates, J. (2011) *Australia's Private Rental Market: The Supply of, and Demand for, Affordable Dwellings*, Final Report no. 168, AHURI, Melbourne.

Wulff, M., Yates, J. and Burke, T. (2001) *Low Cost Renting in Australia 1986 to 1996: How Has It Changed, Who Does It Work for and Who Does It Fail?*, Australian Housing Research Fund Project no. 213, Department of Family and Community Services, Canberra.

Yardney, M. (2012) *Why Negative Gearing should not be Abolished for Property Investment*, http://propertyupdate.com.au/why-negative-gearing-should-not-be-abolished/ (accessed 21 August 2014).

Yates, J (1996) 'Towards a reassessment of the private rental market', *Housing Studies* 11(1): 35–50.

Yates, J. and Milligan, V. (2007) *Housing Affordability: A 21st Century Problem*, Final Report no. 105, AHURI, Melbourne.

Yates, J. and Wulff, M. (2005) 'Market provision of affordable rental housing: Lessons from recent trends in Australia', *Urban Policy and Research* 23(1): 5–19.

Chapter 10
Keynes in the Antipodes: The Housing Industry, First Home Owner Grants and the Global Financial Crisis

Elizabeth Taylor and Tony Dalton

Introduction

> If the Treasury were to fill old bottles with banknotes, bury them at suitable depths in disused coalmines which are then filled up to the surface with town rubbish, and leave it to private enterprise on well-tried principles of laissez-faire to dig the notes up again (the right to do so being obtained, of course, by tendering for leases of the note-bearing territory), there need be no more unemployment and, with the help of the repercussions, the real income of the community, and its capital wealth also, would probably become a good deal greater than it actually is. It would, indeed, be more sensible to build houses and the like; but if there are political and practical difficulties in the way of this, the above would be better than nothing. (Keynes 1936)

One of the ways that Keynes (1936: 136) talked about economic growth during the Depression was to point out that growth could be generated by the state burying money in large holes, and allowing private enterprise to compete to dig it up. Although this would generate employment and economic activity, Keynes of course noted that the economic and social benefits of burying something only to dig it up again were limited. Perhaps it would 'be more sensible to build houses and the like'. In Australia, using the housing industry to stimulate economic activity in the way envisioned by Keynes became a bi-partisan policy tradition during the early post-World War II (WWII) decades. This is evident in the history of government measures, based on the concept of the 'construction multiplier', and the funding of a 'shovel ready' housing industry to rapidly increase new housing output and increase employment.

One way in which this has been done in the owner-occupied sector is through the provision of first homeowner grants (FHOGs) – grants paid directly to households purchasing their first dwelling. Although FHOGs are used elsewhere, their use in Australia is distinct (Dalton 2012). They have become the norm as a policy lever because they are seen to meet two popular policy objectives: supporting entry into homeownership by increasing affordability; and stimulating demand for new housing. There have of course been many other programs such as low interest loans and the sale of public housing. However, FHOGs have endured while many of these other programs have been retired.

This chapter considers how FHOGs have come to feature so strongly in Australian housing policy and considers the strengths and weaknesses of this policy instrument in stimulating housing supply.

The structure of the chapter is as follows. First, we describe the development of FHOG schemes since the 1960s when they first became a feature of Australian housing policy. Second we present an analysis of the recent use of FHOGs between 2008 and 2012 when they were used on an unprecedented scale as a response to the Global Financial Crisis (GFC). Third, we assess the efficacy of FHOGs by examining: the influence on the number and value of new dwelling commencements; the type of housing produced and its location in the context of (Melbourne) metropolitan planning strategy; and the effect on house prices. We argue that FHOG incentives to purchase new housing do stimulate the supply of new housing, but that there are issues about the realisation of other policy objectives concerning the use of resources and urban development and equity in the distribution of housing subsidies.

We conclude that a supply side strategy based on supporting first homebuyers to purchase new outer suburban housing should be reconsidered on two grounds. First, stimulating new housing for first home purchasers does little more than assist in evening out the cyclical nature of housing starts while not addressing the larger issue of continuing undersupply. Second, FHOGs undermine the alignment of new housing production and metropolitan planning strategies aimed at denser cities that improve labour productivity and housing affordability.

FHOGs in Australia

FHOGs are paid directly to households purchasing their first dwelling, and supplement their savings and the mortgage obtained from a financial intermediary to meet the sale price of the dwelling. The Australian Government established the first FHOG in 1964 as the Home Savings Grant Program by providing £1 for every £3 saved up to a maximum grant of £250 for all married or engaged couples under 36 years old saving to purchase a home (Dalton 2012). Since then FHOG programs with similar broad eligibility criteria, but with different names, have operated almost continuously. The Home Savings Grant was phased out from 1973 and replaced with the Home Deposit Assistance Grant in 1976. In 1983 it was replaced by the First Home Owners Assistance Scheme, which ran until 1990. The current FHOG was introduced in July 2000 to 'offset' the cost of the introduction of the Goods and Services Tax (GST). This sequence of FHOGs is presented in Figure 10.1. This program history makes Australia a 'standout' country in the use of first home purchaser grants (Dalton 2012). A further 'standout' feature of FHOGs in Australia is that they are not restricted by age or income, but are available to all who have not previously owned a dwelling.

There have been four changes in FHOG program design. First, the idea that grants could be used to stimulate new housing supply was coupled to the earlier idea that grants would improve first homeowner affordability. The Australian Government made this explicit in March 2001 when it introduced the Commonwealth Additional Grant (CAG), which provided an extra $7000 to grant recipients who were purchasing a newly constructed

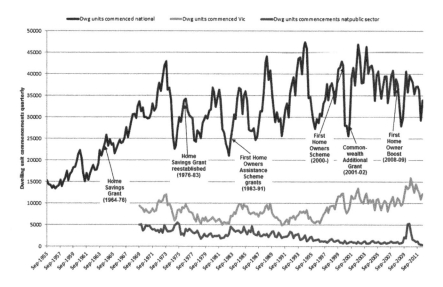

Figure 10.1 Dwelling supply and supply-oriented interventions, Australia

dwelling (Dalton 2012). Second, from 2000 the Australian Government transferred program administration to the states but with continued Australian Government funding (Productivity Commission 2004: 71). Third, some state governments added their own resources to these grant programs, while continuing with stamp duty concessions for first home purchasers. Fourth, some state governments also overlaid a spatial frame by providing additional amounts to householders buying in non-metropolitan regional areas, aimed at encouraging a more decentralised settlement pattern and addressing supply imbalances in metropolitan housing markets.

Underpinning this FHOG program development was the broadly accepted precept that the housing industry should be a focus of demand and supply management. Housing, especially in the early post-WWII decades, became central to Keynesian economic demand management, in the context of increased demand for housing; the politics of earlier housing shortages; and the potential for increased housing supply to buffer cyclical downturns (Berry 1999). This could be achieved by using monetary and fiscal policy to manage demand for housing. Downing (1948: 85) a Keynesian economist, at Melbourne University and advisor to the Australian Government, summed up this thinking.

> The housing problem can be reduced to a few words. If a high and stable output of housing can be maintained – for instance at 60,000 a year – men who might otherwise be idle will get jobs building them. In spending their earnings, they will create jobs for more men. If houses go on being built, a vital section of total effective demand will be stabilized and the problems of full employment correspondingly simplified.

This argument has subsequently been made many times over, particularly at times of low economic growth and rising unemployment. For example, in the early 1980s, the Building

Workers Industrial Union (1982), in the context of a downturn pressed the government to stimulate housing supply.

> It is ... a cruel scandal that the housing industry is being wound down, when more and more people are in need of housing ... there is a huge backlog of neglected housing needs ... by stimulating the housing industry to meet these needs, we will be putting our resources to better use, and helping employment and growth throughout the whole economy ...

Similarly in 1987, the state and territory governments (Walker et al. 1987) restated the case for housing investment in a pamphlet *Housing Makes Sense* that presented evidence on the employment and return on investment in housing.[1]

> The benefits of the proposal put forward in this booklet will be enjoyed throughout Australia ... more jobs per $million invested than any other industry ... and help alleviate housing poverty ... within the context of the present current account deficit, expenditure on housing can be justified because housing is Australian Made ... each dollar invested by the Commonwealth produces a combined savings/revenue benefit of $1.30 to them ...

Similarly, in the wake of the GFC the Housing Industry Association (2010) made this argument based on an ABS analysis of construction industry multipliers.

> ... as activity increases in the construction industry, as well as in the suppliers to that industry and the 'suppliers to the suppliers', there is an increase in wages and salaries to employees throughout this chain. The spending component of these wages and salaries induces a further round of consumption effects.

In sum, Australia has a policy tradition that supports grants to first home purchasers as a way of increasing housing affordability and increasing the demand for new housing particularly during periods of low economic growth and crisis. Of specific interest to this chapter was the change to this program that occurred in 2008. In response to the GFC, the Australian Government made provision of an additional amount to the purchasers of new dwellings on top of a base grant to all purchasers.

FHOGs as a Response to the Global Financial Crisis, 2008–2012

In the December Quarter 2006 and March Quarter 2007, two consecutive quarters of high (1.4%) GDP growth were recorded in Australia. However, by the June Quarter 2008 GDP growth was 0.6 per cent and in the December Quarter 2008, 0.1 per cent. There was the prospect that the Australian economy would enter a recession, similar to those being

---

1   This pamphlet was based on research undertaken by CSIRO researchers (Flood et al. 1984) for the Australian Housing Research Council, an intergovernmental body that commissioned and funded research projects on various aspects of housing.

experienced by many other developed economies, as a result of the effects of the GFC that started in the USA and spread through most developed economies. As this possibility loomed the Reserve Bank of Australia drove down interest rates by lowering the cash rate target from 7.25 per cent in March 2008 to less than half that, 3.00 per cent by April 2009. At the same time the Australian Government launched a $10.4 billion Economic Security Strategy (ESS) so as to 'strengthen the national economy and support Australian households, given the risk of a deep and prolonged global economic slowdown' (Prime Minister and Treasurer 2008). This was followed in February 2009 by the $42 billion Nation Building and Jobs Plan (NBJP) (Treasurer 2009).

Housing was central to the ESS and NBJP for two reasons. First, there was concern that reduced demand for existing housing could create a house price bubble that would 'burst' as demand and prices fell. The spectre of rapid housing price decline, extensive negative equity and flow-on effects, as evident in the US and the UK, was a key factor in the development of economic policy. Fast, direct and large expenditures might maintain confidence in the housing market. Second, expenditures could be used to directly stimulate new residential construction and increase employment in the housing and related industries, in the way that Keynes originally advocated.

There were three Australian Government program responses in the ESS and the NBJP. First, there was the announcement in the ESS which doubled the grant to all first home purchasers from $7000 to $14,000 while purchasers who bought a new dwelling were eligible for $21,000. Second, a commitment was made in the NBJP for more than 20,000 new social and defence housing units (see Chapter 12). The resulting blip in public sector dwelling commencements is evident in Figure 10.1 (above). Third the Australian Government funded a national insulation program by subsidising owners to insulate uninsulated ceilings. All these measures were aimed at maintaining confidence in the housing market and stimulate industry.

State and territory governments have also supplemented the Australian Government grants to first homebuyers while seeking to influence regional housing markets and industry within the Australian federal system of government. In the case of Victoria the government introduced its 'Bonus' as a supplement to the Australian Government funded FHOG in 2004.[2] From a base of $5,000 this was increased for new housing and decreased for established housing. By mid-2009, the government was offering an additional $11,000 for new homes and $2,000 for established homes. It continued to offer $13,000 for purchasers of new homes (plus an additional $3,500 for new homes in regional areas) until mid-2012.

Together the combined Australian Government and Victorian Government support for first home purchasers presented in Figure 10.2 (below) has been substantial. The high point was in late 2009 when purchasers of new dwellings in Victoria were eligible for as much as $36,500 in regional Victoria, or $32,000 in metropolitan Melbourne. At that time, the maximum grant for an established dwelling was $16,000. For the whole period of 55 quarters in Victoria between 2000–2013 grants for new housing were larger than for established homes in 39 quarters, or 70 per cent of the time.

---

2 Randolph et al. (2013) also take a state based approach in their analysis of the first homeowner grants in NSW for the same reason.

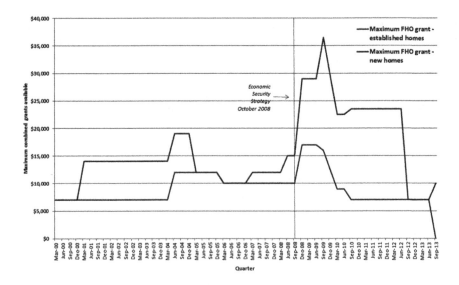

Figure 10.2 First home owner grants, established and new homes, Victoria 2000–2013
Source: Authors' calculations. based on SRO (2014).

The history of grants converted into government expenditures is presented by month for the period 2000–2013 in Figure 10.3. The lower bars show Australian Government programs and the Victorian programs are added from 2004 onwards. The total value of Australian Government and Victorian Government FHOGs in Victoria averaged $26.8 million per month between mid-2000 and October 2008. Between October 2008 and June 2011 the average monthly grant expenditure in Victoria was $57.6 million, more than double the earlier average. In October 2009 the combined value of federal and Victorian expenditure on first homeowner grants subsidies peaked at $97.8 million. In total the Victorian State Revenue Office (SRO) distributed $2 billion in first homeowner grants over the three financial years, 2008–2009, 2009–2010, 2010–2011.

The Efficacy of FHOGs

Activity, Value and Employment

There was a noticeable increase in the proportion of first home purchasers who purchased a new dwelling following the introduction of the FHOG boosts. In Victoria since 2000 approximately 80 per cent of first homebuyers purchased lower priced established housing (SRO 2014). However, the proportion of grants paid to first home purchasers who purchased a new dwelling for the two years 2009–2010 and 2010–2011 indicates an increase in the proportion of first homebuyers purchasing new dwellings. In 2009–2010 and 2010–2011 grants for new housing exceeded established housing and the share of loans to first home purchasers used to finance new housing was more than 40 per cent (SRO 2014).

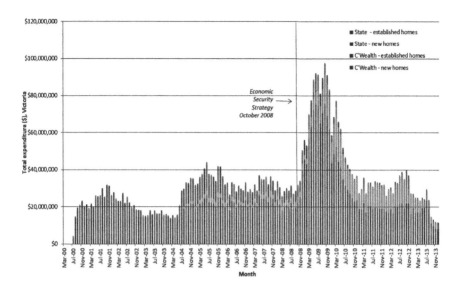

Figure 10.3 First home owner grant expenditure, new and existing dwellings Victoria 2000–2013

Source: Authors' calculations. based on SRO (2014).

It is clear that dwelling construction numbers in Victoria increased soon after the FHOG boosts were introduced. Quarterly private dwelling commencements in Victoria for the period 2003–2012 shown in Figure 10.4 show this increase. After the ESS, the rapid increase in FHOG grant values foreshadows the increase in dwelling commencements, reaching nearly 16,000 in the September quarter 2010. Also, even in mid-2012, with Australian Government grants back to the earlier level but with Victorian bonuses remaining for new housing, dwelling commencements in Victoria were well above the average in the years before the ESS measures were introduced.

Prima facie, the policy objective set for the grants program was achieved. However, there were other changes that prompt further analysis. This has been done by testing the relationship between grants and construction activity with two ordinary least squares regression models. They were used to estimate the extent to which FHOG increases are associated with increased construction output while controlling for other factors, including population growth and interest rate changes. These models can go some way towards identifying the effect of the grant on housing construction activity, especially on new housing, while also taking into account other changes.

It is assumed that relationships between FHOGs and dwelling construction can have a range of effects. For example, it is possible to envisage that an increase in housing industry output was going to happen regardless. Paris (1990: 309) argues that this may have been the case in 1983–1984 when the Labor Government claimed that the First Home Owners Scheme, that the government introduced, had lifted housing industry activity.

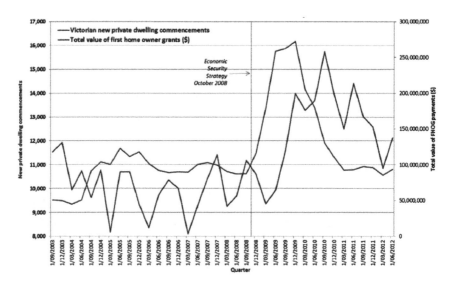

Figure 10.4 Value of first homeowner grant programs and private dwelling commencements

Source: Authors' calculations. based on SRO (2014). and ABS (2012 CAT. 8750).

This possibility is not eliminated here – however, the models do assist in examining the temporal relationships between FHOGs and industry activity.

The scope for the models is 36 quarters for Victoria between September Quarter 2003, and June Quarter 2012. This slightly reduced time frame is due to the lack of continuity across some ABS datasets. Two dependent variables were explored. The first was the number of new dwelling commencements in Victoria, by quarter. The second was the total value of new residential building activity, a more direct measure of the multiplier effect sought by FHOGs than the number of dwellings started. The effect of the FHOG is explored by examining two variables. These are the maximum FHOG grant available in Victoria at that quarter for new dwellings; and the difference between the grant available for newly constructed dwellings compared to established dwellings. This latter measure can be termed 'the incentive for new dwellings over existing dwellings'.

The control variables are: the RBA standard variable home loan interest rate; the change since the preceding quarter in Melbourne's House Price Index (ABS 2013 Cat 6416.0); and the change (generally an increase) in Victoria's estimated resident population (ABS 2013 Cat 3101.0). It is expected that increases in population, and decreases in interest rates, generate demand for housing in addition to the availability of grants. All other things being equal, if supply is elastic, higher prices would presumably lead to greater supply.

Descriptive statistics for variables used in the models are presented in Table 10.1. FHOGs available for new homes ranged between $10,000 and $36,500, with an average of $18,417 available. On average buyers of newly constructed homes were eligible for $8,181, more than for buyers of established homes, although this incentive was as high as $20,500, while in some quarters no additional incentive for new homes was available. Across Victoria the average number of quarterly dwelling commencements was 11,081, ranging from 8,108 to 15,738. On average the quarterly change in the Melbourne house price index was 1.48 per cent, ranging from negative 3.28 per cent to positive 7.45 per cent. The estimated resident population for Victoria increased from 4.9 million to 5.6 million over the period.

Table 10.1 Descriptive statistics, model variables for FHOGs and quarterly new dwelling activity, Victoria 2003–2012

	N	Minimum	Maximum	Mean	Std. Dev.
Max FHOG (new homes)	36	10,000	36,500	18,417	7,097
FHOG incentive for new homes	36	0	20,500	8,181	6,842
New dwelling commencements	36	8,108	15,738	11,081	1,853
Value of new residential building ($000s)	36	1,680,304	4,027,975	2,541,678	658,893
RBA home loan interest rate	36	5.77	9.52	7.41	0.87
Estimated resident population	36	4,887,826	5,632,521	5,234,636	236,900
Melbourne House Price Index change	36	(3.28)	7.45	1.48	2.88

Table 10.2 Regression model results: value of new building activity, Victoria ($000s)

	Value of new residential building ($000s)		
	Coefficient	Standard error	Significance
FHOG maximum ($1,000)	−57.304	18.120	0.004
FHOG incentive for new housing ($1,000)	93.543	24.086	0.001
Home loan interest rates	−2.143	7.387	0.774
Change in Melbourne HPI	21.423	19.128	0.272
Estimated Resident Population (1,000s)	1.393	0.409	0.002
Constant	*(4,334)*		
Adjusted R Square	*0.793*		

Table 10.3 Regression model results: new dwelling commencements, Victoria

	New dwelling commencements		
	Coefficient	Standard error	Significance
FHOG maximum	−235.191	70.304	0.002
FHOG incentive for new housing	430.894	93.454	0.000
Home loan interest rates	0.607	28.662	0.983
Change in Melbourne HPI	97.282	74.217	0.200
Estimated Resident Population (1,000s)	−0.231	1.589	0.886
Constant	12,906		
Adjusted R Square	0.606		

The estimates of the FHOG effect on the value of new building activity in Victoria are presented in Table 10.2. The adjusted R squared value indicates that around 79.3 per cent of variation in quarterly building value is explained. Increases in the FHOG grant for existing dwellings are seen to have a significant negative effect on building activity: with each $1,000 increase in the FHOG associated with a decrease of $57.304 million in quarterly new building activity. At the same time, the effect of the additional incentive for *new* housing is *positive* and significant: each $1,000 additional FHOG for purchasing new housing increases building activity by $93.543 million. These coefficients take into account home loan interest rates (increases which have a negative but statistically insignificant effect) and population change. Each 1,000 population increase is associated with an increase in $1393 million in new building activity. Changes in the Melbourne house price index are also associated with an increase the value of building activity.

The estimates of the FHOG effect on the number of new dwelling commencements are presented in Table 10.3. This model explains slightly less variation in the dependent variable, 60.6 per cent. It shows that each $1,000 additional available for FHOG grants for existing dwellings *reduced* commencements by 235 units per quarter. However, each $1,000 additional incentive given for new housing had a *positive* effect on dwelling commencements, and was associated with 430 additional units. These effects take into account interest rates; and increasing population (neither of which are significant in this model); and changes to house prices — which are positive and significant.

Both models, using different indicators of building activity, suggest that increased FHOG grants for existing dwellings are associated with a reduction in construction activity. In both models, the maximum value of FHOGs for existing dwellings had a significant *negative* effect on construction activity. This effect is true when holding interest rates, population increase, and house price index change constant. The FHOG incentive given for purchasing *new* housing had a significant *positive* effect on both measures of construction activity. The net effect of the two coefficients for dwelling commencements is 195 units, if FHOGs overall are

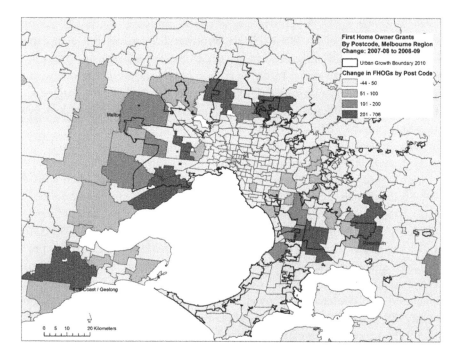

Figure 10.5 FHOG grants by postcode, 2007–2008, Melbourne
Source: Authors' calculations. based on SRO (2014).

increased by $1,000 but an additional $1,000 is made available for new housing. The numbers are small; however an incentive of $14,000 to buy a new rather than established dwelling suggests a net increase of 2,740 commencements over the period, a significant increase.

The conclusion from this analysis is that FHOGs do influence on building activity, but only when additional money is available for new housing. Without this incentive, the effect of grants for existing dwellings on construction appears to be negative.

FHOGs and House Building

Besides the effect on the level of housing industry activity stimulated by FHOG boosts, it is also important to consider where this new housing is located, the conditions under which it is produced and how it contributes to broader housing supply. This is important because in Melbourne, FHOG grants for new housing appears to be associated with an increase in new housing in the outer suburban growth areas.

This association is apparent in Figure 10.5 where the growth in the number of postcodes (between September quarters 2007–2008, i.e. before the ESS, and December quarters 2008–2009, i.e. during the maximum boost period) is greatest in the postcodes near the Melbourne metropolitan growth boundary in the West, North and Southeast. These areas include Truganina, Hoppers Crossing and Tarneit (postcode 3029); Werribee (3030); Mernda and Doreen (3754); Caroline Springs and Deer Park (3023); Craigieburn

(3064) and Cranbourne (3977). This is similar to the outcome of the FHOG boosts in Sydney where Randolph et al. (2013: 71) showed that a 'majority of Boost expenditure was taken up in a spatially targeted way, that is, primarily in lower and moderate value markets' in outer suburban areas. In terms of access to housing by moderate and lower income households, this is a positive outcome because as in Sydney the 'large majority of Boost expenditure was taken up in a spatially targeted way, that is, primarily in lower and moderate value markets' (Randolph et al. 2013: 71).

There are, however, other broader urban outcomes shaped by the FHOG boost program. First, the FHOG boosts disproportionally and thus puts further growth pressures on the urban fringe, which runs counter to broader urban planning urban consolidation objectives. Strategic planning in Melbourne, similar to planning for metropolitan cities in other states, has for some time placed emphasis on encouraging an increasing proportion of new housing to be built in existing urban areas (Buxton and Taylor 2011; Gleeson et al. 2004). This policy is based on the argument that denser cities can be more productive, efficient, fairer, and environmentally sustainable. In many cities, such as Melbourne that are oriented to homeownership and car usage, these objectives remain, in large part, aspirational and also contentious (Downs 2005; Goodman et al. 2010; Randolph 2006). The majority (79.9% in 2011) of Victoria's housing stock is detached housing and in June quarter 2009, 79 per cent of dwelling approvals in Victoria were for detached houses (ABS 2012 Cat. 8750.0).

The FHOG that directly stimulates new build does little to support the development of denser metropolitan cities. The reason is that land developers and house builders on the fringe of metropolitan areas can respond quickly to increased demand from price constrained low and moderate-income first home purchaser households. Together the land developers and builders present display houses in villages and through builder sales teams, purchasers select a house model, buy a block of land from the land developer and sign a contract with the builder for construction (Burke and Hulse 2010; Dalton et al. 2011a). The time taken for this process can be quite short. A marketing manager from a large home building company operating in three Australian capital cities describes how quickly this company can mobilise.

> Yes, you have to be able to respond quickly because generally we get as much notice from the government about first homebuyer grants as Mrs Jones does. And it's always been [the company's] strength to be able to respond very quickly, in terms of house design. We've turned ranges of houses ... around in two weeks to market because you have to be able to if a first homebuyer grant comes out. (Interview by Dalton, Melbourne, 22 November 2011)

This then becomes another element in managing the production of detached dwellings on the fringe, built through an extensive sub-contract system that engages large numbers of sub-contractors (Dalton et al. 2011b). The program leads builders, through their salespersons, to commit to a program of building that may be beyond their capacity to fulfil in a timely way. As a construction manager for a large builder asked somewhat rhetorically: 'When the first home buyers grant came in, how many of them [salespersons] are going, we only need 10 this week, not 30, because we can't sustain the people in the office or the people out on site?' (Focus group, Melbourne, December 1st, 2011). The manager answered by suggesting that no companies turn customers away.

An executive from a larger builder described the nature of the labour market that they draw their labour from when responding to a sharp increase in demand for new housing.

> At the end of the day all us volume builders are all competing for the same group of guys that are in the industry ... relying on – on the one bucket of – of subbies [sub-contractors], suppliers, supply and installers, you know. (Interview by Dalton, Melbourne, 17 March 2011)

A consequence of this additional demand can be increases in average build times. In recent decades the time taken to build suburban detached housing has steadily increased because of systemic issues including, increasingly complex design and detailing, the sequencing of a large number of sub-contracts and poor quality work requiring rework (Dalton et al. 2013). The peaks in demand associated with FHOG boosts can exacerbate these underlying production problems within the suburban house building industry.

Finally, there is the broader issue of housing supply where the evidence is that grants tied to the purchase of new housing increase supply but the effect does not last. Program evaluations suggest the programs stimulate a 'pull through', 'bring forward' or 'pull forward' effect, by encouraging purchasers to come into the market earlier than they otherwise would and, as noted above, convert intending purchasers of existing dwellings to switch to the purchase of a new dwelling (COAG Reform Council 2012: 26; Productivity Commission 2004: 34; Rodrigues 2007: 5). In other words, boost programs that stimulate new housing production do not address the underlying shortage in housing supply that has been well documented by the National Housing Supply Council (2013). Nor do they necessarily address the inelasticities of housing supply that result in Australia having a housing system that responds more poorly than comparable countries to increases in house prices (Andrews 2010: 7).

Effects on Housing Prices

Literature, media, and policy examinations (Randolph et al. 2013: 59; Eslake 2008, 2013; Productivity Commission 2004; Housing Supply and Affordability Reform Working Party 2012) suggest FHOGs grants feed into house price increases and undermine housing affordability particularly in the contest of the broad entitlement nature of the program and the size of the grants. For example, Eslake (2013) argues 'that cash handouts for first home buyers have simply added to upward pressure on housing prices, enriching vendors (and making those who already own housing feel richer) whilst doing precisely nothing to assist young people (or anybody else) into home ownership'. Further, there is a question about whether low-income and low net wealth households who take up an FHOG can sustain homeownership in the longer term because they may be exposed to too much repayment, price, and negative equity risk.

Figure 10.6 shows change in the ABS Melbourne Established House Price Index; the ABS average loan size taken out by Victorian first home owners (based on ABS Housing Finance Statistics, Cat. 5609.0); and the median and first quartile Victorian house prices

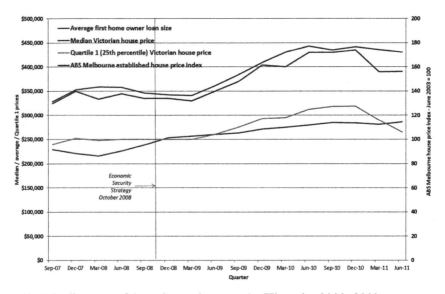

Figure 10.6 Indicators of housing price trends, Victoria, 2003–2010

Source: ABS 2012 (Cat 5609.0), ABS 2013 (Cat 6416.0), authors' calculations based on Valuer General Sales.

(extracted from unit-record sales data). As shown in the graph, prior to the ESS, in the four quarters December 2007 to September 2008 (inclusive), most indicators of housing prices dropped. The Melbourne House Price Index dropped 2 per cent; the median Melbourne house price dropped 4.3 per cent; and the first quartile house price dropped 0.8 per cent. Following the stimulus boost to FHOGs, in the four quarters December 2008 to September 2009 (inclusive), all indicators of housing prices increased, mainly in the latter part of 2009. The Melbourne House Price Index increased by 12.1 per cent; the median house price by 10.4 per cent; and the lower quartile house price by 10 per cent.

We experimented with regression techniques to estimate the effect of FHOG changes on housing prices - measured by the median house price, lowest quartile price, ABS established house price index, average first home owner loan size, while controlling for other factors, including interest rates. The results, however, were not statistically significant which leads to the suggestion that the following factors might be at play. First, the direct effect of FHOG on price may be minimal in the context of the other drivers of housing price increases. Second, there are many interacting drivers of Melbourne house price increases that make the price effects of the FHOG too challenging for this model.

If the focus is narrowed to the association between FHOGs and house prices in the outer suburban growth areas the effect of FHOGs is similarly difficult to discern. The top 10 Victorian postcodes for FHOGs and for FHOG growth were charted along with changes in their median and lower quartile prices. They mirror the overall trends noted above – that is, stagnant prices before the GFC, followed by increases from early 2009 roughly mirroring the period of the FHOG boost. However, it is not possible to say how much of this is because of the FHOG increase, or whether price increases in FHOG stimulated areas are significantly different.

Alternatively what may have happened is that the effect of the FHOG boost, in combination with drops in the mortgage interest rate, was an increase confidence in the housing market, which in turn averted a price drop. In this context it is not possible to point to any causality, or the specific contribution of the FHOG program. Instead it is only possible to point to the corresponding timing of the FHOG boost and housing price increases. In sum, it is not possible to conclude whether or not first homebuyers assisted into home ownership by the boost caused an increase in prices. All we know is that they were entering into a market with rising prices and with higher levels of debt. In Victoria the proportion of mortgage finance increased for first homebuyers from approximately 20 per cent in 2007 and 2008 up to 31.4 per cent in June quarter 2009 (ABS 5609.0 Table 9b). This reflected not only an increased presence in the market but an increase in the average loan from an average of $226,100 in mid-2008 to $279,833 in mid-2010 taken out by first homebuyers in Victoria.

Other research evidence suggests the FHOGs do have a price effect. The Productivity Commission (2004) found a small effect but also found it was dwarfed by other factors. The Council of Australian Governments (COAG) Reform Council (2012) found that the stimulus boost was likely to have inflated prices in Tasmania and Western Australia. Again, this effect was small compared to other factors, but at the same time assisted more first home buyers to enter the market. Randolph et al. (2013: 59) also found that in Sydney, first home buyers appeared to be pulling up lower-end price markets during the boost period. Eslake (2008, 2013) bases his criticism of FHOGs on correlations between house price increases and stagnant homeownership rates. Overall this research seems to suggest that the effects of grants are different in different markets.

FHOG programs can also result in households being exposed to too much negative equity risk. Broadly the data in Figure 10.6 indicate that Victorian homeowners who bought before FHOGs were increased as a response to the GFC benefited from substantial housing equity increases. Those who bought at the peak of the FHOG boosts then went through a period from late 2010 of declining housing prices. Although prices after the FHOG boosts were still higher than before the ESS. Nevertheless, first home buyers who bought during the boost period on average borrowed more and were more highly indebted and were therefore more exposed to the risk of the later price drops and negative equity for those with a low loan to valuation ratio.

Finally FHOGs exacerbate the underlying inequity in the distribution of housing assistance. Because FHOGs are not means tested the benefit is more likely to be sought by higher income and higher net worth purchaser households who are moving from renting to ownership and would make this transition irrespective of a FHOG grant. This assistance overlays a situation where housing assistance favours owner occupier over rental households (Yates 2003, 2009, 2011). In 2005–2006 tax subsidies for owner-occupiers were $45 billion (equivalent to $8,000 per household), larger than $3 billion for renters ($1,000 per household) (Yates 2009). Further, housing assistance favours older, higher income, outright owners rather than younger, lower or moderate-income purchasers or renters. Growing numbers of older households who are not homeowners are also disadvantaged (Yates and Bradbury 2010).

In this context first home purchaser households receiving FHOGs facilitate increased access by first homebuyers, with the proviso that higher income groups are more likely to access home ownership. Adding to the complexity of their distributional effect, the value of FHOGs is offset by increased mortgage and transaction costs and is more likely to impact lower income purchasers. Such deposit gaps and price constraints for home purchasers in lower income households are worsened by a tax bias toward high income households already in home ownership (Yates 2011).

Conclusions

This chapter traced the history of FHOGs and explained why they feature so strongly in Australian housing policy and particularly as a response to the GFC. When viewed in the context of Keynes' discussion of stimulus measures FHOGs can be understood as a 'better than nothing' measure. They are easy to implement, stimulate the housing market and new housing construction and enjoy broad support within the housing industry. Even Eslake (2008), a long term critic of FHOGs, has acknowledged the quick stimulus effect of FHOGs when he noted that the 'trebling of the First Home Owners' Grant for buyers committing to a newly-constructed dwelling during the current financial year will undoubtedly stimulate additional housing activity in the short-term'.

We found evidence, using Victoria as a case study, that FHOGs do have this effect on housing construction. Increases in the size of the grant available for purchasing newly constructed housing are associated with increases in the number and value of new residential building. We however identified three features of FHOGs that show they fail as good policy. First, FHOGs for established housing undermine the objective of increasing housing construction. The modelling showed that increases in these grants were associated with less new construction. Second, the take up of FHOGs supporting new house building tends to result in an increase in outer suburban growth area building. This runs counter to policy emphasising increasing the density of metropolitan cities. Third, there is evidence that the house builders respond quickly by taking orders for new houses but then can struggle to maintain quality and complete houses on time. Finally, based on our modelling and other research, we noted that the link between FHOGs and housing price increases is unclear. However, it is clear that FHOGs do exacerbate the inequality in the underlying distribution of direct and indirect subsidies in the Australian housing system.

An alternative approach to stimulating economic activity through housing construction and demand on the broader housing industry supply chains is investment in social housing. In the post-WWII period, as the public housing system grew, funds provided through the Commonwealth State Housing Agreement to the states and territories varied, often as a counter cyclical measure. However, this policy tradition has waned in Australia in recent decades, although it did feature alongside FHOGs as a response to the GFC (Chapter 12). This preference for FHOGs over funding for social housing as a stimulus is largely attributable to the lack of political support for social housing in Australia (Chapter 11; Dalton 2009). However, even with the unusual return to social housing expenditure in the stimulus package the funds allocated to the FHOG program exceeded the funds expended on social housing.

The potential advantages of direct investment in social housing as a stimulus measure include greater control over the quality of housing, its form and location in established urban areas. Social housing is also more targeted to low and moderate-income groups experiencing declining housing affordability, the effects of the continuing undersupply of affordable housing. The chief disadvantage of stimulating construction through social housing is the time taken to complete planning and procurement processes. Some delays in planning approval can be caused by objections to redevelopment and this includes social housing in these redevelopments (Chapter 12). In the ESS this type of delay was anticipated and funding was made conditional upon the rights of third parties to object being waived by state and territory governments. Projects were 'fast tracked', but not without opposition from neighbouring homeowners (Cook et al. 2012).

In conclusion FHOGs aimed at increasing economic activity in the housing sector were an effective response within the context of the threat that the GFC posed to the Australian economy. However, as a longer-term response to the underlying structural problems in the Australian housing system FHOGs fail. The evidence is that FHOGs do not do contribute to making housing more affordable. First, the best they do is assist a group of households into homeownership. Second, they do not address the underlying undersupply of housing. The only contribution they make is to stimulate demand and 'pull' through a cohort of purchasers so that they become homeowners a little earlier than they would have if there had been no grant. A program with these characteristics, particularly when compared to the advantages of a consistently resourced and planned social housing program, has little merit. A resourced and planned social housing program does have the potential to both improve affordability and address undersupply. It is worth remembering a 2007 Peter Nicholson cartoon. It showed the then Prime Minister, John Howard, with another politician watching a dog slavering after its own tail. The dog is marked 'First Home Owners Grant'. They conclude that 'we need a bigger dog'.

References

Australian Bureau of Statistics (ABS) (2012), 'Dwelling unit commencements Australia', Cat. 8750.0 Canberra, Australian Bureau of Statistics.

ABS (2012), (2013), 'Housing finance Australia', Cat. 5609.0 Canberra: Australian Bureau of Statistics.

—— (2013), 'Australian demographic statistics, estimated resident population', Cat 3101.0 Canberra, Australian Bureau of Statistics.

—— (2013), 'Residential property price indexes: Eight capital cities', Cat 6416.0 Canberra: Australian Bureau of Statistics.

Andrews, D. (2010), 'Real house prices in OECD countries: The role of demand shocks and structural and policy factors', *OECD Economics Department Working Papers*, No. 831 Paris, OECD Publishing.

Berry, M. (1999), 'Unravelling the 'Australian housing solution': The post war years', *Housing, Theory and Society* 16(3): 106–121.

Building Workers Industrial Union (1982), *Housing Australia: Let's get to work!* Sydney: Building Workers Industrial Union.

Burke, T. and Hulse, K. (2010), 'The institutional structure of housing and the sub-prime crisis: An Australian case study', *Housing Studies* 25(6): 821–838.

Buxton, M. and Taylor, E. (2011), 'Urban land supply, governance and the pricing of land', *Urban Policy and Research* 29(1): 5–22.

COAG Reform Council (2012), *Affordable Housing 2010–11: Comparing Performance across Australia*, COAG Reform Council, Sydney.

Cook, N., Taylor, E., Hurley, J., and Colic-Peisker, V. (2012), *Resident Third Party Objections and Appeals against Planning Applications: Implications for Higher Density and Social Housing*, AHURI Final Report. No. 136. Melbourne: Australian Housing and Urban Research Institute.

Dalton, T. (2009), 'Housing policy retrenchment: Australia and Canada compared', *Urban Studies* 46(1): 63–91.

—— (2012), 'First homeowner grants', in S.J. Smith (ed.), *International Encyclopedia of Housing and Home*, Oxford: Elsevier.

Dalton, T., Wakefield, R., and Horne, R. (2011a), *Australian Suburban House Building: Industry Organisation, Practices and Constraints*, AHURI Positioning Paper No. 143, Melbourne, Australian Housing and Urban Research Institute.

Dalton, T., Horne, R., Chettri, P., Groenhart, L., and Corcoran J. (2011b), *Understanding the Patterns, Characteristics and Trends in the Housing Sector Labour Force in Australia*, Positioning Paper No 142, Melbourne, Australian Housing and Urban Research Institute.

Dalton, T., Hurley, J., Gharaie, E., Wakefield, R., and Horne, R. (2013), *Australian Suburban House Building: Industry Organisation, Practices and Constraints*, AHURI Final Report Melbourne, Australian Housing and Urban Research Institute.

Downing, R.I. (1948), 'Housing and public policy', *Economic Record* 24(1): 72–86.

Downs, A. (2005). 'Smart growth: why we discuss it more than we do it' *Journal of the American Planning Association* 71(4): 367(314).

Eslake, S., (2008), 'Spend, spend, spend', *The Adelaide Advertiser*, 15 October.

—— (2013), *Australian Housing Policy: 50 Years of Failure*, submission to the Senate Economics References Committee inquiry into affordable housing, 21 December 2013.

Flood, J., Woodhead, W.D., and Tucker, S.N. (1984), *Evaluation of the Impact of Housing Expenditure on Employment*, AHRC Project 145, Canberra, Australian Housing Research Council.

Gleeson, B., Darbas, T., and Lawson, S. (2004), 'Governance, sustainability and recent Australian metropolitan strategies: a socio-theoretic analysis', *Urban Policy and Research* 22(4): 345–366.

Goodman, R., Buxton, M., Chhetri, P., Taylor, E., Wood, G., (2010), *Planning and the Characteristics of Housing Supply in Melbourne*, Final Report No. 157, Melbourne, Australian Housing and Urban Research Institute.

Housing Industry Association (2010), *Small Business in the Construction Industry and its Linkages with the Economy*, Canberra: Housing Industry Association.

Housing Supply and Affordability Reform Working Party (2012), *Housing Supply and Affordability Reform*, Canberra: Council of Australian Governments.

Keynes, J.M. (1936), *The General Theory of Employment, Interest and Money*, London: Macmillan.

National Housing Supply Council (2013), *Housing Supply and Affordability Issues 2012–13*, Canberra, National Housing Supply Council.

Paris, C. (1990), 'Housing policy', in C. Jennett and R.G. Stewart (eds), *Hawke and Australian Public Policy: Consensus and Restructuring*, Melbourne: Macmillan.

Prime Minister and Treasurer (2008), *Joint Press Conference, Prime Minister and Treasurer, Economic Security Strategy*, Canberra, The Treasury, Australian Government.

Productivity Commission (2004), *First Home Ownership*, Report no.28, Melbourne, Productivity Commission.

Randolph, B. (2006), 'Delivering the compact city in Australia: current trends and future implications', *Urban Policy and Research* 24(4): 473–490.

Randolph, B., Pinnegar, S., and Tice, A. (2013), 'The First Home Owner Boost in Australia: A Case Study of Outcomes in the Sydney Housing Market', *Urban Policy and Research* 31(1): 55–73.

Rodrigues, M. (2007), 'First home buyers in Australia', *Economic Roundup* (Summer 2003–2004: The Treasury).

State Revenue Office (SRO) (2014), 'First home owner statistics', Melbourne: State Revenue Office, http://www.e-business.sro.vic.gov.au/corporate/statistics/faces/fhog/summary.jsp.

Treasurer, Prime Minister and (2009), *$42 Billion Nation Building and Jobs Plan*, Canberra, The Treasury, Australian Government.

Walker, F.J., Wilkes, F., Hemmings, T., and Wilson, K. (1987), *Housing Makes Sense: The Social and Economic Benefits of Housing Investment in Australia* (pamphlet no publisher cited).

Yates, J. (2003) 'The more things change? An overview of Australia's recent home ownership policies', *European Journal of Housing Policy* 3(1): 1–33.

—— (2009) *Tax Expenditures and Housing – Report for the Brotherhood of St Laurence*, Melbourne, Australian Housing and Urban Research Institute.

—— (2011) 'Explaining Australia's trends in home ownership', *Housing Finance International*, Winter: 6–13.

Yates, J. and Bradbury, B. (2010), 'Home ownership as a (crumbling) fourth pillar of social insurance in Australia', Special Issue: Home ownership and Asset-based welfare *Journal of Housing and the Built Environment* 25(2): 193–211.

Chapter 11
The Historical Construction of 'The Public Housing Problem' and Deconcentration Policies

Kathy Arthurson and Michael Darcy

Introduction

From its inception, mass-produced public housing played a major role in the post-World War II (WWII) reconstruction and economic development of Australian cities. At this time public housing estates provided an efficient solution to a number of social, economic and political problems. These included a severe housing shortage, serious affordability issues, and trade skills and infrastructure deficits. Although consistently representing a very small proportion of total housing stock (4% as of 2006, AIHW 2009: 5) when compared to European standards, and while it remained politically contested, up until the early 1990s Australian public housing provided affordable and secure housing for those households who could not afford to house themselves appropriately through owner occupation or private rental (Chapter 9). Some 70 years beyond its inception and despite a similar situation of chronic undersupply of housing in major cities, and the least affordable housing internationally, public housing in Australia is now perceived by many as a highly problematic form of tenure which exacerbates or even produces social problems rather than ameliorating them (Arthurson 2012b). Mass-produced broad-acre estates containing concentrations of public housing are frequently characterised as incubators for crime and anti-social behaviour, residents' unemployment and poor educational outcomes (Pinnegar, Randolph and Davison 2011). Not just the policy of providing assistance through state owned housing, but its actual physical form and location is now widely described as a 'failed experiment' and has emerged as the target of a concerted campaign of reform and redevelopment (Troy 2011).

This chapter examines the historical shift in Australian housing assistance policy with a particular focus on the way in which the geography (especially spatial concentration) of contemporary public housing has come to be conceptualised as destroying its effectiveness. In recent debates the roots of this problem are generally understood as cultural and economic: cultural causes being the reproduction of poverty brought about by lack of sufficient role models of 'good citizens' and the 'bad side' of social capital, allied with popular prejudice and stigmatisation of public tenants; economic mechanisms are related to work disincentives and poverty traps directly arising from the structure of housing assistance. Given the depictions of spatial concentration as an underlying cause of these issues, the solutions are also frequently couched in terms of the geography of public housing, that is to say, dispersal.

Drawing on Australian empirical and participatory research conducted in three states over recent years, we provide an alternative account of Australian social housing provision to the one which underlies most contemporary policy debate about processes of residualisation and concentration. We argue that, rather than focusing on a simple explanation about proximity of tenant households as a cause of problems, reduced supply and various forms of tighter targeting have impacted on the demographic mix of tenants to increase stigmatisation, and exacerbate housing related poverty traps. The international research findings on the practices of housing authorities designed to de-concentrate public housing are also called upon to help assess the likely success of policies designed to address social problems through relocation of tenants and implementing small scale geographic tenure mix.

Historical Context

Deconcentration and tenure mixing has emerged over recent decades as the preferred strategy of public housing managers across the industrialised world, in particular in the USA and UK (Darcy 2010). Housing authorities in all Australian states, supported and encouraged by Federal funding agreements, have pursued a program of demolition and redevelopment of estates aimed at 'de-concentrating' public housing and dispersing public tenants amongst mortgage-paying, or at least private rent-paying, neighbours. New developments arising on former public housing sites are designed to achieve 'social mix' – often of no more than 30 per cent subsidised tenants – which, it is argued, will offset the stigma and prevent the cultural reproduction of negative values and behaviours which compound the disadvantage of poor households (Coates and Shepherd 2005). As in the U.S. (Imbroscio 2008; Chaskin and Joseph 2011), this policy has sparked considerable research and academic debate (Arthurson 2002; 2008; Darcy 2010; Ware et al. 2010) but apart from some changes to tenant consultation and participation practices, has continued substantially unaltered for a decade.

Despite the similarity in the contemporary diagnosis of public housing problems and chosen intervention strategies, the history, sociology and geography of Australian public housing is distinctively different from its international counterparts. As in the US and UK, the earliest examples of public housing in Australia emerged in the early 20th century and were associated with slum clearance or 'social hygiene' strategies. The design of estates such as Dacey Gardens in Sydney sought to move poor households away from the overcrowded inner city to lower density suburban sites. Dacey Gardens was constructed following World War I but was never completed. Somewhat ironically, this 'garden suburb' was planned partly as means of reducing anti-social behaviour associated with the inadequate housing conditions of poor households in inner city areas. Within just a few years, it was widely described as a failure and the Housing Board set up to administer it was abolished (Pugh 1976). Troy (1997: 16) accounts for these events with reference to insufficient funds provided by the incoming conservative State government in 1922, and 'ill-founded criticism ... [and] critical attitudes similar to those expressed 50 years later by opponents of public housing programs'.

Despite these early problems, because of its multiplier effects in creating increased demand and employment in allied building and urban development industries, in times of crisis public housing construction has regularly been enlisted in pursuit of achieving national economic objectives (see Chapter 9). This aim was explicit in the Commonwealth Housing Commission report in 1944 and featured in subsequent Commonwealth State Housing Agreements (CSHA) through the second half of the 20th century. Nonetheless, political discourse surrounding public housing has consistently framed it as an inferior form of tenure, not in a legal sense but in a social one where 'the private home rather than public housing was seen as ... the font of civic virtues' (Murphy 1995). As summarised by Ruming et al. (2004: 235):

> Housing policy over the last 50 years has been structured around a politically initiated ideology of home ownership as normal and beneficial, and public housing as an inferior form of tenure.

From the late 1950s through to the 1970s, public housing dwellings were mass-produced in relatively large scale concentrated projects developed as part of the stimulatory strategy of the Keynesian/modernist welfare state, to provide affordable housing for the low income urban industrial workforce. As opposed to the high density, high rise, form which dominated US and UK public housing in the 1960s, and later became the focus of deconcentration policy in those countries, the bulk of Australian public dwellings were single family dwellings and low-medium density row housing on greenfield suburban and urban fringe sites. Unlike the UK and European experience, public housing in Australia never exceeded around 6 per cent of housing stock, except in South Australia where housing policy was explicitly deployed as a strategy to attract investment in manufacturing industry through downward pressure on wage costs, and where it reached as high as 10 per cent of dwellings in the 1980s (Marsden 1986).

Even during the Fordist 'long-boom' years with expansionary Keynesian economic policies in full swing, public housing never enjoyed unequivocal support. Paris et al. (1985) argue that there have always been at least two competing discourses of social housing in Australia which they characterise as *'public* housing' and *'welfare* housing', with the latter achieving clear dominance in public policy debates for at least the last quarter of a century. They argue that,

> It is incorrect ... to suggest that an established tradition of public housing has only lately been undermined. Rather, during the 1970s we witnessed the consolidation of the traditional conservative welfare approach. (Paris et al. 1985: 107)

Housing Estates

Around half of public housing dwellings in Australia are located in geographically concentrated developments, or 'estates', of between one hundred and several thousand units, the bulk of which were constructed in the 1960s and 1970s on 'greenfield' sites at

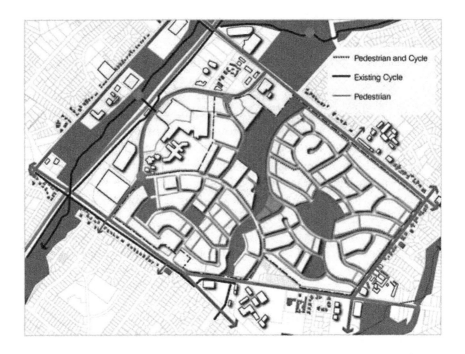

Figure 11.1 Radburn style estate with cul de sacs at Bonnyrigg Estate in NSW
Source: NSW Government Premiers Council for Active Living, Case Study Bonnyrigg Living Communities Project, http://www.pcal.nsw.gov.au/case_studies/bonnyrigg_living_communities_project/descriptioncontext.

the urban fringe. These usually comprise a mix of detached and row housing, walk-up apartments, and a small number of medium rise (up to 10-storeys) blocks. Less than 10 per cent of dwellings nationally are located in high-density tower blocks and walk-up apartments close to centres of large cities.

Greenfield development allowed housing authorities to experiment with urban design, and in NSW planners of suburban estates embraced the principles used to develop the planned community of Radburn, New Jersey in 1929. These principles sought to create new kinds of spaces for social interaction and community life 'in the motor age' (Stein 1957) by separating pedestrian and vehicular traffic, replacing the traditional grid street pattern with

> houses grouped around small cul-de-sacs, each of which has an access road coming from the main roads ... The living and sleeping sections of the houses face toward the garden and park areas, while the service rooms face the access road ... to further maintain the separation of pedestrian and vehicular traffic, a pedestrian underpass and an overpass, linking the superblocks, were provided. The system was so devised that a pedestrian could start at any given point and proceed on foot to school, stores or church without crossing a street used by automobiles. (Gatti, n.d.: 1)

This typical arrangement for a Radburn Estate is illustrated in Figure 11.1.

As with the 'garden cities' of an earlier age, Radburn style estates sought to bring about cultural and behavioural changes amongst tenants through their geographical and design features. By the mid-1990s, these estates had experienced decades of chronic under-investment in maintenance of dwellings and public spaces. Increasingly stringent allocation policies had focused on the most needy; local drug dealers frequented poorly lit pedestrian underpasses; and, large poorly maintained common areas became 'no-man's-land'. Confusing cul-de-sacs with houses placed back-to-front were easily identified and stigmatised as places of last resort housing for workless, welfare dependent households, and this 'experiment' in public housing 'design' was widely deemed by many as a failure.

Deconcentration Debate

While over time the concentration of public housing in estates has come to be depicted as destroying its effectiveness, historical analysis shows that key contributors to the problems experienced in public housing are not its design or specific geography but progressively tighter targeting for entry coupled with reductions in funding, and the effects of economic and industry restructuring. The latter factor led to large-scale losses of jobs particularly in manufacturing industries on which many public housing tenants relied for their livelihood. Initially public housing was targeted to assist low income working families but gradually over time the demographic makeup has transformed through targeting increasingly higher need and complex groups, such as ex-prisoners, and people experiencing homelessness and substance abuse issues. As such public housing is now considered a residualised tenure targeted to the most high need and complex groups, and low income alone does not guarantee access.

The Henderson Commission of Inquiry into Poverty conducted in the mid-1970s also played an inadvertent role in the development of this situation. The report identified that the most impoverished groups tended to reside in private rental rather than public housing (Commission of Inquiry into Poverty 1975). Based on this finding the inquiry recommended implementing new forms of income redistribution, for instance, cash transfers, targeted specifically to private renters. This group varied significantly from the low-income working tenants then in public housing. As Peel (1994) has pointed out, while the proposal was non-housing specific it would have allowed the housing authorities to charge market based rents and recover their costs making the system financially viable. But in practice the findings of the Inquiry were used selectively to argue that better off public tenants were being subsidised to the detriment of more impoverished groups that were thus unable to access public housing. These contentions bolstered support for the idea that public housing should be targeted only to people with the greatest need. Soon after the CSHA (Commonwealth of Australia 1978) proposed implementing market level rents to encourage 'better off' public tenants to move into private rental, although as a concession the States agreed to set 'market related' rents (Troy 1997: x).

At the same time as Federal Government direction under the CSHA moved to implement tighter targeting of admission to public housing, the negative effects of economic change were impacting on the delivery of public housing and existing tenants. A series of economic recessions in the 1970s and 1980s led to loss of jobs in manufacturing industry that coupled with the narrower targeting resulted in estates with high levels of public housing increasingly becoming characterised by concentrations of residents with low incomes, poverty and high unemployment rates.

The issues of administering to an increasingly complex tenant group and maintaining ageing public housing stock was exacerbated by major declines in funding levels for public housing provision and renewal. According to Hall and Berry (2007), sustained reductions in the real value of capital investment in new social housing over the 30 years up to 2007, and consequent decline in the proportion of housing stock it represents, leading to stricter targeting of allocations and reduction in security of tenure have produced a generally less viable and harder to manage public housing sector. Between 1989 and 2001 the reduction in funding for public housing equated to around 26 per cent (Jacobs et al. 2013). The net effect of this process has been to reinforce the perception of failure – not just of policy, but of whole communities – and thus to instil a profound sense of public tenants as 'failed citizens' who are unable to produce the conditions for a standard of everyday life such as that enjoyed by owner occupiers (Jacobs et al. 2011).

Notwithstanding a one-off injection of funds as part of the 2008/2009 Federal stimulus package in response to the Global Financial Crisis (GFC), the lack of funding has meant virtually no net additions to public housing stock over several decades (see Chapter 12). Consequently attention turned to issues of how to fund the ongoing maintenance and renewal of the existing ageing post-war housing stock mostly built in the 1950s and 1960s. The first attempts at renewal of public housing estates in Australia commenced in the 1990s as a response to escalating management issues along with emerging problems of anti-social behaviour on some housing estates. In response to these issues and considerable attention from tabloid media, Housing NSW pioneered a program of 'Neighbourhood Improvement' which included community development activities, public space upgrades, closing off pedestrian walkways and fencing front (or back) yards, in an attempt to 'de-Radburnise' some estates. The program was popular with tenants and resulted in a marked drop in transfer applications and refusals of housing offers in those areas where it was implemented (Bijen and Piracha 2012). Nonetheless it was soon discontinued for lack of funds, and before the decade was out had been superseded by a far more radical form of intervention.

Whereas initially the focus was on physical renewal of ageing public housing assets, as awareness increased that physical design changes made little difference to behavioural and other social problems experienced on the estates, attention turned to concentration of public housing as the problem and 'social mix' policies aligned with physical renewal as a solution.

In contemporary Australian estate regeneration policy, social mix strategies have become the preferred means to create more viable communities. These social mix strategies are couched in terms of deconcentration, diversifying housing tenure and socioeconomic mix of existing social housing estates and interspersing social tenant households with homeowners, homebuyers and private renters. The idea is that through interaction with homeowners public housing tenants will be provided with models of exemplary behaviour that lead to other positive outcomes such as access to employment and educational opportunities. Social mix approaches also usually incorporate an important housing design element: whereas the aim is to disperse social housing tenants amongst private market neighbours, housing designers and managers frequently stress the need for the dwellings themselves to be indistinguishable, although this is not always achieved (Arthurson 2012a). Just as they were in the original design of estates, the spatial geography and design of social housing are being employed to produce changes in the culture and behaviour of tenants.

Neighbourhood Effects

A consistent narrative has been deployed to explain the social conditions which are observed in urban areas dominated by public housing tenure and to justify deconcentration and dispersal of public tenants. This locates the roots of poverty in the behaviour and values of the poor themselves which are believed to be reproduced and reinforced by local cultural dynamics arising from the geographic concentration of their homes. This theory of 'neighbourhood effects' draws on a few seminal texts such as Wilson's (1987) *The Truly Disadvantaged* and Venkatesh's (2009) *American Project*. A growing body of work in the social sciences seeks to develop methods to prove and measure the effect of local social geography on social and economic outcomes for poor households (van Ham and Manley 2010). Yet more research is focussed on understanding the dynamics of social interaction in newly developed 'mixed-income' developments which replace concentrated public housing (Allen et al. 2005; Chaskin and Joseph 2011; Graves 2010).

Despite Wilson's (1987) emphasis on the consequences of de-industrialisation, and his rejection of the cultural causation of poverty, urban managers and policy-makers have focussed almost exclusively on the 'concentration effects' which, Wilson (1987) argued, isolate poor communities from economic opportunities. Rather than confront the macro social and economic forces which, under the banner of the free market, divide large cities, they have reverted to a former explanation of urban disadvantage, found in the 'social hygiene' and slum clearance movements of the late industrial revolution and Oscar Lewis' (1961) 'culture of poverty'. The first step in addressing poverty is thus to disperse poor households amongst the self-reliant working population of homeowners where 'successful' cultural patterns can be observed and learned, and the cycle interrupted.

It is not possible here to adequately review the many deconcentration and dispersal programs which have emerged in North America, Europe and Australia since the mid-1990s (see Porter and Shaw 2009). However, it is fair to say that isolating the impact of the local neighbourhood from the urban conditions which lead poor households to live in them, and from the effects of housing quality, access to jobs and services, and a myriad of personal and family characteristics, has proved to be an elusive goal, while the benefits to poor tenants of being removed to mixed income neighbourhoods are highly contested, not least by tenants themselves.

Public Housing from Solution to Problem

Through the lens of neighbourhood effects, public housing, once promoted by government as a solution to urban poverty, now appears in social research and urban policy as a cause of it. The theory of cultural reproduction of poverty through 'neighbourhood effects' provides the necessary social justification for returning publicly owned land to the market by claiming that relocation of tenants is in their own best interest. The media has added fuel to these ideas, particularly high rating 'tabloid' television current affairs programs that frequently and enthusiastically report any incidents of anti-social behaviour or perceived irresponsible or undeserving tenants, as evidence of fundamental problems inherent in subsidised and state managed housing (Arthurson 2012b). In enthusiastically adopting the theoretical notion of neighbourhood effects as a rationale for breaking up estates researchers, policy makers and housing managers have focussed attention on the perceived deficiencies of social housing communities and the malign effects of disadvantaged households residing in proximity to each other. Policy and consultation documents produced to justify specific redevelopment projects usually refer to selected indicators to present a narrative of community life in need of urgent intervention (Darcy 2010).

Nevertheless, the evidence is equivocal and several reviews that assess the overall research findings conclude that notwithstanding their living near to each other, the limited interaction that occurs between home owners and social housing tenants is unlikely to lead to the supposed potential benefits ascribed to these policies (Smith 2002; Holmes 2006; Arthurson 2012a). Considered by some just as spurious is the idea of role model effects in relation to employment opportunities or the expected raising of life aspirations for public housing tenants (Holmes 2006). In their study van Ham and Manley (2010) found that although living in a deprived neighbourhood is negatively correlated with labour market outcomes this was largely so for homeowners but not public housing tenants.

As Luxford (2006: 3) points out, 'it is not necessarily the concentration of public housing *per se* that creates stigma. Rather, it is the allocation of housing to only those who are the most disadvantaged in our community. Indeed, in Australia, Ruming (2011) has shown local opponents of dispersed social and affordable housing projects have frequently adapted the definition of 'concentration' to encompass anything more than one or two dwellings in a hundred. In Ruming's (2011) study, local residents demonstrated little appreciation or interest in the subtleties of new management structures or subsidy arrangements, they simply associated subsidised or affordable housing projects with public housing, often referring to all projects as 'Housing Commission' thus invoking the historical discourse of inferiority and the undermining of civic values and community life. Goetz (2004: 7) warns that under conditions such as this, strategies to address poverty by dispersing social housing may be counterproductive:

> the deconcentration argument provides the basis for low-poverty neighbourhoods to continue to oppose subsidized housing, by linking social pathologies to concentrated poverty, and concentrated poverty to subsidized housing. In the end, there is something perversely uniting about the deconcentration argument – it leads to almost universal resistance to subsidized housing.

While the development of social and affordable housing in the form of smaller dispersed projects is undoubtedly preferable to large poorly located and under maintained estates, the legacy of previous practices means that new developments must be carefully managed to avoid recreating the conditions of stigma and exclusion that currently apply to estates, albeit at a smaller and more personal scale. As Ruming et al. (2004: 238) caution, places of social mix may become new spaces for social exclusion through identification of 'us' and 'them' due to the unequal material conditions experienced by public housing tenants whereby they represent some of the disadvantaged social groups in contemporary society.

We now examine how some of these ideas about neighbourhood effects and deconcentration policies have worked in practice in Australia through drawing on some research vignettes of Carlton (Victoria) and Bonnyrigg (NSW) estates. The redevelopment of Carlton Estate (Lygon Site) in Melbourne was originally planned to break down social barriers between housing tenure groups through a mixed income development implemented as a 'salt and pepper' model of social mix where public and private units were situated in the same buildings. Financial constraints of the GFC and pressure from the private sector partner (the developer) meant that the Department of Human Services and the Office of Housing instead agreed to construct a complex of three buildings segregated by housing tenure (one public housing building and two private buildings) with separate secured entrances and car parks. The development includes an enclosed courtyard garden that is enclosed by and visible from all three buildings but only accessible to residents in the two private buildings. In addition a wall was constructed that not only physically but also symbolically separates public and private residents from each other (Levin et al. 2014).[1] This situation poses the key question of how the social integration aspects of the project will be achieved.

Likewise in the larger showpiece Bonnyrigg redevelopment project west of Sydney, Housing NSW set out to demonstrate best practice in many key aspects of deconcentration policy. The aim was to replace approximately nine hundred public housing dwellings, which made up 90 per cent of the estate, with a new suburb of more than two thousand units, only 30 per cent of which would be subsidised social housing and the remainder privately owned and occupied. This was to be achieved through a public-private partnership under which responsibility for physical redevelopment, sale of new dwellings and management of continuing social tenancies would pass to a private consortium (Rogers 2013). Importantly, the consortium involved not just a developer and facilities manager, but also a non-profit housing association that would manage tenancies and conduct community development and consultation activities. Exterior design of social housing dwellings was to be indistinguishable from private dwellings. Transfer of the management of tenancies to a non-government landlord also contributed to the financial viability of social housing on the site since unlike tenants of State Housing Authorities, Housing Association tenants who qualify for Commonwealth pensions and benefits can also receive rent assistance. However, rather than increasing the income of tenants, Commonwealth Rent Assistance payments are added in their entirety to the rent payable to the Housing Association, thus effectively capturing Commonwealth funding for the project which would not otherwise be available.

---

1 For more detailed information, additional resources and analysis of the Carlton Redevelopment project see the VicHealth website for a full research report (http://www.vichealth.vic.gov.au/).

At the time of writing, more than half a decade after the commencement of the redevelopment, the Bonnyrigg project illustrates some of the structural issues inherent in this approach. Firstly, the social mix objective of the project relies on the idea that owner-occupiers, as mortgage holders, will be stable neighbours with a stake in the area and will underwrite an aspirational local culture based on employment. However, as the financial viability of the project relies on sales, buyers are not constrained to actually live on the estate and up to half of the private dwellings sold to date are not owner occupied but privately rented. Research is still being conducted into the impact of the mix strategy on outcomes for tenants, but this certainly calls into question some key features of the rationale deployed to justify the project. Far more significantly, sales have not met expectations and the private development company that was the lead player in the private consortium responsible for the project, has now declared insolvency (Rogers 2013). Given the chronic undersupply of well-located housing in Sydney, and the fact that new houses in Bonnyrigg were offered at prices well below similar property in surrounding areas, it is clear that the stigma associated with public housing remains a factor, even where it represents only 30 per cent of households.

Conclusions

In current debates public housing concentration is linked to reproduction of a culture of poverty whereby public housing tenants are depicted as rejecting employment for a life on the dole. As such public housing concentration is depicted as an obstacle to successful welfare reform. However the issues are more complex than this and as such appear unlikely to be resolved by simply drawing on public housing geography as a solution.

An alternative explanation for the concentration of unemployed tenants is that the move to narrower targeting, which began in the late 1990s has resulted in concentrations of households in public housing that have fewer opportunities in the labour market. Consequently it is not surprising that households in public rental compared to other housing tenures have low rates of economic participation. They may also lack skills or have lower levels of training and education or be unsuccessful in seeking employment due to lack of transport and stigma associated by some employers of living in public housing. In addition due to targeting to high need groups, public housing tenants are often unlikely to seek paid employment due to ill health, old age, disability, and carer responsibilities for children (Wood et al. 2009).

There is little question that current rent-setting formulas provide a disincentive for employment and a poverty trap. Tenants' rent increases or benefits such as income support reduce if they take up paid employment or increase their hours of employment or they may have to exit public housing. In many instances they only have access to low paid employment, which creates welfare or poverty traps whereby there may be no financial benefits from taking up paid employment. These outcomes are supported by research illustrating that recipients of housing assistance are more likely to be in unskilled or casual work with low rates of remuneration (Wood et al. 2009).

Owner-occupiers often perceive public housing households as bad neighbours and in mixed tenure communities often attribute problems, such as inappropriate social behaviour, as due to the presence of public housing in the local neighbourhood (Bretherton and Pleace 2011; Arthurson 2012b). The negative associations of public housing tenants are reinforced by insensitive portrayals on television and in print media. It is not uncommon for public housing estates to be portrayed as sites of crime and disorder, such as the characterisations of 'Sunnyvale Estate' as depicted in the SBS television program 'Housos' (Arthurson, Darcy, and Rogers 2014). Jacobs et al. (2011) identified that few positive stories about public housing are reported in the media, as negative stories are more likely to appeal to mass audiences. Thus in reality there is considerable pressure for journalists to deliver negative stories. Reports focusing on public housing estates typically document neighbour disputes drawing on sensationalist reporting, and utilising particular phrases such as 'neighbours from hell'. These media reports presenting a pejorative narrative of public housing estates are rarely challenged (Hastings 2004). The way housing policy issues are reported can be instrumental in setting political agendas to address the problems. Many of the narratives about socially disadvantaged groups in the media maintain that individuals are to a large degree responsible for their own disadvantage. The causes and effects of structural inequality are largely overlooked within mainstream media discourses, discounting structural explanations of disadvantage and compounding the negative effects of stigma.

Poverty deconcentration programs in the US and Australia are almost exclusively focussed on public housing neighbourhoods. Of course this is because government authorities 'own' the land and the dwellings and so they can intervene with relative ease. Many poorer households not living in public housing are driven by the market to concentrate in the least expensive parts of the city, the same market forces cause the value of certain areas to change and poor households to move on. Public housing concentration, however, is the product of policy rather than market forces, and so requires policy intervention in order to allow the realisation of changing urban land value. The theory of cultural reproduction of poverty through 'neighbourhood effects' provides the necessary social justification for returning publicly owned land to the market by claiming that relocation of tenants is in their own interest. So despite the equivocal evidence, housing managers and policy makers have enthusiastically adopted the theoretical notion of neighbourhood effects as a rationale for radical programs of dispersal of tenants and large-scale redevelopment of land.

As has been shown, public and social housing in Australia has historically been politically contested and has incorporated multiple and sometimes conflicting objectives. The simple aim of providing low income households with secure affordable housing outside the uncertainties of the private market has existed alongside an agenda which sought to use housing as a tool of social engineering designed to improve the situation of poor people by changing their behaviour. From the slum clearance and garden suburbs of the early 20th century, through the Radburn estates of the 1970s to contemporary deconcentration projects, housing location and design was expected to improve tenants social networks and behaviour, to make them healthier, more motivated or more responsible. The perception of public housing estates as a 'failure' does not arise from their failure to securely and affordably house people (which has more to do with decades of under investment) but the failure to turn public tenants into responsible citizens who work and pay their own way rather than relying on taxpayer assistance.

Despite this somewhat dire analysis, secure affordable housing, even in the context of social housing concentrations, continues to be the most important factor underwriting the ability of poor households to participate in community life, including education and even employment. But in the early 21st century, public housing tenure has reached a stage of crisis. The gradual narrowing of targeting to only high need and complex tenants, reduced supply of public housing and insufficient funding in the past and leading up to now has meant the sector lacks a long term investment plan to enable public housing to grow and be better configured to meet current and future tenant needs. State Housing Authorities have not made the case for the funding and support needed to address the long-term viability, growth and provision of stronger connections with support services in homelessness education and health. Within the sector there is recognition that a new approach is needed but also pessimism about the future and fear that it is ill equipped to deal with the challenges of demographic change and demand for housing (Jacobs et al. 2013). Public housing does not have the political clout of other sectors such as health to fall back on. Given the complexity of these issues it seems incongruous if not counterproductive to focus on public housing concentration as the main problem.

References

Allen, C., Camina, M., Casey, R., Coward, S., and Wood, M. (2005) *Mixed Tenure, Twenty Years On*, Chartered Institute of Housing/Joseph Rowntree Foundation. Sheffield Hallam University, Coventry.

Arthurson, K. (2002) Creating inclusive communities through balancing social mix: A critical relationship or tenuous link?, *Urban Policy and Research* 20(3): 245–261.

—— (2008) Australian public housing and the diverse histories of social mix, *Journal of Urban History* 34(3): 484–501.

—— (2012a) *Social Mix and the Cities: Challenging the Mixed Communities Consensus in Housing and Urban Planning Policies*, Sustainable Cities Series, CSIRO Publishing, Clayton.

—— (2012b) Social Mix, Reputation and Stigma: Exploring Residents Experiences of Neighbourhood Effects, in M. van Ham, D. Manley, N. Bailey, C. Simpson and D. Maclennan (eds), *Neighbourhood Effects Research: New Perspectives*, London: Springer.

Arthurson, K., Darcy, M., and Rogers, D. (2014) Televised territorial stigma: how social housing tenants experience the fictional media representation of estates in Australia, *Environment and Planning A* 46(6): 1334–1350.

Australian Institute of Health and Welfare (2009) *Housing Assistance in Australia* June, Cat no HOU 236, AIHW, Canberra.

Bijen G., and Piracha A. (2012) Evaluating the urban design and community life in public housing in Australia, *Australian Planner* 49(4): 349–360.

Bretherton, J. and Pleace, N. (2011) A Difficult Mix: Issues in achieving socioeconomic diversity in deprived UK neighbourhoods, *Urban Studies* 48(16): 3429–3443.

Coates, B. and Shepherd, M. (2005) Bonnyrigg Living Communities Project. A Case Study in Social Housing PPPs presented to National Housing Conference Perth, Western Australia.

Chaskin, R. and Joseph, M. (2011) Social Interaction in mixed-income developments: Relational expectations and emerging reality, *Journal of Urban Affairs* 33(2): 209–237.

Commission of Inquiry into Poverty (Henderson Report) (1975) *Poverty in Australia, First Main Report, Volume 1*, AGPS, Canberra.

Commonwealth of Australia (1978) *Housing Assistance (Form of Agreement) Determination 1978*, AGPS, Canberra.

Darcy, M. (2010) De-concentration of disadvantage and mixed income housing: A critical discourse approach, *Housing, Theory and Society* 27(1): 1–22.

Gatti, R. (n.d.). *Radburn: The Town for the Motor Age*, The Radburn Association.

Goetz (2004) The Reality of Deconcentration, *Shelterforce Online* 138, National Housing Institute.

Graves, E. (2010) The structuring of urban life in a mixed income housing 'community', *City and Community* 9(1): 109–131.

Hall, J. and Berry, M. (2007) *The Financial Impact of Welfare Targeting in Public Housing*, AHURI Research and Policy Bulletin 89, November.

Hastings, A. (2004) Stigma and social housing estates: beyond pathological explanations, *Journal of Housing and the Built Environment* 19(3): 233–54.

Holmes, C. (2006) *Mixed Communities, Success and Sustainability*, York: Joseph Rowntree Foundation.

Imbroscio, D. (2008) '[U]nited and actuated by some common sense of passion': Challenging the dispersal consensus in American housing policy research, *Journal of Urban Affairs* 30(2): 111–130.

Jacobs, K., Arthurson, K., Cica, N., Greenwood, A., and Hastings, A. (2011) *The Stigmatisation of Social Housing: Findings from a Panel Investigation*, AHURI Final Report, Melbourne.

Jacobs, K, Berry, M. and Dalton, T. (2013) 'A dead and broken system?': 'insider' views of the future role of Australian public housing, *International Journal of Housing Policy* 13(2): 183–201.

Levin, I., Arthurson, K. and A. Ziersch (2014) Social mix and the role of design: the Carlton Public Housing Estate redevelopment, Melbourne, *Cities* 40: 23–31.

Luxford, L. (2006) Housing assistance and disadvantaged places, *AHURI Research and Policy Bulletin* 85 November.

Marsden, S. (1986) *Business, Charity and Sentiment: The SA Housing Trust 1936–1986*, Netley S.A.: Wakefield Press.

Murphy, J. (1995) *The Commonwealth State Housing Agreement of 1956 and the Politics of Housing in the Cold War*, Working Paper No 50. Canberra: ANU Urban Research Program.

Paris, C., Williams, P., and Stimson, R. (1985) From public housing to welfare housing, *Australian Journal of Social Issues* 20(2): 105–117.

Peel, M. (1994) Empowering a version of the future: The 'Great Housing Debate' revisited, *Shelter-NHA* 10(2): 16–21.

Pinnegar, S., Randolph, B., and Davidson, G. (2011) *Feasibility Study tTo Undertake a Multi-Year Research Project – Addressing Concentrations of Social Disadvantage*, Melbourne: AHURI.

Porter, L., and Shaw, K. (eds) (2009) *Whose Urban Renaissance. An International Comparison of Urban Regeneration Strategies*, London: Routledge.

Pugh, C. (1976) *Intergovernmental Relations and the Development of Australian Housing Policies*, Centre for Research on Federal Financial Relations, Australian National University, Canberra.

Rogers D, (2013) Urban and Social Planning through Public-Private Partnerships: The Case of the Bonnyrigg Living Communities Project, Sydney Australia, in J. Colman and C. Gossop (eds) ISOCARP Review 09: Frontiers of Planning: Visionary Futures for Human Settlements, Brisbane, Qld.: 142–155.

Ruming, K. (2011) Understandings of social mix and community opposition to social housing constructed under the nation building economic stimulus plan. *State of Australian Cities (SOAC) Conference*, Melbourne, November.

Ruming, K., Mee J., and McGuirk, M. (2004) Questioning the rhetoric of social mix: Courteous community or hidden hostility? *Australian Geographical Studies* 42(2): 234–248.

Smith, A. (2002) *Mixed-income Housing Developments: Promise and Reality*, Cambridge, MA: Harvard University, Joint Center for Housing Studies.

Stein, C. and Mumford, L. (1957) *Toward New Towns for America*, Cambridge, MA: MIT Press.

Troy, P. (1997) Introductory Remarks to the Forum: The End of Public Housing, 25 October 1996 in R. Coles (ed.), *The End of Public Housing? A Discussion Forum Organised by the Urban Research Program held on 25 October 1996*, Urban Research Program, Australian National University, Canberra, ix–xii.

—— (2011) *Accommodating Australians: Commonwealth Government Involvement in Housing*, Sydney: The Federation Press.

van Ham, M., and Manley, D. (2010) The effect of neighbourhood housing tenure mix in labour market outcomes: A longitudinal investigation of neighbourhood effects, *Journal of Economic Geography* 10(2): 257–282.

Venkatesh, S. and Venkatesh, S. (2009) *American Project: The Rise and Fall of a Modern Ghetto*, Cambridge, MA: Harvard University Press.

Ware, V., Gronda, H., and Vitis, L. (2010) *Addressing Locational Disadvantage Effectively*, AUHRI, Melbourne.

Wilson, W. (1987) *The Truly Disadvantaged: The Inner City, the Underclass, and Public Policy*, Chicago, IL: University of Chicago Press.

Wood, G., Ong, R., and Dockery, A. (2009) The long run decline in employment participation for Australian public housing tenants: an investigation, *Housing Studies* 24(1): 103–126.

Chapter 12

Reviewing the Social Housing Initiative: Unpacking Opportunities and Challenges for Community Housing Provision in Australia

Kristian Ruming

Introduction

Australia is characterised by a complex and shifting social housing landscape (see Chapters 9 and 11). Despite the residualised nature of social housing, the election of a social democratic Commonwealth government in 2007 marked a renewed interest in housing (and urban) policy. Important policy interventions included the introduction of the National Affordable Housing Agreement (NAHA) and the National Rental Affordability Scheme (NRAS).[1] While these policy initiatives represented significant and long overdue Commonwealth engagement with housing, such programs were disrupted by the 2007-2009 Global Financial Crisis (GFC). The GFC saw Commonwealth supported housing initiatives transformed from broader social equity objectives (albeit couched within language of economic productivity) to a mechanism to stimulate the economy. The Social Housing Initiative (SHI) was introduced as part of the Nation Building Economic Stimulus Plan (NBESP) which sought to address the risk of a collapse in house prices and loss of construction and finance industry jobs (Milligan and Pinnegar 2010). The SHI represented the single biggest investment in social housing in recent decades and acted as a catalyst for restructuring social housing provision by supporting a fledgling community housing sector. According to the Council of Australian Governments (COAG 2009a: 7), the SHI would 'drive significant reform of social housing through consolidation of waiting lists, growth of the not-for-profit sector, funding reform and reduction of concentrations of disadvantage'.

This chapter explores the *delivery*, *management* and *lived experience* of housing provided under the SHI. While it is broadly acknowledged that the NBESP played a vital role in

---

1 A subsidy scheme which provides a grant or tax incentive to the private sector and to community organisations to build and rent new dwellings to low- and moderate-income households at 20 per cent or more below market rates for 10 years (Yates 2013: 117). NRAS ceased to operate in 2014 following budgetary cut-backs following the September 2013 election of a new Federal Coalition Government.

the Australian economy weathering the worst of the GFC (McDonald and Morling 2011; Murphy 2011), a series of issues and challenges arose which offer important insights for future funding, delivery and management of social housing. This chapter draws on fieldwork undertaken in New South Wales (NSW) and highlights a series of important issues emergent from the SHI, which should inform future community housing provision.

A qualitative research methodology was adopted to trace: the implementation of the SHI; local community opinion; tenancy management and delivery challenges; and, the lived experience of new tenants. Fieldwork was conducted in four local government areas[2] where community opposition had been recorded. Interviews were undertaken with: residents surrounding SHI developments, local planning officers and elected councillors, planning officials and state government employees, and staff of Community Housing Providers. The project also explored the experience of new tenants via a survey and interviews. In total 5,339 surveys were administered,[3] 536 surveys were returned (10%), and 152 interviews were conducted (Table 12.1).

Table 12.1   Interviews conducted

Group	Residents surround development	Local council staff	Elected councillors	State government employees	Community Housing Providers	New tenants	Total interviews
Number of interviews	93	11	3	3	6	36	152

Source: Kristian Ruming.

Social Housing, Global Crisis and New Provision

Social Housing in Australia

Social housing in Australia accounts for just 4.7 percent of total housing stock (ABS 2011) and represents the tenure of 'last resort' for some of the most disadvantaged individuals in society. This residualisation has been driven by the dual processes of budgetary constraint and increasingly focussed allocation policy (Jacobs et al. 2010). Historically social housing has been built and managed by the states with the bulk of funding provided by the Commonwealth government through agreements such as the Commonwealth-State Housing Agreement (CSHA) (1945–2008) and the NAHA (2009–present). The NAHA adopts a broader housing policy agenda with the objective that: 'all Australians have

---

2   Ryde, Wollongong, Lake Macquarie and Wyong.
3   A *Government Information (Public Access) Act 2009* request was lodged with the NSW Department of Finance and Services for the postal address of *SHI* dwellings. 6,095 postal addresses were provided. 756 surveys were returned to sender due to incorrect addresses were removed from the sample.

access to affordable, safe and sustainable housing that contributes to social and economic participation' (COAG 2008). The NAHA also envisages a substantially increased role of the community housing sector in delivering affordable housing. While the most recent NAHA provided some new initiatives, there remains an undersupply of social housing. The nine years to 2007/2008 saw the national funding provided to Social Housing Authorities (SHAs) fall by 25 percent in real terms (Productivity Commission 2009, cited in Pawson and Gilmour 2010). Between 2001 and 2010 the total stock of public housing fell by 6.6 percent, only partially offset by an increase in community housing. Nationally, in 2010 there were 383,316 social housing dwellings with a combined waiting list of 248,419 households (Shelter NSW 2011).

Together the reduced funding and focussed allocation has worked to define social housing as problematic in both policy rhetoric and public consciousness (Chapter 11). The responses to these problems have been diverse, but have increasingly centred on large urban/estate regeneration projects (Arthurson 2010a). At the centre of these projects sit two ideological policy presumptions. First, that 'mixing' social tenants with populations in other tenures can address the challenge of social housing (Arthurson 2010b; Ruming et al. 2004). The second, and related, policy approach embedded in the urban/estate regeneration model is the use of private finance and developers to deliver change. The absence of sufficient departmental budgets has seen a rapid growth in the Public-Private Partnership (PPP) model (Gilmour et al. 2010). Together policies of social mix and urban/estate regeneration are emblematic of a neoliberal urban policy environment which works to promote the virtues of the private market in terms of both the social/cultural values of homeowners (social mix) and the value of the private market as an appropriate delivery/funding mechanism (PPPs) (Milligan and Randolph 2009). However, the GFC challenged the dominant social housing redevelopment model and acted as a catalyst for new investment and modes of delivery/management, such as an expanded community housing sector.

The management of the social housing sector has been diversifying from the early 1990s with the growth of Community Housing Providers (CHPs). Australia has a long history of CHPs, however the total stock they manage is small compared to countries such as the UK (Pawson and Gilmour 2010). Traditionally CHPs have been small and confined to niche markets which has acted as a barrier for growth (Yates 2013; Gilmour and Milligan 2012). Over the past decade there has been a call for the introduction of significant stock transfer programs which would see existing SHA stock transitioned to CHPs (Jacobs et al. 2013; Milligan 2013). The supposed benefits of this transfer include the provision of more housing choice and the increased capacity for CHPs to leverage these assets (Groenhart 2013; Arthurson 2012). According to Blessing (2012: 190), the appeal of such organisations is that they use limited state resources and mobilise existing assets to 'lever private development capital and to pursue commercial profits for social ends'. CHPs were identified as part of the Rudd Labor government's broader housing policy agenda (Gilmour and Milligan 2012). As then Federal Housing Minister, Tanya Plibersek, (2009: 6) identified: 'Over the next five years, I would like to see more large, commercially sophisticated not for profit housing organisations emerge and operate alongside the existing state and territory housing departments.'

The Minister went on to argue that CHPs would provide the, 'flexibility and commerciality we need to transform our social housing system' (Plibersek 2009: 6).

The NAHA outlined an overall objective of up to 35 percent of social housing managed by CHPs by 2014 (Australian Government 2010). While the push for community housing emphasised the capacity to leverage private funds, the capacity to access state funds was equally important in the early stages of the transition. The transition of SHA stock to CHPs was also promoted at the state level. For example, Housing NSW (2007: 5) established the following target, a 'growth in community housing from 13,000 to 30,000[4] over the next 10 years'. However, due to the introduction of the NRAS and the SHI, the target was projected to be met in 2012/13 (Housing NSW 2010).

The Global Financial Crisis and the Nation Building Economic Stimulus Package

The SHI represented an unprecedented injection of funds into the social housing sector. The NBESP was introduced in 2009 as a response to impending global recession. The NBESP was a two-year, AU$42 billion plan seeking to 'support jobs and invest in the long term growth of the Australian economy' (COA 2009: 7; see also Chapter 10). A significant proportion of stimulus funds were directed to large public works programs. Construction was identified as a trigger for economic growth and a means for circulating and multiplying Commonwealth funds through the economy (Murphy 2011; McDonald and Morling 2011). According to KPMG (2012: 2) for every $1.00 of construction activity spent under the SHI, $1.30 in total turnover was generated in the economy (see Chapter 10).

Within the context of the National Partnership Agreement of Social Housing (COAG 2009b), the SHI provided AU$5.2 billion for the construction of 19,200 social housing dwellings (NSW Government 2009). Nationally, this target was exceeded (KPMG 2012), with SHI (and NRAS) funded dwellings responsible for the net increase in social housing dwellings between 2006-2011 (Groenhart 2013). SHI funds were provided directly to state governments, who were responsible for managing the expenditure, planning and development processes within Commonwealth timelines. In promoting the Commonwealth objective of expanding the community housing sector, one of the additional criteria outlined in the National Partnership Agreement of Social Housing was that projects support the growth of the not-for-profit sector. Following the removal of the cap on stock transfer under the NAHA, there was commitment that up to 75 percent of dwellings constructed under the SHI be transferred to CHPs (COAG 2009b). Although the 75 percent target was not achieved, the SHI did see the largest transfer of state owned housing assets to the not-for-profit community housing sector in Australia's history. The SHI also worked to restructure the sector with 75 percent of properties allocated to large, well performing providers (Gilmour and Milligan 2012).

The key rational for the transfer of stock to the community housing sector was that these assets would work to facilitate access to private development capital which in turn

---

4   Consisting of previous SHA stock transferred to CHAs and new build dwellings funded under the NRAS.

could deliver affordable housing options (Blessing 2012). The ability of CHPs to generate revenue via state-subsidised rental payments (Commonwealth Rental Assistance, CRA) also worked to position community housing as a more financial viable alternative to state-funded models (Pawson and Gilmour 2010). The capacity for CHAs to charge higher rents than SHAs, generate third party contributions, attract tax benefits and undertake commercial activities is also identified as vital in generating more financially viable social housing provision (Yates 2013). The push for private finance and management arrangements also led to internal restructures of CHPs with a push for commercialisation, employment of private sector managers, the professionalisation of boards and a greater emphasis on economic outcomes (Gilmour and Milligan 2012).

The Social Housing Initiative in New South Wales

Under the SHI the NSW government was allocated AU$1.9 billion. In addition, the NSW government provided a further AU$1 billion (NSW Government 2009). 6,330 dwellings were to be constructed, the bulk of which would be produced on publically owned land. The redevelopment of existing Housing NSW[5] sites was preferred as it facilitated more expedient and cheaper development and allowed construction to occur in locations where the cost of land was prohibitive to new purchase. An additional 91 sites were acquired via private tender. A cost threshold of AU$300,000 per dwelling was implemented, with the final selection of sites driven by value for money, yield and speed of delivery.

NSW adopted a hybrid planning model. This approach was facilitated in three key ways. First, NSW was the only state to implement special purpose planning legislation. The Nation Building and Jobs Plan (NBJP) set out the broad framework for how the state would meet budget and delivery criteria. Under the NBJP new legislation was adopted – the Nation Building and Jobs Plan (State Infrastructure Delivery) Act (NBJP Act). The NBJP Act overrode existing planning frameworks for the period of the NBESP. The NBJP Act was administered by an Infrastructure Coordinator General (ICG) who had ultimate approval delegation for NBESP projects. The ICC was assisted by a specially appointed Taskforce of planners. The NBJP Act and the ICC were only used where existing assessment structures were seen as unable to meet project timelines (Shepherd and Abelson 2010). Second, Housing NSW was able to 'self-approve' projects under the State Environmental Planning Policy Affordable Rental Housing) 2009 (AHSEPP). The AHSEPP was designed to facilitate faster approval of certain types of dwellings in an effort to address ongoing housing affordability concerns. Finally, dwellings could be approved by local councils. The emphasis on fast delivery left little room for detailed local planning (Ruming 2013). The remainder of this chapter explores the delivery, management and lived experience of social housing provided under the SHI before exploring some opportunities and challenges for CHPs.

---

5   The State government agency responsible for managing social housing in NSW.

Implementing the *Social Housing Initiative* in New South Wales

Delivery Tensions: Local Opposition

The delivery of the SHI in many sites was controversial. While controversy and public opposition came to represent the public image of the SHI in most states (Davison et al. 2013) this conflict was confined to a relatively limited number of sites. Given that the SHI was the most significant program of new social housing construction in decades, a level of community opposition was not unexpected. Public perceptions of social housing have progressively been developed within a policy framework that has worked to ostracise social housing, and which often mobilised stereotypical, problematic representations of tenants as deviant (Arthurson et al. 2014). Concerns over social housing have manifest themselves in resident fears over the changing nature of their neighbourhood and community, increasing social issues, stigmatisation, and falling property values. In response to the SHI local residents around specific sites mobilised complex resistance strategies that challenged simplistic 'not-in-my-backyard' (NIMBY) categorisations. Detailed analysis of community opposition is provided elsewhere (Ruming 2013; 2014). The purpose of this section is to highlight the main themes of local opposition as a means of informing contemporary and future debates around social/community housing provision.

First, the bulk (although not all) of residents who actively opposed the SHI claimed to be supporters of social housing. By claiming to support social housing, local residents claimed a level of legitimacy by adopting a broadly social justice/welfare framework that identified social housing as a valuable social infrastructure. These residents positioned social housing as necessary to support 'deserving' parts of society, such as elderly residents who 'worked their entire life', persons with disabilities, and people who were 'down on their luck'. The exact definition of the latter category is open to debate. Where guarantees could be made that these groups would be housed in SHI dwellings, resistance was reduced. For opponents, 'underserving' residents were responsible for their situation, often characterised as single mothers and/or drug addicts/dealers.

Second, opponents mobilise a complex understanding of policy to challenge development. The SHI was positioned as inconsistent with existing planning frameworks, with residents challenging the level of information provided, the legitimacy of local planning decisions being made by the state government, and the speed of planning and development (Ruming 2013). For opponents, the NSW planning framework was positioned as undemocratic; removing local input expressed via the local planning frameworks and elected councillors. In addition, residents challenged the planning logic of the SHI by attempting to position development as the antithesis of contemporary social housing policy: social mix (Ruming 2014). According to residents, the type of development constructed under the SHI constituted 'estate' development, promoted concentrations of disadvantage and would create social problems.

Finally, residents challenged the built form of dwellings. On the one hand, the dwellings were seen as inconsistent with existing built form, often identified as the first medium/ high density developments in particular locations. Opponents claimed that SHI dwellings could be easily identified, subjecting tenants to a higher level of stigmatisation. Further, opponents claimed that many SHI developments were inappropriately located, away from local shops and social services. Access to public transport was an oft-cited critique. On the other hand, residents mobilised the needs of future tenants to oppose the built form. In particular, opponents claimed that the (small) dwellings were inappropriate for elderly tenants or those with disabilities. In this sense, opponents could position themselves as advocates for future (deserving) tenants. The extent to which new tenants themselves supported these claims is explored below.

It is important to recognise that the employees of Housing NSW and the SHI Taskforce challenged the claims raised by local opponents. In some locations minor changes did occur, however, for the bulk of locations SHI dwellings were implemented as planned. Nevertheless, community opposition offers a series of important insights for future planning and management of social/community housing covered later in the chapter.

Management: Community Housing

The SHI was an unexpected catalyst for a fledgling community housing sector. The rapid development and stock transfer, the need to fill tenancies, and the limited input into the planning process resulted in a number of teething problems for CHPs.

First, and echoing Milligan and Tiernan's (2011) claim that the new Commonwealth housing agenda exposed the public sector as underprepared and ill-equipped to address housing policy, the size and speed of the SHI program represented a significant challenge to CHPs organisational capacity and experience. The community housing sector was small, with little experience of large community housing provision or stock transfer. Despite the changing nature of staff identified by Gilmour and Milligan (2012), many CHPs identified staff experience as a barrier to management and development. Although the growth of the sector via the SHI was supported, all CHPs claimed to be understaffed. The lack of qualified and experienced staff was a challenge to tenant management, but also around maintenance, funding models and future development. These issues were compounded for CHPs new to the sector. In most cases these were large not-for-profit charities that identified community housing as an important extension of their social welfare role. These organisations had limited, if any, experience of community housing and were required to implement new institutional structures and hire staff responsible for housing provision and management. While many of the staff hired by these CHPs had histories in project management, residential development or social housing management (many coming from SHAs), it was recognised that there would be extensive on-the-job training required as the organisation and staff responded to the task of providing community housing.

Second, tensions around staffing levels and tight timelines also represented a challenge to the allocation and management of new tenancies. While working from a single waiting list with Housing NSW (Housing Pathways), CHPs sought, as much as possible, to 'match' new tenants with properties. The capacity to better 'match' tenants to properties has been identified as one of the advantages of community housing and was seen by CHPs to generate more cohesive developments. The capacity for CHPs to 'select' tenants, seeking to avoid tenants with problematic housing histories was identified as a major advantage. This was primarily the case for seniors dwellings. While potentially creating more harmonious developments, this process also has the potential to further residualise tenants being allocated to stock managed by SHAs. Further, the capacity to select tenants was identified as a tool for engaging (sometimes hostile) local communities. In the face of local opposition, CHPs sought to highlight their ability to mediate who moved into their properties. In most cases, CHPs attempted to align their tenants with those outlined as deserving by the local community (primarily elderly residents).

Nevertheless, according to CHPs, both the short timeframe for delivery and, in some cases, the lack of experience limited their capacity to 'select' appropriate tenants for individual developments. The 'matching' process was made difficult given that developments were new – CHPs could not 'match' an existing tenant profile. There was a belief that this 'matching' process would be improved in the future. Further, the SHI timeline limited the extent to which CHPs could engage with local residents. This was due to the fact that the state government managed the development process, limiting CHP involvement to the final stages. CHPs were limited in their capacity to influence the design of the developments or inform local communities of the benefits of community housing and their organisation in particular. CHPs only become involved with individual developments in the final stages of development, after a tender process and, in some cases, after significant local protest. CHP engagement with local communities after tenants had moved in tended to emphasis this 'selection' process and ongoing management, while simultaneously attempting to differentiate community housing from housing managed by Housing NSW. Nevertheless, it should be noted that some CHPs overstated their capacity to select tenants in their engagement with local communities. The primary strategy mobilised by CHPs was to liken community housing to private rental. CHPs were also keen to emphasis their capacity to manage problematic tenancies, highlighting their greater capacity to evict tenants compared to private landlords.

Third, in some ways echoing opponents, a number CHPs raised concerns around the form and quality of the dwellings themselves. While there was general agreement that SHI dwellings were of a good design, some developments were problematic. The main design concerns centred on the proximity of dwellings to each other and/or the purpose/ use of shared spaces. In these instances, the design of the dwellings was identified as a factor potentially increasing tensions between tenants and between tenants and neighbours. Further, within the context of a expenditure threshold, the quality of SHI developments was questioned by CHPs. Building quality issues raised by CHPs included: faulty plumbing and hot water systems; mould and damp; poor quality flooring; and, poor kitchen and bathroom fittings. Many CHPs suggested that if they been responsible for the developments, they would have been built to a higher standard. In cases where defects were not covered by warranties, CHPs were responsible for fixing the problems. Given that many CHPs had limited financial resources, the need to invest funds in to repairing new SHI dwellings was identified as an unexpected cost and a significant barrier to the management and expansion of their portfolio. For CHPs, issues around design and quality were seen to be the result of tight development timelines. CHPs also expressed longer term concerns about future costs as warrantees expired.

Finally, while stock transfer and the leveraging of assets to fund new construction have been advocated by many, the processes initiated under the SHI raised a number of challenges for CHPs. There was an expectation, as outlined in the stock transfer agreement, that successful CHPs would provide new dwellings. The purpose here is not to explore in detail the various financing models (such as housing supply bonds) which might be mobilised to the facilitate construction as this is covered elsewhere (Lawson et al. 2010). There was a broad belief from CHPs that they would be able to leverage their assets to facilitate construction. However, all CHPs expressed concerns over their capacity to secure private finance. Most recognised the difficult economic conditions and the reluctance of banks to lend to CHPs. In the short-term, CHPs emphasised tenant management and an ongoing reliance on state funding. The (now defunct) NRAS was identified by participants in this research as the principle source of ongoing funding. While leveraging private funds to facilitate future construction was a goal (and condition of receiving SHI properties), this was a long-term objective that was not possible in the immediate post-NBESP environment. These findings support a series of recent studies which question the extent to which CHPs are able to leverage assets for the purpose of securing construction finance (Yates 2013). Indeed, one of the ongoing tensions is the need to maintain affordable rents for tenants and the need to generate revenue to support expansion. Yates (2013) concludes that existing financial analysis demonstrates the limited capacity of CHAs to leverage their assets to generate (private) funding. The SHI was a catalyst for change, but was not itself the solution to all challenges facing the sector.

Lived Experience: Tenant Reflections

Despite public opposition in some locations and the fact that the impact of the NBESP was largely measured against macroeconomic matrices, the lived experience of new tenants provides an equally valid measure of success. While responding to the GFC was the principal catalyst for the NBESP, within the SHI was a broader social justice agenda tied to addressing disadvantage in social housing and rapidly growing waiting lists. In particular, the SHI sought to 'support the economic and social participation of tenants' and 'improve social inclusion' (COAG 2009b: 14). Broadly, from the perspective of SHI tenants, these goals were being achieved.

In NSW the SHI was delivered in an attempt to address issues of homelessness (target of 40% of dwellings going to homeless persons) and work to realign social housing stock with the tenant profile by moving existing tenants in under occupied dwellings into smaller dwellings (30% of dwellings) (Shepherd and Abelson 2010). Of the participants involved in the study, only 38.7 percent (206 responses) moved from social housing. The single largest previous tenure was private rental with 40.6 percent (216 responses). Given the complex definition of homelessness, it was difficult to assess how many participants had been homeless prior to moving into SHI dwellings. Nevertheless, the sample illustrated a very high proportion of tenants who had been homeless at some point in their life – 25 percent of participants. The majority of tenants moving into SHI dwellings from private rental had been on the social housing waiting list at some point. Across the sample, the SHI was meeting its broader social justice objectives by housing the disadvantaged while providing new stock and facilitating movement of tenants out of under-occupied dwellings. Although most tenants moving into SHI dwellings were satisfied, there was a small proportion of residents who were upset that their previous dwellings had been demolished. In most cases the concerns centred on the loss of social support networks which fell apart as friends and family moved away as a result of the SHI development process.

Importantly, many of the challenges raised by local opponents did not receive support from new tenants. The majority of tenants identified their neighbourhood as being characterised by a mix of tenure types (if not dominated by 'private' tenures) and well serviced. While opponents claimed that the sites were inappropriate in terms of providing services to disadvantaged tenants, this was not echoed in the experiences of new tenants. For new residents the list of perceived benefits was long and included: access to shops (71% of tenants surveyed), access to public transport (63%), access to open space and parks (58%) and access to educational facilities (57%). Further, the majority of residents agreed that their local area was a good place to live (74%) and liked living in their neighbourhood (67%). For those moving into social housing from private rental, the security of tenure and affordable rent were the most significant.

With so many new dwellings being delivered it is to be expected that some locations were identified as poor. In most cases these were problematic sites owned by Housing NSW, and where concerns around local facilities and services were long-term challenges, in particular appropriate activities for children and teenagers. Equally, the bulk of tenants recounted stories of problematic tenants, emphasising illegal activity.

Although most participants emphasised the benefits of SHI dwellings, an interesting tension was observed in some developments between groups who have previously owned their homes (or who had been in private rental) and others who had been long-term social housing tenants. To some extent this tension repeated the support for 'deserving' tenants by local opponents. For some moving to social housing from home ownership or private rental, being offered a home was seen as a privilege – a vital service when they needed it most. Rehearsing discourses of the superiority of private housing, these tenants position themselves (and others with similar histories) as responsible and respectable. In contrast, while they currently lived in social housing, stereotypical representations of long-term social housing tenants were mobilised – particularly where certain tenants had been disruptive. Such tenants were positioned as irresponsible, difficult and repeated common themes (crime, drug use, single parents). Nevertheless, many also identified the diversity of tenants living within their developments as an advantage. Many were keen to point out the wide range of tenants in terms of their histories, education and professions. In doing so, many of the participants sought to differentiate themselves from other forms/locations of social housing. The capacity to 'selectively' allocate tenancies (within the confines of allocation policy) was seen as a positive by tenants as it was seen as a mechanism by which the impact of disruptive tenants could be minimised. Equally, the capacity of CHPs to manage (and evict) problematic tenants was a positive.

The majority of tenants acknowledged that their building was different to those in their neighbourhood. In most cases the buildings were identified as being of a superior quality. The buildings were seen as modern and a model for future development in the area. While these developments were different to existing properties, this difference in appearance was not an issue for most tenants. Rather than working to identify them as social housing tenants, as claimed by opponents, the fact that the dwellings did not resemble historical/

stereotypical social housing was seen as a major advantage by new tenants. The experiences of SHI residents suggest that the built form of the dwellings did not act as a significant barrier to interaction with the local community.

Some issues of built form were raised by tenants. The most common concerns centred on the level of privacy and car parking. Car parking was a central issue raised by opponents (Ruming 2013). Despite continued claims by Housing NSW that social housing tenants have lower rates of private car ownership, in the majority of developments tenants raised concerns about the amount of parking. In some cases the lack of adequate parking spaces had led to conflicts between tenants and concerns of crime when residents were forced to park on the street. However, the bulk of tenants were overwhelmingly happy with their dwellings.

Discussion: Opportunities and Challenges

The SHI was a success in terms of both providing much needed resources to the social housing sector and as part of a broader stimulus plan which sheltered the Australian economy from the worst of the GFC. The program also improved the lives of some of the most disadvantaged sections of the community, particularly citizens at risk of homelessness and those experiencing housing stress in the private rental market. Recent developments in housing policy have positioned Australia on a similar trajectory as other Western nations which increasingly position the not-for-profit housing sector as central in delivering affordable housing, providing innovation, diversity and flexibility of housing form/location and alternative funding mechanisms (Milligan 2013). Although this transition has been long in the gestation period, the SHI (along with the NRAS) worked to accelerate this process. The case of the SHI supports the call from Blessing (2012) that community housing should not be viewed as the 'magical solution' to issues of housing affordability. Despite claims by the COAG (2009a) that the SHI would act as a catalyst for reform of the social housing sector in Australia, this has only partly been the case (Pawson and Gilmour 2010). Administrative and structural reforms around the funding, management and delivery of social housing via the public sector (SHA) remain absent. Indeed Groenhart (2013) notes that even with the substantial growth in social housing provided under the SHI, social housing supply has not kept pace with demand, with a series of new challenges now facing the sector. In returning to the title of this chapter, this final section draws out some of the opportunities and challenges for community housing based on reflections of the SHI in NSW.

Opportunities

1) Growth of the community housing sector
Pawson and Gilmour (2010) support a phased approach to the transition of housing stock currently managed by SHAs to CHAs. The SHI represented a significant, and somewhat unexpected, catalyst for growth in the community housing sector. The SHI prompted expansion of the sector in terms of number of providers (especially large providers),

level of stock transferred, number of tenants, and number of employees working in CHPs. As a first stage of the transition to CHPs, the SHI represented an opportunity to quickly promote the skills and knowledge of CHPs to manage large stock portfolios into the future.

2) New housing identity

Given the fledgling community housing sector, there is considerable scope for promoting a new housing identity which differentiates community housing from public housing. Evidence from the SHI illustrated that both the general public and potential tenants were unaware of the purpose or nature of community housing. This is an opportunity that has the potential to address issues of stigma associated with social housing. In this sense, SHI properties might be mobilised as an exemplar of an effective alternative housing tenure. Promoting community housing is not the sole responsibility of CHPs, but also their advocates (Community Housing Federation of Australia), broader social housing and social services advocates (Shelter and the ACOSS), the media, government and academics. The success of the SHI, and the fact that new tenants are not ashamed to be identified as community housing tenants, represents a potentially powerful tool for addressing tenure based stigma at multiple scales.

3) Private financing

The growth of the community housing sector, via the SHI and NRAS, is a vital opportunity to present alternative funding/investing possibilities for affordable housing. However, for many CHAs, the ability to secure private finance to fund expansion was a major challenge. Indeed, Milligan et al. (2015) note that institutional finance (such as banks and superannuation funds) for NRAS (identified as the primary source of post-SHI funding by CHAs in this project) had been lacking. Nevertheless, the scheme was well subscribed by small-scale investors (family trusts, self-managed super funds and not-for-profit organisations). As the private sector becomes more familiar with community housing, it is possible that private investment might increase, thereby expanding the supply of social housing and position it as an appealing investment (Milligan et al. 2013). Ultimately, the willingness of private sector finance to invest in community housing (and affordable housing more broadly) rests upon the regulatory and investment frameworks established by the government (Milligan et al. 2015).

Challenges

1) Reduced state funding

While one of the central objectives of the SHI was to leverage private funds for future housing provision, the sector has traditionally relied heavily on state funding. Much of the initial post-SHI expansion was funded via the NRAS with CHPs actively engaging in partnerships to provide new dwellings. The former Labor Commonwealth government committed $AU622.6 million annually from 2008/9 to 2015/16 (Jacobs et al. 2013). However, in a shifting political and economic environment, governments are seeking to wind back this support – evidenced by the decision of the current Federal Coalition

Government to cease the NRAS program in 2014. In its place, government needs to implement alternative regulatory and funding arrangements which, first, make investment in affordable housing an appealing investment to the private sector, and, second, maintain government funding via the NAHA. CHPs need to adopt alternative financial models in the wake of reduced state funding. One alternative funding source for the expansion of affordable and community housing might be the rollout of the National Disability Insurance Scheme (NDIS) (Milligan et al. 2015).

2) Staff capacity
The SHI represented a somewhat unexpected catalyst for growth in the community housing sector. This expansion resulted in a number of 'growing pains'. Both CHPs and new tenants involved in this project identified a need to develop staff capacity and experience as central to the future of the sector. According to CHPs, staff needed more experience in finance and development models used to facilitate growth in the sector. According to residents, tenant management skills needed to be improved to be able to manage the complex array of social and economic issues confronting tenants. Both of these challenges, in part, arose from the rapid expansion of the sector under the SHI and must be addressed if the community housing sector is going to prosper in the future.

3) Lack coordinated social housing policy
Milligan and Pinnegar (2010) in their review of the re-engagement of the Commonwealth with housing policy suggest that the post-2007 initiatives under the Labor government worked as an effective short-term intervention, however, they failed to adequately acknowledge or address long-term strategic and structural challenges faced by the social housing sector. There is a need for social housing issues to be better integrated into broader urban policy and governance. The ascendance of neoconservative state governments represents a challenge for a coordinated and coherent social housing policy agenda. For example, in NSW, following the 2011 election of the O'Farrell Coalition government, the social housing portfolio was split between Housing NSW (within the Department of Family and Community Services) which was responsible for tenancy management and Department of Finance and Services which managed estate regeneration, maintenance and, in its latter stages, the SHI. These divisions need to be addressed if many of the challenges facing social housing (including community housing) are to be resolved.

4) Management of community housing tenants
As the stock of community housing grows, it is likely to draw on a wider set of tenants than those historically applying for public housing. As was evidence in the case of the SHI, tensions can arise between tenants new to social housing and those with longer histories. To some degree these tensions are an expression of 'deserving' versus 'undeserving' tenants played out across social housing literature. Given that these tensions will be played out within individual developments, CHPs need to adopt allocation policies and management practices which balance new and long-term tenants and develop the skills of housing managers to address such tensions.

5) Residualisation of public housing stock

While the expansion of the community housing sector offers a number of potential advantages associated with reducing the stigma of social housing, stock transfer and new development programs need to be rolled out in a way which limits further residualisation of public housing. Presenting community housing as an alternative to state managed public housing potentially works to further identify public housing as an illegitimate and problematic tenure. Locations, communities and individuals which remain in public housing are likely to be further stigmatised. This process is likely to be perpetuated by the fact that the early stages of stock transfer will focus on less problematic stock and tenants, leaving the more difficult and troublesome properties in the management of the state. In addition, although working from a single waiting list, the capacity for CHPs to be more selective in their allocation policy means that high demand or problematic applicants are likely to remain in the public housing system. These are concerns which need to be addressed across the whole social housing system.

6) Development challenges

In addition to challenges around finance, future development needs to address a number of issues emergent under the SHI. First, the design of dwellings needs better consideration. Concerns around privacy and car parks are particularly important. Car parking is likely to be an increasing concern as CHPs address housing needs of middle income households who are more likely to own private vehicles. Second, were future development requires the demolition of existing dwellings, thought needs to be given to managing how existing tenants are managed. Efforts should be made to ensure that residents have the option to return to the new dwellings or choose to live near friends and families who may also have moved. These are also challenges currently being encountered at large-scale estate regeneration projects. Smaller-scale redevelopment by CHPs is better placed to manage these issues. Third, in locations of new construction, early consultation is required with existing residents in an effort to overcome opposition to the development and potential long term community tensions. This consultation should emphasis the nature and purpose of community housing. Where appropriate, community input into the design of the development could be used to overcome tensions and integrate developments into existing locations. In an effort to reduce local conflict, new community housing development should, as much as possible, align with local planning frameworks. State-based planning tools for affordable housing are essential in facilitating new developments; however, CHPs should exercise caution in uncritically mobilising such tools which might generate local conflict and potential destabilise many of the social benefits of community housing (Davison et al. 2013).

As a one-off policy response to global financial pressures the SHI met many of its objectives around housing affordability and addressing homelessness in NSW. Tenants identified the affordable and secure housing as a significant factor contributing to improving their quality of life and optimism for the future. In addition to providing new stock to a sector which had experienced significant disinvestment in recent decades, the SHI provides a series of insights for the future of the community housing sector. Beyond just assets, the SHI offers the community housing sector lessons on funding, planning, developing and managing future stock. Whatever the future for the community housing sector, it will owe much to the SHI.

References

Arthurson, K. (2010a) Operationalising social mix: Spatial scale, lifestyle, stigma as mediating points in resident interaction, *Urban Policy and Research* 28(1): 49–63.

—— (2010b) Questioning the rhetoric of social mix as a tool for planning social inclusion, *Urban Policy and Research* 28(2): 225–231.

—— (2012) *Social Mix and the City: Challenging the Mixed Communities Consensus in Housing and Urban Planning Policies*, Collingwood: CSIRO Publishing.

Arthurson, K., Darcy, M. and Rogers, D. (2014) Televised territorial stigma: how social housing tenants experience the fictional media representation of estates in Australia, *Environment and Planning A*, 46(6): 1334–1350.

Australian Bureau of Statistics (2011) *Australia Basic Community Profile Cat. no. 2001.0*, Canberra: ABS.

Australian Government (2010) *Regulation and Growth of the Not-For-Profit Housing Sector: Discussion Paper*, Canberra: Australian Government.

Blessing, A. (2012) Magical or monstrous? Hybridity in social housing governance, *Housing Studies* 27(2): 189–207.

Council of Australian Governments (COAG) (2008) *National Affordable Housing Agreement: Factsheet*, Canberra: COAG.

COAG (2009a) *Special Council of Australian Governments Meeting. Nation Building and Jobs Plan, Communique*, 5 February, Canberra: COAG.

—— (2009b) *National Partnership Agreement on the National Partnership and Jobs Plan: Building Prosperity for the Future and Supporting Jobs Now*, Canberra: COAG.

Commonwealth of Australia (COA) (2009) *Nation Building Economic Stimulus Plan: Progress Report to 30 June*, Canberra: Dept of Prime Minister and Cabinet.

Davison, G., Legacy, C., Liu, E., Han, H., Phibbs, P., van den Nouwelant, R., Darcy, M. and Piracha, A. (2013) *Understanding and Addressing Community Opposition to Affordable Housing Development*, Melbourne: AHURI.

Gilmour, T., Wiesel, I., Pinnegar, S. and Loosemore, M. (2010) Social Infrastructure Partnerships: A firm rock in a storm?, *Journal of Financial Management of Property and Construction* 15(3): 247–259.

Gilmour, T. and V. Milligan (2012) Let a hundred flowers bloom: Innovation and diversity in Australian not-for-profit housing organisations, *Housing Studies* 27(4): 476–494.

Groenhart, L. (2013) Reflecting on a decade of Australian social housing policy: Changes in supply and geography, 2001–2011, *Geographical Research* 51(4): 387–397.

Housing NSW (2007) *Planning for the Future: New directions for Community Housing in NSW 2007/08–2012/13*, Sydney: Housing NSW.

—— (2010) *Factsheet: Community Housing Sector, April 2010*, Sydney: Department of Family and Community Services.

Jacobs, K., Atkinson, R., Spinner, A., Colic-Peisker, V., Berry, M. and T. Dalton. (2010) *What Future for Public Housing? A Critical Analysis*, Melbourne: AHURI.

Jacobs, K., Berry, M. and Dalton, T. (2013) 'A dead and broken system?': 'insider' views of the future role of Australian public housing, *International Journal of Housing Policy* 13(2): 183–201.

KPMG (2012) *Social Housing Initiative Review*, Report for the Housing Ministers Advisory Committee, September.

Lawson, J., Gilmour, T. and Milligan, V. (2010) *International Measures to Channel Investment Towards Affordable Rental Housing*, Melbourne: AHURI.

McDonald, T., and Morling, S. (2011) *The Australian Economy and the Global Downturn: Part 1: Reasons for Resilience*, Canberra: Australian Treasury.

Milligan, V. (2013) Not-for-profit affordable housing providers: All dressed up and ready for a bigger role, *Parity* 26(6): 40–41.

Milligan, V. and S. Pinnegar (2010) The comeback of national housing policy in Australia: First reflections, *International Journal of Housing Policy* 10(3): 325–344.

Milligan, V. and Randolph, B. (2009) 'Australia', in V. Gruis, S. Tsenkova and N. Nieboer (eds), *Management of Privatised Housing: International Policies and Practice*, Chichester: Wiley-Blackwell.

Milligan, V. and Tiernan, A. (2011) No home for housing: The situation of the Commonwealth's Housing Policy Advisory Function, *Australian Journal of Public Administration* 70(4): 391–407.

Milligan, V., Yates, J., Weisel, I. and Pawson, H. (2013) *Financing Rental Housing Through Institutional Investment – Volume 1 Outcomes of an Investigative Panel*, Melbourne: AHURI.

Milligan, V., Pawson, H., Williams, P. and Yates, J. (2015) *Next Moves? Expanding Affordable Rental Housing in Australia through Institutional Investment*, Sydney: City Future Research Centre, UNSW.

Murphy, L. (2011) The global financial crisis and the Australian and New Zealand housing markets, *Journal of Housing and the Built Environment* 26(3): 335–351.

NSW Government (2009) *Fact Sheet: Nation Building Economic Stimulus Plan – Building Housing NSW*, Sydney: NSW Government.

Pawson, H. and T. Gilmour (2010) Transforming Australia's social housing: Pointers from the British stock transfer experience, *Urban Policy and Research* 28(3): 241–260.

Plibersek, T. (2009) *Room for More: Boosting Providers of Social Housing*, Canberra: Australian Government.

Ruming, K.J. (2013) 'It wasn't about public housing, it was about the way it was done': Challenging planning not people in resisting the Nation Building Economic Stimulus Plan, Australia, *Journal of Housing and the Built Environment* 23(1): 39–60.

—— (2014) Social mix discourse and local resistance to social housing: The case of nation building economic stimulus plan, Australia, *Urban Policy and Research* 32(2): 163–183.

Ruming, K.J., Mee, K.J. and McGuirk, P.M. (2004) Questioning the rhetoric of social exclusion: Courteous community of hidden hostility, *Australian Geographical Studies* 42(2): 234–248.

Shelter NSW (2011) *Housing Australia Factsheet*, Sydney: Shelter NSW.

Shepherd, N., and Abelson, P. (2010) *Review of Implementation of the Nation Building and Jobs Plan in NSW and Potential Applications for Other Projects*. Report prepared for the NSW Government, Sydney: NSW Government.

Yates, J. (2013) Evaluating social and affordable housing reform in Australia: Lessons to be learned from history, *International Journal of Housing Policy* 13(2): 111–133.

Chapter 13
Homelessness, the 'Housing First' Approach and the Creation of 'Home'

Hazel Blunden and Gabrielle Drake

Introduction

Homelessness is a severe and persistent feature of Australian society. Historically, homelessness was understood to be the result of personal failings and policy responses were largely focused on managing homelessness, including the provision of welfare services and temporary accommodation. However, since the 1980s there has been greater recognition of the structural aspects of homelessness and acknowledgment of the diversity of how homelessness is experienced and who experiences it. In a major turning point in how homelessness was conceptualised and approached in the policy arena, the Australian Government (2008) released the first *White Paper on Homelessness: The Road Home*. Optimistically, the Rudd Government undertook to 'halve homelessness by 2020' (Australian Government 2008: viii). However, in the years that have followed the announcement of this ambitious target, homelessness grew by 17 per cent between 2006 and 2011[1] (ABS 2012b). Currently there are more than 105,000 people experiencing homelessness in Australia (ABS 2012b).

In what appears to be an increasingly dire picture of homelessness in Australia there exist some glimmers of success. One of these stories of achievement in homelessness policy in Australia has been the high success rates shown by individual 'Housing First' programs (measured by tenancies being maintained). A Housing First approach emphasises unconditional and rapid provision of permanent housing to persons who are homeless. This chapter is particularly concerned with homelessness's ontological meaning. We define homelessness in its broadest sense as a lack of 'home'. That is not just a roof over one's head but a deficit of ontological security. Access to ontological security is underlined by the material provision of housing but also impacted upon via the background of individuals who may have been born into or moved into circumstances that have led to radical insecurity. The very act of providing access to permanent and unconditional (rather than transitional and behaviourally conditional) housing is a precondition for 're-homing' as possibility, however 'homelessness is more than houselessness' (Seager 2011). The Housing First model seeks to address both of these aspects. The aim is not only to provide homeless persons with permanent housing, without conditionality (such as requiring sobriety or ability to live independently), but to also provide wraparound support – this is

---

1   The overall Australian population increased by only 8 per cent.

not an added 'extra' – but rather key to the model, and to the 're-homing' process (Seager 2011) allowing people to live in permanent, secure and affordable housing and access the other services they need to address their physical and mental health issues.

In this chapter we examine the Housing First programs in Australia within the wider context of homelessness policies and programs. First, we examine the definitions of homelessness in Australia, in particular the classification of homelessness into 'primary, secondary and tertiary' types (Chamberlain and MacKenzie 2003) and the Australian Bureau of Statistics (ABS) definition. We then go onto examine concepts of 'houselessness and homelessness' and how programs have evolved to find their impetus in an aspiration to end primary homelessness (in particular to house rough sleeping persons) by offering permanent housing and support. We then review the evolution of the 'Housing First' approach in Australia and some of the findings from evaluations of 'Housing First' programs. Through examining these case studies we conclude that most 'Housing First' programs show success rates (usually measured as the number of persons who maintain a tenancy for a specified time interval – usually 12 or 24 months) of 77–92 per cent of the Australian Housing First programs that have been evaluated and this is broadly in line with other studies (see Johnson et al. 2012: Johnson and Chamberlain 2013). We conclude the chapter by looking at how a sense of 'home' can be constructed after a person is physically housed, based on interviews with recently housed persons who have participated in two Housing First programs.

Defining Homelessness in Australia

In recent years there has been an increased focus on developing consistent definitions that capture the 'scope and scale' of homelessness in Australia as well as enabling comparative, cross-national analysis (ABS 2012a). Within the Australian context, there are two main definitions that inform policy and practice: Chamberlain and McKenzie's 'Cultural definition of homelessness' (1992) and the 'Statistical definition of homelessness' developed by the Australian Bureau of Statistics (2012a).

Cultural Definition of Homelessness

In the early 1990s, Chamberlain and McKenzie (1992) introduced, what is known as, 'the cultural definition of homelessness'. They argued that homelessness and inadequate housing 'are socially constructed, cultural concepts that only make sense in a particular community at a given historical period' (Chamberlain and MacKenzie 1992: 290).

The cultural definition comprises three tiers of homelessness:

- *Primary homelessness*: people without conventional accommodation (living on the streets, in deserted buildings, improvised dwellings, under bridges, in parks, etc.).
- *Secondary homelessness*: people moving between various forms of temporary shelter including friends, emergency accommodation, youth refuges and hostels.
- *Tertiary homelessness*: people living in single rooms in private boarding houses without their own bathroom, kitchen or security of tenure (Chamberlain and MacKenzie 2003: 5).

Australian Bureau of Statistics (ABS) definition

In recent years the ABS 'statistical definition of homelessness' has expanded to include not only those who are homelessness because of 'rooflessness'. 'Homeless persons', according to the ABS definition, are persons that are 'in a dwelling that is inadequate; or has no tenure, or if their initial tenure is short and not extendable; or does not allow them to have control of, and access to space for social relations' (ABS 2012a). The ABS maintains that a person is considered to be homeless if they do not have 'suitable accommodation alternatives'. An important aspect of the ABS definition is the inclusion of people experiencing violence and abuse, such as women and children experiencing domestic and family violence. However, it has been argued (and acknowledged by the ABS) that the ABS relies on Census data which is an unreliable and inappropriate tool for capturing the housing vulnerability of women and children experiencing domestic violence. This is because they may be staying with others on Census night and be undistinguishable from other visitors or may not be disclosed on Census forms due to concerns about their safety (Chamberlain 2012; AIHW 2013: 7).

Both definitions are useful as they go beyond 'houselessness'. The 'three tier' definition of Chamberlain and Mackenzie is useful as a typology. However, the ABS inclusion of factors such as temporary or insecure tenure and lack of alternatives gives a broader meaning to 'homelessness' as more than 'houselessness'.

Housing and Home: The Non-material Aspects of Homelessness

Increasingly there has been an emphasis on non-material aspects of homelessness. While it is absolutely the case that persons can only be housed if there is access to affordable, secure housing (for example, social housing) and that this is fundamental as a precondition to reducing or ending homelessness (as Parsell put it, 'housing is required to experience home' (2010: 160)), the inability to 'settle' or have one's basic needs met can also affect home-making. Seager (2011) argues that approaches to homelessness can be overly material (focusing on 'a roof over ones' head') to the detriment of the basic psychological needs of persons – simply that 'a house is not a home' and re-homing relies on basic human needs (to be loved, to be listened to, to belong, to achieve and to have meaning and hope) (Seager 2011: 184 citing Seager and Manning 2009).

Homeless persons may refer to being 'outside' and 'inside' and having a 'roof over one's head' (for example, comments from rough sleepers in Darcy et al. 2014a) – that is, refer to a physical environment rather than to 'home' This suggests housed homeless persons who are newly housed have not yet done 'home making' work in their own minds, and a sense of impermanence can persist post housing.

Homelessness is most certainly not 'a choice' as a police officer once suggested to one of the authors. It is a physical and psychological state. While it may be claimed that rough sleepers who do not or cannot conform to the rules of accommodation providers, or who want to avoid other homeless persons that stay in that accommodation, may 'choose' to sleep rough – as Parsell and Parsell (2012) point out, this 'choice' needs to be understood within a context of opportunities and consequences; rough sleeping may be the 'least worst' option (especially for people fleeing violence). Social housing waiting lists can be up to two years even for those accorded 'priority' status (Darcy et al. 2014b).

Importantly Housing First approaches seems to recognise both the material and non-material dimensions of homelessness. It does this by addressing two aspects of homelessness: 1) providing physical housing (the materiality of home and housing), and 2) responding to broader needs via support services (building an inherent recognition within the approach that a home is more than a house).

What is a 'Housing First' Approach to Homelessness?

A Housing First approach emphasises unconditional and rapid provision of permanent housing to persons who are homeless. This consumer-driven approach focuses on supporting people who have experienced chronic homelessness to move from 'street to home' without conditions or expectations of abstinence from drugs and alcohol, as well as 'stable' mental health. Within this approach housing is understood as a human right; not something that must be earned through sobriety or addressing mental health issues. A Housing First approach is consistent with a treatment first or continuum of care approach (Padget et al. 2006). Key to a Housing First approach is the provision of secure, stable, ongoing and sustainable housing – conditional only on meeting basic tenancy requirements (City of Melbourne 2007).

Johnson et al. (2012: 5 citing Tsemberis 2010) characterise the Housing First approach as having five key elements:

1. *Rapid access to permanent housing*: Housing First approaches usually emphasise the importance of offering *permanent* housing with support, as opposed to transitional or emergency accommodation or mainstream tenancy with no support. Housing is dispersed, although there are some congregate models such as 'Common Ground' (see Common Ground 2013) with support services nearby or even on site.
2. *Consumer choice*: Persons actively choose to participate. There is no conditionality attached to housing (in relation to complying with treatment or engagement with support services).
3. *Separate support services*: Support services are provided by different organisations to those who provide the housing. Support services are also individually focussed. Support is provided in a holistic manner – casework, clinical, legal, specialist counselling, and other services based on individuals' needs. Importantly support is not time-limited. Rather, it is assumed that support will need to be ongoing or at least available in the long-term.
4. *Recovery as an ongoing process*: Housing First approaches to homelessness understand housing to be the first step in recovery. Housing is not conditional upon engagement with treatment and support services and there is a recognition that recovery takes time.
5. *Reintegration into the community*: The final key feature is the integration of Housing First housing into the community. Housing First housing should be located in 'normal' neighbourhoods, rather than being separated. Central to the 'reintegration into the community' is the ancillary goal of Housing First programs of moving people into employment or education.

The Housing First approach has now been adopted and integrated into national and state policy and implemented in all of Australia's major capital cities. There are two main approaches – the 'Pathways to Housing' and 'Common Ground' models. 'Pathways' emphasises the dispersed housing model while 'Common Ground' offers congregate[2] housing. This approach is now the default policy setting in Australia[3].

Housing First as a Response to Growing Homelessness in Australia

The Housing First approach originated in the United States and in this section we provide an overview of its evolution in the U.S. and importation into Australia. The Australian versions wholly or partially follow the North American models, sometimes uncritically adopting wholesale the overseas innovation and seeking to directly transplant it here, or purport to but omit basic elements (for a discussion of this see Parsell et al. 2013b; Murphy 2014).

The 'Housing First' approach was pioneered in the U.S. by Pathways to Housing, founded by Dr Sam Tsemberis in New York in 1992. Given other approaches were clearly not reducing homelessness, the Housing First approach was to first offer chronically homeless people housing and then offer assistance (if the person so desired) with other issues such as mental illness and addictions.

The continuum of care or step approach to homelessness based on conditional assistance demands certain rules be followed prior to (temporary) housing being given. Such services typically provide meals, medical services and overnight accommodation in dorm-style facilities. Homeless persons with mental health or drug and alcohol problems may not be deemed 'ready' for a tenancy of their own. This conditionality was part of the impetus for the Housing First approach: 'Consumers who are homeless regard housing as an immediate need, yet access to housing is not made available unless they first complete treatment' (Tsemberis et al. 2004: 651).

There are a number of examples from the United States of America (USA) of effective Housing First programs. Some evaluations focus on tenancy outcomes, and others on cost-benefit. For example, the US program, Pathways to Housing, housed more than 600 tenants and achieved an 85 per cent retention rate. Similarly Common Ground[4] reduced street homelessness by 87 per cent in the 20-block Times Square neighbourhood, and by 43 per cent in the surrounding 230 blocks of West Midtown (Common Ground n.d.). Larimer et al. (2009) studied persons who were housed and persons on a wait list (control group) in a Housing First program called 1811 Eastlake in Seattle, USA. The study found that for 'chronically homeless individuals with high service use and costs, a Housing First program was associated with a relative decrease in costs after six months. These benefits increased

---

2   Although in the Common Ground Camperdown program there are mixed income tenancies.
3   See Parsell et al. 2013b for a critique of the wholesale adoption of the Common Ground model in Australia.
4   Common Ground (a congregate supported Housing First model offering housing options including transitional and permanent) began in New York in 1991.

to the extent that participants were retained in housing longer' (Larimer et al. 2009: 1). Another evaluation by Perlman and Parvensky (2006) indicated that the relative cost of housing someone is less than servicing their homelessness (including higher levels of hospitalisation and incarceration). These (seemingly) impressive results were disseminated to evidence-based policymakers in a variety of other countries including Australia.

In the 1990s, Australians working in the housing sector started hearing about the Housing First approach from the US and formed a 'Common Ground Alliance' (Parsell et al. 2013b: 10). US practitioners such as Rosanne Haggerty – the founder of Common Ground in New York – visited Australia and launched Australia's first Common Ground project in Adelaide in 2008. The approach also filtered into government strategies. In December 2008, the Australian Government released its White Paper on homelessness, *The Road Home*, which adopted two main goals: to halve the rate of homelessness by 2020; and to offer supported accommodation to all rough sleepers who need it (Australian Government 2008: viii). Housing First approaches were identified as key strategies within this policy for reducing, and ending, homelessness.

The Housing First approach has now been adopted and integrated into national and state policy and implemented in Australia's major capital cities (for example, the Common Ground project in five Australia cities, 'Project 40' in Western Sydney and the '50 Lives 50 Homes' project in Brisbane). Indeed many Australian programs take their names directly from US programs. As Parsell et al. (2013b: 8) notes the Common Ground approach (despite a lack of evidence) took hold partially because it was seen as 'new and innovative' and involved public-private-community partnership with commercial developers prepared to build at cost which created its own impetus.

Although there has been widespread articulation of the Housing First approach in homelessness strategies, from the National, State and local government level (see for example Parramatta City Council's Homelessness Strategy 2011), and despite the written policy commitment, the implementation of the Housing First approach has been partial. In most cases it has been small-scale, 'experimental' or pilot projects, some of which were not provided with adequate access to designated housing stock (Phillips et al. 2011). These programs have relied on the existing social housing stock rather than 'new build' housing and/or headleasing. Access to suitable housing is regularly reported as a key barrier to success in evaluations and reports (Johnson and Chamberlain 2013).

Another drawback is the limitations imposed by funding. A numerical target may be set (for example, 'Project 40' had the initial aim of housing 40 homeless persons). The target may not be based on need, but rather on available funding and staff time. After the 'target' number of persons are housed, demand for assistance may exceed the supply of housing and staff time, or funding is insecure.

Despite the above limitations, there are numerous examples and evaluations of Housing First programs in Australia. The outcomes are summarised below.

HomeGround, Melbourne

An evaluation conducted on two cohorts of Street to Home participants found that after 12 months over three-quarters (77%) were housed (Johnson and Chamberlain 2013: 2).

In addition there were 'marked improvements in the participants' physical health and emotional well-being' and a reduction in drug and alcohol use after a 24 month period of being housed (Johnson and Chamberlain 2013: 3).

Way 2 Home – Inner Sydney

The initial assessment of the program based on a baseline survey with 39 Way to Home participants found that 'housing was the primary positive change that people noted' (Parsell et al. 2013a: xii). By 2013, the City of Sydney claimed 189 people had been helped into permanent accommodation via the program (ABC 2013). By August 2014 this had increased to over 200 people.[5]

Project 40 – Western Sydney

Project 40 initially had funding for 37 tenancies (including the actual housing and support services). At the end of June 2013, the project was managing 45 tenancies. As of November 2013 this had grown to 56 tenancies. Evaluations found that 92 per cent of tenancies had been maintained for 12 months or more. The attrition rate is low – two tenancies could not be maintained, and four tenants passed away after being housed.[6]

Common Ground – Camperdown, Sydney.

The six-storey building houses a mix of 50 per cent formerly homeless persons, 10 per cent social housing tenants and 40 per cent low income earners (104 in total). An evaluation was underway at the time of writing.

Street to Home – Parramatta.

The program followed eight persons before and after housing, over a two year period. The program recorded a 100 per cent success rate (however the sample size is too small for these results to be robust). After approximately two years, all participants were still in situ in their housing. Three were in employment and two entered into some sort of education or training, and voluntary work. Participants all reported an improvement in wellbeing and/or health (Darcy et al. 2014a).

In summary from the early evidence available from Australian programs, tenure stability is achieved by using the Housing First approach. We now turn to participants' experiences of moving in to permanent housing and how they create or (or sometimes fail to create) 'a feeling of 'home'.

---

5   Michele Maitland, Neami National, personal communication.
6   Kerry Dolaghan, Wentworth Community Housing, personal communication.

Home Creation amongst Participants in Two 'Housing First' Programs in Sydney, Australia

As mentioned previously, while housing is an absolute condition of ending homelessness, it is just one step on a person's journey of constructing a sense of 'home' (and this is not to say that those traditionally defined as 'homeless' do not experience a sense of 'home' even when roofless). Homelessness, as well as not having access to affordable and permanent accommodation, is 'an inability to be at home, to feel some connectivity through house, neighbourhood and wider community' (Robinson 2001: 8). Thus while being housed is a precondition for the establishment of a greater sense of security, feeling 'at home' is much more complex.

Between 2011–2014 research on two Housing First style programs in Sydney a 'Street to Home' program targeted at rough sleeping males in Parramatta and a 'WorkFast' pilot program involving persons from the 'Way 2 Home' program, in inner Sydney was conducted. The participants of these projects had experienced homelessness and had been rehoused.

The 'Street to Home' Parramatta research involved a series of interviews over an 18 month period in 2011–2012 with eight participants who were about to be housed or had been recently housed. The interviews focused on wellbeing, health, their housing situation, and expectations and aspirations for the future. The interviewees were all male, and aged between 31 and 58. The lead organisation was Parramatta Mission, and the University of Western Sydney conducted the evaluation.

The 'WorkFast' inner city research involved two interviews over a 6 month period with three participants, two of whom were housed and one who was sleeping rough. Interviewees were all male, aged between 30 and 55, living in inner Sydney and had been (or still were) rough sleeping, or in emergency or temporary accommodation. The interviews focused on employment aspirations in particular as the pilot program sought to assist persons not only access housing, but also employment, education and training. The lead organisation was Neami National, and the University of Western Sydney conducted the evaluation.

Both programs were based on assertive outreach, housing and support. The housing stock that was accessed by the participants was drawn from a mixture of social housing providers including Housing NSW and community housing organisations.

Eleven participants' interviews from these two Housing First style programs have been utilised for this paper. In the analysis of these interviews, four key themes that relate to the rehoming process were identified across both programs: 1) furnishing and hosting; 2) control and gatekeeping; 3) safety; and 4) permanency. These four themes and associated practices can be understood as part of the process of 'settling' and creating a sense of 'deservedness' and permanency, post-housing allocation. The identities of the participants have been anonymised and will be referred to in shorthand (P1, P2, etc.).

1. Furnishing and Hosting

One's home is an expression of self. It is a person's space and this space can be extended to visitors in acts of hospitality. We examined this by looking at how interviewees who are housed via Housing First began offering their home for hospitable purposes and how this was identified as a part of 'home creation'.

Part of establishing a home includes deciding what items to place in the new abode. Basic domestic items are required (refrigerators, washing machines, etc.) as well as items that express the resident's personal needs and tastes. Housing First programs often include funds for house set up such as white goods and furnishings. In order to assist in the work of home-making, new occupants in the Parramatta Street to Home program were encouraged to shop for their own furnishings purchasing kitchenware, bedding and other household items. This provided them with the opportunity to choose items that suited their needs and tastes. Following the establishment phase one participant added to the décor by making curtains and putting items on lay-by for future purchase. Those who were satisfied with their abode became 'house proud' and enjoyed showing off their place to others, as one participant commented:

> ... yeah I've had friends around, I walk around, show them the verandah. (P1)

Another part of home creation was sharing the space with others. One interviewee offered his flat for other homeless persons to stay in:

> You just can't separate yourself from the people on the street that you've lived with ... Of a night, let 'em come up cos you know what it's like out there. (P5)

Another participant imagined the opportunity his home would provide to 'play host' when the food services in Parramatta were not operating:

> I'd just come in on the weekends [to Parramatta] and 'hello boys, come back [to my place]', cos there's no food on the weekends, you've only got your breakfast, then there's nothing ... I'd just get two of me mates, 'come on, come back, we'll have a good feed at home', you know what I mean, have a feed, few beers. (P2)

For another (in recovery from a drug addiction), assisting family members by sharing his space was a source of both pride and family reconciliation:

> He said [his brother] 'Can I use your garage?' ... not a problem. He bought a new stereo for his car and he just wanted to use the garage to work out of. I haven't been able to do something like that for my family forever .... (P3)

The desire to 'play host' – offer hospitality – can be a way of extending good fortune to others that are less lucky and that one has an obligation to – evidenced by the desire expressed by Participant 5 to assist those 'still on the street' and also a way of returning favours to family members as a way of making recompense for previous behaviour. As Dikec et al. (2009: 12) state 'every act of hospitality gives space' – the home space and the host's time can be extended to others and is a gift to others.

2. Control and Gatekeeping

Identity formation is a process of controlling boundaries (Dikec et al. 2009: 7). Territorial boundaries can create a safe space for those trying to move away from the 'homeless' identity and this can mean excluding others that threaten to re-immerse the person back in a previous identity or lifestyle.

In a study conducted by Darcy et al. (2014a), participants who had been housed often used re-identification mechanisms to move away from 'the homeless label' as one ex-rough sleeper put it. This included avoiding places where persons experiencing homelessness gather (food vans, public spaces in shopping centres), and gatekeeping (controlling access to their home by keeping their address secret from certain associates). These strategies of home making were designed to avoid their former associates coming over and using drugs or alcohol, or creating a risk factor for sustaining the tenancy:

> I haven't got time to … have people in my home that would only push me to a point of eviction. I don't – and that's because they don't want to let the party go. The party stopped many years ago. The party stopped the day when I became homeless. (P4)

Homed persons may see their house as a haven, a place to be themselves, free of others:

> It's given me a sanctuary, to sort of hide out in, get away from all the people who are up in your face every 2 minutes. (P5)

A former rough sleeper articulated a changing relationship to 'homelessness' and this meant physical and symbolic distance:

> [did you do Street Count?] Nah. I'm trying to break that homeless flaming … homeless label, I'm trying to break that homeless bullshit label, you know. Trying to stay away from it. (P5)

One risk in 'gatekeeping' for those who had been housed was isolation and a tendency to socialise less, as people could lose contact with (or chose to remove themselves from) their street associates. Participants were aware of this and some set goals for themselves such as doing courses or training and doing voluntary work.

As described above, 're-homing' might mean setting limits on who can enter the homes, and limit hospitality (conditional and necessary to preserve sense of self and home – sovereignty). "Thresholds are the very scenes for the drama of responsiveness, hospitality, and responsibility" (Dikec et al. 2009: 9) – limiting access was an act of responsibility to themselves.

3. Safety

People experiencing homelessness are vulnerable to environmental, random and symbolic violence (Robinson 2010: 14) and close to half experience violent victimisation (Larney et al. 2009: 349, cited in Robinson 2010). Having a space that is delineated, private and lockable can create a greater feeling of safety and security. In relation to wellbeing, many of the participants had suffered injury or experienced a severe health problem when living on the streets. Examples included having acts of violence committed against them or getting serious infections such as pneumonia, caused by living outdoors in cold and wet conditions. Being housed protects against the hazards of sleeping outdoors and the stress of being constantly alert:

> [I don't have to] worry about sleeping with one eye open … don't have to spray myself so I don't get bitten. (P3)

However although being housed reduced the risk of danger, trauma experienced in the past could still resurface:

> Yeah I don't have that fear of being attacked. But yes, I've got to choose what I watch on TV, because [it] triggers nightmares. (P4)

In this sense the home is a protective, lockable space which provides a haven for the development of self. Being free from the threat of violence or attack and relatively safe in a space that can be closed to others and the rest of the world is a basic function of a 'home'. However this was tenuous and subject to controllable and uncontrollable factors. While freedom from physical danger is sometimes achieved, relationships with others who inflicted violence was a struggle for those who felt they could not escape or exclude these persons. Those with episodic mental illnesses generally reported being better than they were when rough sleeping and had regular contact with their doctor.

4. Permanency

In her discussion on homelessness and home, Moore reflects on the tensions within home and homelessness, between staying and moving: 'Home and homelessness both contain a central tension between movement and rest, rootlessness and rootedness, nomadism and sedentariness' (2007: 147). Getting used to being in one place can be a challenge to people who are used to moving and have little sense of permanency. This restlessness can be a challenge once permanent housing is obtained.

> The only thing that concerned me about the stability was that, after being, having to look around for someplace different to go to, being on the move all the time sort of thing, the feeling of being at ease with stability was hard to get used to. I'd still wake up and think to myself 'right where am I going to go today' you know. (P7)

Disbelief or a feeling of not quite 'deserving it' was also common:

> But since I've been housed I still sometimes – like at first I really had a hard time coming to grips, is this for real? I still even have moments … like that now. (P4)

Some people who had been rough sleepers found it hard to sleep in a bed and continued to sleep on the floor for a period:

> Couldn't get used to being in a house for the first couple of weeks. Had to get out and sleep on the floor, couldn't sleep on the bed. (P6)

There was a period of adjustment and often the word 'house' or home' was not used rather an inside/outside distinction was made:

> I'm getting used to staying inside. (P5)

Another participant described day-to-day living as a process of habituation, as finding a place in society:

> … as you realise, as the day to day reality becomes part of habit, you realise hey I have control over my environment. I have a position in this society. (P3)

After having been housed for a period of time, one person who slept rough for years declared:

> [Q: Is there anything that could lead to the loss of this tenancy?]
>
> My life. They'd have to shoot me at the moment. Think I like being out on the street? (P5)

A sense of permanency, that they could stay in the place, was both difficult to accept and a basis for growing ontological security.

Once housed, a sense of home can begin to be constructed. However it is only the beginning. Some participants, while they stayed physically housed, did not see their dwelling as a home:

> … this ain't a place. It's nothing ideal it's just you know as I say it is a bedsitter [in fact the dwelling was a spacious, one-bedroom, near-new apartment].
>
> [Q: Do you feel like it's not a home?] No. Too late for anything to call home. (P8)

Coming to feel 'at ease' in one place is a process and due to key elements lacking the place could not be a home, in the case of the interviewee (P8) above. Even when housed, and established, participants still had another idealised 'home' in their minds – a place in the country, a place at the coast, owning a dog, having a partner. One participant highlighted Seager's (2011) observations on the elements necessary to construct 'home':

> When I moved into my bedsit I thought 'my life's complete, it's about complete now'. I've got a place to live, all I needed was another three things in my life and my life would have been complete. And that was love, happiness and a partner to share the rest of my life with. (P6)

It is important to recognise that there are two aspects to homelessness, physical provision of dwellings and the more complex and lengthy work of home creation that is essentially a territorial, psychological and emotional process. By combining permanent housing and ongoing support Housing First provides the platform for this work.

Conclusion

This chapter has discussed homelessness in Australia and the adoption of 'Housing First' models as one mechanism of addressing homelessness in both the short- and long-terms. The chapter was oriented around the idea of 'home' and its relationship to homelessness. Using research from two case studies of Sydney-based Housing First projects, the chapter illustrated aspects of this creation of a sense of home, post-housing. The authors join with Parsell and Jones (2014) and concur that the Housing First model, although having been somewhat uncritically adopted in Australia, has provided good results for those in such programs. However, such findings should be tempered by the fact that overall there is little evidence that these programs can counterbalance other structural factors (such as a dearth of affordable housing in Australia) that are making housing more expensive and less accessible.

Although it would seem to be obvious that providing safe, secure, affordable and accessible housing is key to reducing or ending homelessness, the biggest limitation of Housing First approaches in Australia is the inadequate supply of suitable housing. Most programs are reliant on social housing stock as the key (or only) source of housing. Allocation of this housing can take time – often months. This is not the 'rapid rehousing' envisaged in Housing First philosophy.

For those who are housed, the key to 'home' creation is the wrap-around support provided by Housing First programs. While there is acknowledgement that permanent housing is essential to maintaining tenancies creating a sense of 'home' is also vital (see Robinson 2001, 2005; Moore 2007). This means allowing persons ongoing access to support, in an individually tailored and flexible manner.

Organisations working with people experiencing homelessness need to take the right approach. Seager warns on the danger of inconsistency and precarity on those who services are trying to assist (Seager 2011: 186). Outreach and support workers need to be consistent however there is a large turnover of staff in these jobs, and funding and program changes.

Due to the time limited nature of funding for Australian Housing First programs individual support and case management are often prematurely reduced or ended altogether. This is due mainly to government funding cycles rather than agency workers preferences. The Housing First philosophy is that the level of support should be ongoing and based on the needs of the individual, not an arbitrary cut off point.

While still in their infancy, Australia's Housing First programs have been extraordinarily successful if tenancy retention rates 12 months from first being housed are a gauge of success. Where implementation of the Housing First model wholly or mostly follows the four key elements including street outreach, housing, support, and integrated services (Johnson et al. 2012), available Australian evidence outlined previously shows tenancies being maintained at rates of 77 per cent (Home Ground – Street to Home) to 92 per cent (Project 40) at 12 months. Further, there is evidence of reduction in illness, increase in wellbeing and health, and reduction in recidivism (Johnson et al. 2012; Johnson and Chamberlain 2013; Darcy et al. 2014a). This concurs with US research and should provide a strong evidence base for expanding Housing First style programs in Australia.

This chapter has shown that Housing First approaches are creating secure housing outcomes, and that with housing and support, 'home creation' can occur amongst some who had previously been deemed 'unable to sustain a tenancy'.

Acknowledgements

The authors would like to thank the program participants, Neami National and Parramatta Mission.

References

ABC News. 2013. Homeless numbers continue downward trend in inner Sydney. *ABC News.* Accessed on: 8 August 2013. Available at: http://www.abc.net.au/news/2013-08-08/homeless-numbers-continue-downward-trend-in-inner-sydney/4873456.

Anglicare. 2014. *Rental Affordability Snapshot 2014: Greater Sydney and the Illawarra* (prepared by Byron Kemp, Zoe Paleologos, Sue King and John Bellamy), Sydney: Anglicare. Available at: http://www.anglicare.org.au/sites/default/files/public/2014%20Rental_Affordability_Snapshot%20FINAL.pdf.

Australian Bureau of Statistics (2012a). 2049.0.

Australian Bureau of Statistics. 2007. *National Survey of Mental Health and Wellbeing,* ABS, Canberra. Available at: http://www.ausstats.abs.gov.au/ausstats/subscriber.nsf/0/6AE6DA447F985FC2CA2574EA00122BD6/$File/43260_2007.pdf

Australian Bureau of Statistics. 2012a. *4922.0 – Information Paper – A Statistical Definition of Homelessness, 2012.* ABS, Canberra. Available at: http://www.abs.gov.au/ausstats/abs@.nsf/Latestproducts/4922.0Main%20Features22012?opendocument&tabname=Summary&prodno=4922.0&issue=2012&num=&view=.

Australian Bureau of Statistics. 2012b. *105,000 people homeless on Census night 2011.* Media release, ABS, Canberra. Available at: http://www.abs.gov.au/ausstats/abs@.nsf/latestProducts/2049.0Media%20Release12011.

Australian Government. 2008. *The Road Home: A National Approach to Reducing Homelessness.* Australian Government, Canberra. Available at: https://www.dss.gov.au/sites/default/files/documents/05_2012/the_road_home.pdf.

Australian Institute of Health and Welfare 2013. *Australia's Welfare 2013.* http://www.aihw.gov.au/WorkArea/DownloadAsset.aspx?id=60129544561.

Chamberlain, C. 2012. Homelessness: Measurement questions, in Susan J. Smith et al. (eds) *International Encyclopedia of Housing and Home,* Vol. 3, Oxford: Elsevier, pp. 36–41.

Chamberlain, C. and MacKenzie, D. 1992. Understanding contemporary homelessness: Issues of definition and meaning. *Australian Journal of Social Issues* 27(4): 274–297.

―――― 2003. *Counting the Homeless 2001*, Australian Census Analytic Program, ABS Cat. No. 2050.0.

City of Melbourne. 2007. *Homelessness Research Project Stage 2 Final Report*. City of Melbourne, Melbourne. Available at: https://www.melbourne.vic.gov.au/CommunityServices/SocialSupport/Documents/researchproject_homelessness_stage2.pdf.

Common Ground. 2013. Available at: http://www.commonground.org/.

Darcy, M., Drake, G., Blunden, H., and Steinwede, J. 2014a. *Rough Sleepers in Parramatta: From Street to Home – Final Report*. Sydney: Urban Research Centre, University of Western Sydney.

Darcy, M., Blunden, H., Hall, N. and Piracha, A. 2014b. *Unintended Consequences: The Impact of Delivery Systems on Homelessness in the Nepean/ Blacktown Region Final Report*. Sydney: Urban Research Centre, University of Western Sydney.

Dikec, M., Clark, N. and Barnett, C. 2009. *Extending Hospitality: Giving Space, Taking Time*. Paragraph 32:1, pp.1–14. DOI: 10.3366/E0264833409000376.

Dolaghan, K. (pers comm.) June 2014. Kerry Dolaghan is the Project 40 manager at Wentworth Community Housing.

Johnson, G., Parkinson, S. and Parsell, C. 2012. *Policy Shift or Program Drift? Implementing Housing First in Australia*. AHURI Final Report No.184. Australian Housing and Urban Research Institute, Melbourne.

Johnson, G. and Chamberlain, C. 2013. *Evaluation of the Melbourne Street to Home program: 12 Month Outcomes*. Government Department of Families, Housing, Community Services and Indigenous Affairs, Canberra.

Larimer, M., Malone, D., Garner, M., Atkins, D., Burlingham, B., Lonczak, H., Tanzer, K., Ginzler, J., Clifasefi, S., Hobson, W., and Marlatt, A. 2009. Health care and public service use and costs before and after provision of housing for chronically homeless persons with severe alcohol problems. *Journal of the American Medical Association* 301(13): 1349–1357. doi:10.1001/jama.2009.414.

Moore, J. 2007. Polarity or integration? Towards a fuller understanding of home and homelessness. *Journal of Architectural and Planning Research* 24(2): 143–159.

Murphy, L. 2014. *Houston, We've Got a Problem': The Political Construction of a Housing Affordability Metric in New Zealand*. Housing Studies, DOI: 10.1080/02673037.2014.915291.

Padgett, D., Gulcur, L. and Tsemberis, S. 2006. Housing first services for people who are homeless with co-occurring serious mental illness and substance misuse. *Research on Social Work* 16(1), 74–83.

Parsell, C. 2010. 'Homeless is what I am, not who I am': Insights from an inner-city Brisbane study. *Urban Policy and Research* 28(2): 181–194.

Parsell, C., and Parsell, M., 2012. Homelessness as a choice. *Housing Theory and Society* 29(4): 420–434.

Parsell, C., Tomaszewski, W., and Jones, A. 2013a. *An Evaluation of Sydney Way2Home: Final Report*. Brisbane: University of Queensland.

Parsell, C. Fitzpatrick, S., and Busch-Geertsema, V. 2013b. *Common Ground in Australia: An Object Lesson in Evidence Hierarchies and Policy Transfer*. Housing Studies, DOI: 10.1080/02673037.2013.824558.

Parsell, C. and Jones, A. 2014. Bold reform or policy overreach? Australia's attack on homelessness: 2008–2013. *International Journal of Housing Policy* 14(4): 427–443. DOI: 10.1080/14616718.2014.967923.

Parramatta City Council. 2011. *Parramatta City Council Homelessness Policy*. Parramatta: Parramatta City Council.

Perlman, J. and Parvensky, J. 2006. *Denver Housing First Collaborative Cost Benefit Analysis and Program Outcomes Report*. Denver: Colorado Coalition for the Homeless.

Phillips, R., Parsell, C., Seage, N. and Memmott, P. 2011. *Assertive Outreach*. (Positioning Paper. Australian Housing and Urban Research Institute, Queensland Research Centre, Brisbane.

Robinson, C. 2001. *House or Home? The Difference Belonging Could Make*. TASA 2001 Conference Proceedings, 13–15 December 2001, Sydney: The University of Sydney.

—— 2005. Persistent homelessness/persistent trauma. *Parity* 18(7): 4–5. Council to Homeless Persons, Melbourne.

—— 2010. *Rough Living: Surviving Violence and Homelessness*. UTS Shopfront Monograph Series No 6, UTS ePress, Sydney.

Seager, M. 2011. Homelessness is more than houselessness: A psychologically-minded approach to inclusion and rough sleeping. *Mental Health and Social Inclusion* 15(4): 183–189.

Tsemberis, S., Gulcur, L., and Nakae, M. 2004. Housing First, consumer choice, and harm reduction for homeless individuals with a dual diagnosis. *American Journal of Public Health* 94(4): 651–656.

Western Sydney Housing First, n.d. http://www.westernsydneyhousingfirst.org.au/.

Chapter 14
21st-Century Australian Housing: New Frontiers in the Asia-Pacific

Dallas Rogers and Rae Dufty-Jones

Introduction

> The Asian Century is an Australian opportunity ...
> (Australian Government 2012a: 1)

In Western Anglophone countries the role of individual foreign investment in residential real estate has a history that stretches back into the mid-20th century. In the 1980s and 90s, the economies of the Four Asian Tigers (i.e. South Korea, Singapore, Hong Kong and Taiwan) and Japan experienced rapid growth. What followed was a sharp increase in Japanese investor activity in the United States (US) and Australian real estate markets and Hong Kong investors in Canadian real estate markets (Edgington 1996; Hajdu 2005; Ray et al. 1997). More than a decade into the 21st century a similar trend appears to be developing around the rise of Brazil, Russia, India, Indonesia, China, and South Africa (i.e. the BRIICS countries). As the economies of the BRIICS countries grow their citizens have quickly become experienced domestic and foreign real estate investors. The global investment practices of BRIICS citizens are beginning to change the real estate landscapes of several Western Anglophone countries (Dorling 2014; Hay 2013). The rise of the BRIICS countries and the continued influence of the Four Asian Tigers is also rupturing the conceptual landscape for understanding international real estate relations (Ren 2013; Wu et al. 2007).

More often than not 'race' and 'citizenship' frame the domestic debate around individual foreign real estate investment (Rogers et al. 2015). For example, in 1993 Mitchell (1993) demonstrated that Hong Kong investors in the Canadian real estate market faced local resident resistance and parochial, perhaps even racist, protectionism because the property sales had been advertised and secured in Hong Kong. Similarly, in the late 1990s, Ray et al. (1997: 76) discussed the role of housing in enabling place-based racism and Hage (1998) argued that Anglo-Celtic whiteness was a hegemonic and fixed reference point from which to judge the intruding non-White *Other*. In the early 21st century in Melbourne, Australia, Fincher and Costello (2005: 203) argued, 'integral to the "production" of a new housing form is the development of new narratives about it ... narratives include interpretations of new dwellers' ethnicities'. For almost a decade Fincher's work has focused on how the 'host' Australian society understands the impact of immigrant 'outsiders' on a static White-colonial notion of Australian society.

More recently, Rogers and Bailey (2013) have shown the purchase of real estate by non-citizens has a high affective value because citizenship status has typically been understood as being tied up with and 'bounded by' a state's territory. Rogers and Bailey (2013) argue that colonial/Anglo-Celtic ideas about the territorial claims of White citizenship are threatened by the idea that non-citizens can hold legal claims to real estate in Australia. In the short-term and perhaps even longer, the role Asian actors, and Chinese investors in particular, might play in increasing construction capacity or diversifying housing markets in Australia will remain contentious political issues locally (Rogers et al. 2015). Notwithstanding the politics, this is a discussion the Australian housing research and policy communities, and the general population, will be forced to have – not least because a set of broader geopolitical and regional restructuring forces lay behind these changes.

The shift in political and economic power from Europe and the US toward China has facilitated changes in city formation and housing provision that are without precedent in human history (Jacques 2012; Wu et al. 2007). When the Peoples' Republic of China was established in 1949 only 10 per cent of the national population lived in cities (Ren 2013). By 1978, a time of major market reforms, that figure had only reached 20 per cent. In the last 35 years China has implemented an uncompromising urbanization process by adding more than 400 new cities with hundreds of millions of people moving from their historically agrarian communities into new urban environments (Ong 2011; Wu et al. 2007; Ren 2013). In 2010 it was estimated that 50 per cent of the national population now lived in cities (Ren 2013). Subsequently, Chinese property developers – both private and state-owned – have become experienced housing providers and Chinese nationals have quickly become experienced housing investors in national and international markets (Buckley et al. 2010a). Buckley et al. (2010b: 119) argue, China has been the focus of much inward foreign direct investment (FDI) research. But as of 2010, less empirical attention had been paid to China's outward FDI following the global financial crisis (GFC) and very little empirical attention was given to outward individual FDI from China into foreign residential real estate, Australia bound individual real estate investment included (Buckley et al. 2010a).

Individual foreign investment in residential real estate has the capacity to intersect with almost every housing issue and tenure form discussed in this edited volume. Indeed, it already is intersecting in some cases. Edgar Liu et al. (Chapter 2) show how the shift from European to Asian and African migration over the last half-century is changing the cultural landscapes of Australian cities. They argue that many of these migrants come from societies where multigenerational co-residence is common. Furthermore, not only do most new arrivals to Australia spend a substantial period in rental housing after arrival, many face racist protectionism while searching for housing (Chapter 3). Compact (Chapter 8) and sustainable (Chapter 4) living arrangements in Australian cities further increase the spatiotemporal tensions (e.g., the spatiality of cooking smells or the temporality of shift work) between different cultural groups in strata environments. As Habibis (Chapter 5) highlights, these challenges are further compounded for Indigenous people who face an additional layer of historical, structural and cultural discrimination.

For Anglo-Australians, many without the inbuilt familial networks of multigenerational households, Bosman (Chapter 7) argues that aging boomers do not expect their children to support them as they age. Stone (Chapter 6) and Taylor and Dalton (Chapter 10) show that many baby boomer children are facing increasingly unaffordable housing landscapes, and that the mid-20th century housing logics that worked so well for many baby boomers are failing younger Australians. With pent up frustration about housing affordability problems, combined with what Hulse and Burke (Chapter 9) have termed 'housing policy inertia', foreign investors are cast by the Australian media, often incorrectly, as one of the key drivers of housing affordability problems. Meanwhile, Darcy and Arthurson (Chapter 11) show how public housing tenants are being evicted from Australian cities to make way for the new global citizen, and the foreign real estate investor is certainly part of this global citizenry (Rogers and Darcy 2014). Homeless Australians are perhaps even more disadvantaged and equally excluded from any global city visions (Blunden and Drake, Chapter 13). Ruming (Chapter 12) shows how global financial crises only served to bolster the disadvantage experienced by low-income Australians. In the post-GFC foreign real estate investment landscape, 'distressed', or more accurately 'repossessed' housing is promoted, to quote one international real estate professional, as a great way to 'profit in real estate in the new economy' (Grubisa 2014: 85).

We often understand and study housing within a national or sub-national context. However, as the above reflections on the role of FDI in Australia show, at the beginning of the 21st century, housing (like so many other dimensions of our socio-cultural, economic and environmental lives) is far more porous and less constrained by these geopolitical boundaries. A feature of housing in the 21st century, both in Australia and beyond, is its increasing global relationality (Acuto and Curtis 2013; Rogers et al. 2015). By way of conclusion for this edited volume, the remaining three sections of this chapter will focus on one aspect of this broader issue of global real estate relationality and its impacts on Australian housing; namely, the rise of China and the subsequent increase in Chinese investment in Australia housing. As a step toward comprehending and responding to this fluid and transitional period, within which the Australian housing sector will increasingly be encompassed, this chapter offers some initial thoughts on Australian housing in the so-called 'Asian Century' (Australian Government 2012a).

Changing Geopolitical and Housing Landscapes

The scale and speed of the cultural, economic and political rise of China has taken many real estate professionals, government policy makers and urban academics by surprise in Australia (Buckley 2010; Fincher and Costello 2005; Jacques 2012; Ren 2013; Wu et al., 2007). All three sectors are now scrambling to make sense of these changes in the short-term. Meanwhile, little is known about the medium- to long-term opportunities and challenges that the rise of China, and the continued rise of Asia more generally, might introduce. Little is known about the housing policy and industry settings that might be required to maximize the benefits or to ameliorate the challenges of changing Asia-Pacific real estate relations.

In terms of local housing politics, as one observer put it, 'Today, Chinese money makes up the fastest-growing segment of the real estate market in Australia' (Taylor 2012: 1).

Over the last 5 years the changing nationalities of the foreign nationals investing in residential real estate in Australia has garnered considerable political and media attention. Indeed this change has been both rapid and significant. After 2012 much of the attention has been focused on Chinese investors and has been negative in orientation (Rogers et al. 2015). At the time of the Asian Financial Crisis in 1998, 24 per cent of global individual FDI from China was in foreign real estate (Buckley et al. 2010a: 247). According to the Australian federal government's Foreign Investment Review Board (FIRB), which sits within Treasury, approved foreign investment in Australian real estate by Chinese investors was A$12.4billion in 2013/14, $5.9billion in 2012/13, A$4.2billion in 2011/12 and A$712million in 2006/07 (Australian Government 2012b). While there are well-reported limitations with these data (Gauder et al. 2014) one government estimate put the growth rate of individual Chinese investment in residential real estate in Australia at well over 400 per cent between 2006 and 2012, with approved foreign investment more than doubling between 2014 and 2013 (Australian Government 2012b; 2014a). The 2014 FIRB figures indicate overall individual foreign investment, as well as Chinese investment, in residential real estate in Australia will grow further (Australian Government 2014b). It is certainly the case more detail reporting is required about the type, scale and scope of individual foreign investment in residential real estate in Australia (Standing Committee on Economics 2014). Furthermore, it will be important to look beyond these data to the broader geopolitical and economic forces that are at play in the region. Indeed, to even position Australia at the centre of this debate – as a continent by which to measure the rise of Asia – rightly opens the discussion up to a charge of Euro-centrism (Said 1978). Provocatively, Martin Jacques (2012) prompts a different type of regional imaginary in his book 'When China Rules the World'. Jacques argues, while China is set to become the central economic, cultural and political player in the region the Chinese will not achieve this by becoming more 'Western'. Geopolitically, the rise of China may well challenge some of Australia's most cherished political, economic and cultural ideals: the dominance of Western style nation states and democracy are chief amongst them.

Unlike some European and US housing markets, which were exposed to the extensive sub-prime default mortgage debt crisis following the GFC, comparatively, Australian and Asian real estate markets made rapid recoveries (Buckley 2010; Ye and Sun 2011; Berry et al. 2011). Berry et al. (2011: 130) argue the Australian housing sector was 'spared the worst effects' of the GFC. Ye and Sun (2011: 230) argue that 'after February 2009, China's real estate market revived rapidly', and similar rapid recoveries were recorded in Hong Kong and other Asian countries (Yip 2011).

After the post-GFC housing market recovery – and with the housing (and other) market cycles of the Asia-Pacific region and the US displaying different post-GFC recovery trajectories – the Australian government moved to bolster its position in the Asia-Pacific region. In 2012 the federal Gillard government released the *Australia in the Asian Century* white paper. The white paper set out a clear strategy for strengthening Australia's economic, technological and social ties with many Asian countries (Australian Government 2012a). For those who had been following the rise of Asia, and China in particular, for many years the white paper seemed reactionary at best. The geopolitical roots of this document are varied, but in terms of party politics it can certainly be traced to a 1971 telegram from the then leader of the Australian opposition Labour party, Gough Whitlam, to the then Premier of the Republic of China, Zhou Enlai. The telegram reads, 'Australian Labour Party anxious to send delegation to People Republic of China to discuss the terms on which your country is interested in having diplomatic and trade relations with Australia' (Freudenburg 2013: 7).

This telegram was sent at a turbulent geopolitical time. The next year, in 1972, Chairman Mao Zedong opened the door to US president Richard Nixon and thereby signalled to the world a policy shift toward a more open China. Deng Xiaoping's 1978 Open Door policy was followed in the early 1980s with the Hawke Labour government's *pro-Asia* geopolitical discourse (Hajdu 2005), which was further revived and referenced in the Gillard government's 2012 *Australia in the Asian Century* white paper. Thus, in terms of international relations, a surprisingly consistent *pro-Asia* geopolitical discourse worked its way through the foreign policy positions of successive Australian federal governments, from both sides of policies, from the 1970s well into the early 21st century.

Thus, it should not be surprising that one of the central tenets of the *Australia in the Asian Century* document was that 'Asia is a changing world ... The Asian Century is an Australian opportunity ... [and that] Within only a few years, Asia ... will also be home to the majority of the world's middle class' (Australian Government 2012a: 1). As the Four Asian Tigers and the rise of the BRIICS countries demonstrates, the expanding middle class from former, or even current, socialist states have strong commitments to private property investments (Coase and Wang 2013).

What the Australian government failed to state in 2012, or indeed, perhaps failed to comprehend, was that in many ways – and certainly with regard to housing – Australia was already in the Asian century and had been so for decades. In the 1980s the foreign investment practices of Japanese real estate investors had gained considerable media attention. For example, in the early 1980s one Australian media outlet was reporting, 'Our Asianisation is gaining pace' (*The Sydney Morning Herald*, Robinson 1983: 57) and by the late-1980s there were media reports about, 'The new Asian invasion: how Australian property is being sold off' (*The Bulletin*, 29th Septmeber 1987, cited in Hajdu 2005). In 1980s Australia, much like the early 21st century, some people believed that the rise in Asian investment in Australian real estate 'was a prime cause of ... property inflation', which resulted in 'increasing financial difficulties being faced by first home buyers' (Hajdu 2005: 177). Hence, at several points between 1970s and the early 21st century, argues Hajdu (2005: 178), the 'rise in anti-Asian sentiment was the last thing' the federal government wanted when they were 'trying to persuade the public that Australia's future lay with Asia'.

However, there are important differences between the 1980s and the early 2000s. First, large Asian financial and property development companies are increasingly providing capital and technical expertise in the Australian housing sector. Second, there has been an intensification and integration of Australian/Asian real estate relations, often facilitated through advancements in electronic communication technologies (Rogers, in press). For example, Australian and Asian real estate companies are increasingly partnering with each other, and at times with property developers, to sell Australian real estate to investors across Asia. Third, China's internal economic and housing policies are 'pushing' Chinese investors to source new foreign investment, including real estate, opportunities overseas (Rogers et al. 2015).

The contribution of housing markets to national economies is widely recognised as central to public policy concerns for governments across and beyond the Asia-Pacific region. However, little is known about the relationships and interactions between national real estate actors and markets, and how these interactions and economic relations might be shaping international real estate practise (Rogers et al. 2015). Even closer to home, the rapidly changing interrelationships between Australian and Asian housing production and consumption patterns are not well understood. Therefore, in the following section we identify some (but certainly not all) initial research directives that might begin to capture this relationality in Australian housing research. We start with the constitutional tension between the federal and state/territory governments, then we question the usefulness of the foreign investment data, we discuss Asian/Australian real estate collaborations, we highlight several cultural profiling technologies and we finish with the geopolitical repositioning of the Asia-Pacific region and local parochialism in Australia.

New Directions

In 2012 the Australian federal government positioned itself to actively build financial, political and cultural relationships with several Asian countries over the coming years, stating that the government would,

> Work with partners in the region on 'behind the border' initiatives to build an integrated and resilient regional economy and open up market opportunities for Australia, especially in our areas of expertise such as infrastructure, agriculture and food, education, health and aged care, finance and regulation of services. (Australian Government 2012a: 22)

These types of statements suggest the federal government expects Australia to 'export' their technological expertise in infrastructure, and perhaps even housing, provision to Asian countries. However, with the rapid globalisation of the real estate and financial industries over the last decade the opposite is already occurring. Singaporean and Malaysian property developers and financial institutions in particular are already exporting their technical knowledge and financial products to Australia. Property developers and financiers with Asian-Australian links continue to be heavily involved in Australian property development and real estate markets.

The challenge for the Australian government will be how to regulate these sectors to achieve their housing outcomes into the future. This will be a challenge because many of the policy levers for engaging with 'Asian' nationals and business, such as visa programs, foreign investment rules and taxation systems, are under the mandate of the Australian federal government. In terms of housing provision this is complicated by the constitutional demarcations of power in Australia, which allocate the constitutional power regarding public/social housing and planning policies to the state and territory governments. Taken together, these federal/state/territory visa programs, foreign investment rules, taxation settings and public/social housing policies represent a complex suite of policy tools that could be used to guide the production and consumption of Australian housing. When Chinese and other Asian investors, as well as large property development companies, increased their activities in the Australian housing sector, especially in Australia's biggest cities such as Sydney, Brisbane and Melbourne from the early 2000s, their actions brought to the surface, in a very public way, the policy tensions between the state/territory governments' urban and housing agendas and the federal government's immigration and foreign investment agendas (Rogers et al. 2015). These policy tensions are still to be fully acknowledged and understood.

These policy tensions have been further complicated by the local media commentary about the sale of Australian real estate to Chinese and other 'Asian' nationals. In 2014 the Australian Liberal federal government announced that the House of Representatives Standing Committee on Economics would undertake an *Inquiry into foreign investment in residential real estate* (The Inquiry). The Inquiry acknowledged the role that growing public disquiet about Chinese investment in Australian housing played in its establishment. After six public hearings and over 90 submissions the committee handed down its report in November 2014 (Standing Committee on Economics 2014).

The Inquiry found the rules and regulations governing individual foreign investment in Australian residential real estate sufficient. However, the Committee strongly argued for better and more transparent data collection in relation to this type of FDI. The Committee was particularly critical of Australian government agencies, primarily the Foreign Investment Review Board (FIRB, which is supported by the Foreign Investment and Trade Policy Division of Treasury (FITPD)) that are responsible for the collection of such data and the enforcement of the rules and regulations governing individual foreign investment in Australian residential real estate. The government responded to the Committee's report by introducing new fees[1] and a register to track offshore owners of Australian property. The Inquiry process demonstrated that it would be hard to uncouple Australian real estate from global capital flows, no matter the political will. It is no longer accurate to think about Australian land assets in closed national state terms and successive Australian governments have repeatedly championed foreign investment. In 2014 the Australian Prime Minister reconfirmed this commitment by stating, 'As a general principle we support foreign investment. Always have and always will' (Hutchens 2014).

The Need for Better Foreign Investment Data

As The Inquiry identified there is little reliable FDI data for the domestic housing market. As a consequence research into direct foreign investment from China to Australia has largely focused on Chinese public and private multinational companies (Buckley et al. 2010a; Buckley et al. 2010b). Buckley et al. (2010b) argue that little research has focused on the scale and scope of individual Chinese (and other Asian nationals') FDI into Australian

---

1 At the time of writing, these fees were proposed as follows: at least $5,000 for foreign buyers of Australian residential real estate under $1 million; and for properties over $1 million there will be an additional $10,000 for every extra million dollars in the purchase price.

housing (also see: Berry et al. 2011; Buckley 2010). Buckley et al. (2010b: 121) demonstrate that several factors drive outward individual FDI from China: the competitive advantage offered by the host country; the cultural and social conditions at the external site; the role of the home and host countries governments; cultural and geographical distance between the home and host countries; and international relations policies such as China's 1999 'Go Global' and Australia's 'Asian Century' policies (Jacques 2012).

In Australia, it has largely been the Australian federal government (2012b) (through the FIRB), the major financial institutions and property development consultancy corporations that have commissioned research into individual foreign investment into residential real estate. In 2013 The National Australia Bank (NAB) (2013) reported that foreign investors account for around 13 per cent of all new residential property purchases in Australia. But as noted above, there were well-reported limitations with Australia's FDI data (Gauder et al., 2014). In any case, the NAB's chief economist stated, 'Asian investors (mainly Chinese) have been driving this trend according to the latest data from the Foreign Investment Review Board' (Schlesinger 2013b: 2). At the same time, an Australian-Chinese media commenter wrote, 'To buy property is in our bones. So [when] you have the money but you don't have property to buy, the [Chinese] investor will start to look overseas' (Zhou 2013: 1). These types of cultural profiling media debates, which started around 2009, were ongoing when this book was published.

Within this media landscape, the FIRB have come under heavy critique in The Inquiry. Tasked with managing the policy frameworks that guide direct foreign investment into Australian real estate, the FIRB has pointed to the fraught politics of foreign investment by stating,

> the general presumption is that foreign investment proposals will serve the national interest ... The Government has decided that some types of investment in real estate are contrary to the national interest. The Policy outlines this as well as the types of real estate that foreign persons may buy. (Australian Government 2012b: 7)

In 2014, the legislative framework for foreign investment in residential real estate in Australia attempted to direct foreign investment into new dwellings to increase construction activity to boost housing supply (Australian Government 2012b; Gauder et al. 2014). Taylor and Dalton (Chapter 10) call this the 'concept of the "construction multiplier", and the funding of [a] "shovel ready" housing industry to rapidly increase new housing output and increase employment'. These laws allowed: foreign developers to build new residential dwellings for sale to domestic and foreign buyers; individual foreign investors and temporary residents to purchase new dwellings; and temporary residents with visas – which extended beyond 12 months and included many foreign student visas – to purchase one established home provided it was used as their principal place of residence while in Australia and was sold when they left the country.

The changing cultural profiles, and the scale and scope of individual foreign investment in residential real estate in Australia, calls for a suite of different research tasks. First, parties with particular commercial and political interests are undertaking the bulk of the research into direct foreign investment from Asia to Australia for residential real estate. These data are opaque and are being deployed in highly politicised ways, such as within media, policy and public discussions that endorse particular ideological, political or commercial positions. This means that housing customers, businesses and the broader Australian public and policy communities have mediated access to this type of FDI research data. Second, the empirical data that covers individual FDI in Australian residential real estate is currently of poor quality. As The Inquiry goes some way to identifying, more needs to be done to determine what types of data need to be collected, and when and where this data is collected. Furthermore, the collection of these data will most likely require the government data collective agencies to change their collection practices. Third, any critical debate about if and how foreign investment might be used to achieve certain housing outcomes, such as boosting affordable housing, needs to occur (at the least) within the context of the federal and state/territory governments' visa programs, foreign investment rules, taxation settings, and public/social housing and planning policies.

Asian/Australian Real Estate Collaborations

A complex interrelationship between Australian- and Asian-based property development companies, and Australian- and Asian-based real estate agents, is developing. Australian, Chinese and Singaporean property development companies operating in Australia are enlisting sales offices across Asia to advertise and procure housing sales to Chinese and other Asian nationals (Wang 2013). For example, 'Knight Frank' an global real estate company, 'has created a special sales team specifically targeting wealthy Chinese investors following the introduction of the significant investment visa … the 888 visa – colloquially called the 'Golden Ticket' visa – favours Chinese investors' [sic] (Walsh 2013a: 1). Tallman and Shenkar (1994) demonstrate that financial and investment corporations often act as intermediaries for technical, political and legal information flows. Scott (2002) argues the ability to exploit these types of 'culturally-dependent relational assets' between countries, such as those that are enabled by language or cultural linkages, can provide a competitive commercial advantage. The housing producer can pass on some of these advantages to the customer by 'customising particular technologies, products and processes' (Buckley et al. 2010b: 122), which allows them to act as a cross-cultural link between the home and host countries. Buckley et al. (2010b: 123) argue that strong cultural/language similarities – what they call 'relational capital' – between international actors has resulted in countries with strong cultural/language links between home and host achieving significant FDI. Javorcik et al. (2011) argue, cross border cultural/ethnic networks increase FDI because they facilitate information flows about market structures and local conditions, consumer preferences, business ethics and commercial and legal regimes. The Australian cities of Sydney and Melbourne have large Chinese speaking communities and attract significant numbers of Chinese students (Colic-Peisker et al. 2012). In fact, the Australian Bureau of Statistics reported in 2012,

> Recent years have seen China continue as the largest single nation contributor to the international student population in Australia. In 2010–11, one fifth of all student visa applications lodged and granted were from China (18% and 20% respectively).

Chinese students have become important intercultural intermediaries and they might be providing capital pathways for foreign investment into real estate, but these investment pathways have yet to be explored in a systematic way.

Another set of culturally-dependent relational assets, which are central to foreign real estate investment and are in need of further investigation, are the multi-language and international real estate websites (Rogers, in press). Rogers et al (2015) analysed the international real estate website Juwai, which claims to operate 'behind the Chinese government firewall' (Schlesinger 2013c: 1) and has an agreement with the Australian real estate company LJ Hooker. They found, 'Juwai utilises culturally-dependent relational technologies, such as translating real estate advertisements from English into Mandarin, in an explicit effort to make their website "Asia ready" to attract Australian real estate companies to advertise through their website'. Similarly Xiao (2013: 1), an Australian-based real estate agent, argued that understanding and communicating local housing knowledge across cultures is central to securing international sales.

Real estate tourism is also an emerging area for research. For example, some Chinese real estate companies provide 'tours' to Australia to purchase real estate. Equally, representatives of real estate company Landmark Harcourts travelled to Beijing, Shanghai and Hong Kong 'on a 10 day tour' to 'market the benefits of owning property in Australia by speaking and marketing directly to the prospective customer' (Walsh 2013b: 1). Across Asia, the *International Property Expo* is held in several countries (e.g., China, Singapore, Hong Kong) and is advertised as an 'ideal platform for overseas companies offering real estate, land, immigration investing projects to the wealthy Chinese market' [*sic*] (Wang 2013).

These changing electronic communications, real estate travel and international property showcase events are important sites for further research. Studies of these embodied and electronic 'mediating technologies' will allow researchers to track how government regulations, visa controls and property investment information is mediated and translated through international media, property development and real estate networks (Rogers, in press). As highlighted in The Inquiry, little is known about how the actors *themselves* are implicated in the interpretation, circulation and manipulation of the formal laws and practices of the respective national governments.

Cultural Profiling of Customers and Market Profiling of Products

Following on from the last set of possible research directions, a suite of new cultural and market-profiling technologies has been enabled through the networking of Asian-Australian culturally-dependent housing practices (Fincher and Costello 2003; 2005). For example, one real estate journalist provided information to the real estate industry on 'Pressing the right Chinese button for Australian real estate sales' (Chancellor 2013: 1). The cultural profiling of prospective Chinese housing purchasers is common in Australia and China (Fincher and Costello 2005; Xiao 2013). One Australian property agent, Xiao (2013: 1), stated 'most Chinese buy property in Australia because they would like to send their kids here to study in the future, or they would like to migrate to Australia'. Ho (2011: 1) argues 'Many Asian migrant families in particular are famously anxious about their children's academic performance'. Purchasing a house to accommodate a son or daughter who is studying in Australia satisfies Australia's foreign investment rules for 'non-resident' real estate purchases (Australian Government 2012b; 2012c). Real estate agents are using the complicated linkages between educational, visa and foreign investment information to market properties overseas.

With more than a hint of Orientalism (Fincher and Costello 2005; Said 1978), a KPMG demographer advised property developers that new 'ethnicities' were changing the 'shape [of] the Australian residential property market' to 'absorb the cultural preferences and predispositions of these ethnic influences' (Schlesinger 2012: 1). More research is needed about if and how property developers are changing their housing products to suit foreign buyers. Any change in building practices could have possible urban planning and built form implications. As Australian-based sales agent Corbett stated 'vendors believe the Chinese have the money for these properties right now, while Australian's don't' (Schlesinger 2013b: 1). Equally, Chinese-based property developer Wang identified that 'investing in property in Australia was attractive for its lifestyle, a good return on investment and – importantly – because its regulatory system was transparent' (Schlesinger 2013a: 1). Furthermore, these types of statements raise questions about the 'pull forces' of Australia's foreign investment and taxation settings and the 'push forces' resulting from the local policy settings in countries like China.

Finally, the financial professionals, real estate agents and property developers from many countries (including China and Australia) are central to promoting and developing the relationships between the Chinese and Australian real estate sectors. However, in terms of the long-term sustainability of these relationships, it is the new middle class and High Net Worth individuals – the global rich and super rich (Dorling 2014; Hay 2013; Paris 2013) – who increasingly populate the financial spaces that are created by these actors, and these translocal spaces require further critical attention (Acuto and Curtis 2013; Coase and Wang 2013). It is also unclear how the complex relationships between the Australian and Asian housing sectors are mediating information about culture and class. In terms of the media debate, much of the discussion has focused on the cultural dimension of foreign investment (Rogers et al. 2015). For example, the assumption with a statement such as *to buy property is in the Chinese investors' bones*, which was positioned as one of the driving forces behind the increase in FDI for real estate in Australia, needs to be exposed to further critical review. More research is also needed about how the cross-cultural links between Asian and Australian countries are constructing or silencing different cultural identities and/or class ideals. Surprisingly, the class question was little mentioned in the foreign investment media debate in Australia, and Rogers (et al. 2015; in press) posited a counter-question, *is it in the middle class investors' rather then the Chinese investors' bones to buy property?*

Regional Geopolitics and Local Parochialism

Many in the business and government sectors are keen to present 'Chinese investment [as] an opportunity, not a threat' (Brumby 2011: 1). But the Australian government will need to manage an increasingly fraught public debate that pitches the rationalism of 'freeing up' international trade against the jingoistic concern of 'protecting Australians' from foreign investment. A cultural politics is rapidly taking shape around Chinese foreign investment in

Australia at two levels. The first is around individual foreign investment into commodities such as residential housing. The second is around institutional investment – including foreign state-owned companies – into large mining and agricultural assets and business.

Real estate agents and politicians have taken steps to mitigate local fears about increasing numbers of Chinese investors in Australian housing (Brumby 2011). These debates are further politicised when they involve visa programs and offer investors education and immigration pathways to Australia. For example, the introduction of the Significant Investment Visa by the former Gillard government allowed the private financial sector to create special purpose investment vehicles in an attempt to allow Chinese investors to use property trust purchases to secure these visa types (Macquarie 2013). These types of federal government regulation changes quickly circulate through media, property development and real estate networks.

Finally, an important research task will be to compare public perceptions in Australian cities about Asian FDI into real estate with impartial individual FDI data. Early work by Rogers (et al. 2015; in press) has demonstrated that a commonly held view, which the real estate and property development sectors promoted via their respective industry publications, was that 'Chinese investors' are dominant in major Australian cities. However, public perceptions may not discriminate between Australian-Chinese (Australian nationals) and mainland Chinese (Chinese nationals) and this can feed into protectionist and xenophobic discourses. At stake in this type of research agenda are questions about White Australia's recent history and discourses, for example, that occasionally emerge from marginal groups about a so-called 'Asian invasion' (Jayasuriya and Pookong 1999). Equally, if individual FDI into Australian real estate continues to grow from the emerging middle class of Asia and beyond, this could have very real social, political and economic implications; most obviously to housing affordability in cities. Therefore, closer analyses of the policy frameworks that are guiding FDI into Australian real estate, and their aims and efficacy, could provide revealing insights about how to use FDI taxations regimes to provide more affordable housing. However, this type of discussion is unlikely within the parochial, perhaps even racist, discursive space that currently surrounds Chinese investment in Australian housing.

Conclusion

Explicitly in this chapter, and indeed more implicitly in this edited volume, we set out to examine what Australia's location in changing local, national, regional and global landscapes might mean for thinking through Australian housing in the 21st century. For much of the latter half of the twentieth century in Australia housing has been central to defining what it means to be 'Australian' (Kemeny 1983). The relationship linking housing to citizenship was and continues to be very much bound to the geopolitical construct of the nation-state. For much of the last century the Australian government sought to influence, through both direct and indirect means, how housing in Australia is financed, constructed and purchased. At the beginning of the 21st century the nation-state still wields a great deal of power when it comes to defining what it is to be Australian, and housing still pays an important role in the construction and challenging of Australian identities. However, accompanying the broader geopolitical restructuring in the region is a radical reconfiguration of the relationships between housing, citizenship and identity at the local and national levels. The nation-state is no less relevant when it comes to understanding Australian housing, but through new globalising connections that increasingly define and construct the production and consumption of housing in Australia, the future of Australian housing will be undeniably different.

The new forms of regional and global relationality are evidenced by the development of new global financial tools and the role that FDI plays in generating fresh flows of capital to facilitate the purchase of homes. It is also present in the multinational companies that are involved in the production of these homes and the multinational financial institutions that bankroll foreign investors. The porousness of traditionally nationally-bound housing markets can also be seen at the microscale, with the use of a new suite of cultural stereotypes that are employed by real estate agents to either appeal to or contest the ideal of the new globally mobile urban citizen. Nevertheless, it would be a mistake to write the national out of such reflections. Governments still design the nation's visa rules, regulate financial markets, create housing and planning frameworks and approve development applications. Governments set these policy mechanisms and can manipulate these policies to suit changing geopolitical and socio-economic contexts. Thus, the centrality of government for determining Australian housing futures should not be underestimated; it is up to Australian governments, not local, national or global markets, to manage the delicate and dialectic interdependence of foreign investment, national economies, living standards and housing outcomes.

Thus, conceptually, we argue that Australian housing researchers and policy makers will increasingly need to accommodate globalising understandings of housing issues. Relational approaches might allow researchers to prioritise the collection of data in ways that capture the new connections athwart different socio-cultural dynamics, economic forms, housing tenures, geographical scales and timelines. Such a project could encompass all the housing and market forms discussed in this edited volume, including: changing household formations (Chapter 2); radicalised housing practices (Chapter 3); compact (Chapter 8) and sustainable (Chapter 4) living arrangements; Indigenous housing and discrimination (Chapter 5); changing housing careers across generations (Chapter 7); changing government policies (Chapter 10) and housing policy inertia (Chapter 9); the historical rise, decline and renationalisation of collectives forms of housing provision (Chapter 11 and 12); and the plight of Australia's homelessness (Chapter 13).

References

Acuto, M. and Curtis, S. (2013) Assemblage thinking and international relations. In: M. Acuto and S. Curtis (eds) *Reassembling International Theory*. New York: Palgrave Macmillan.
Australian Government. (2012a) Australia in the Asian Century. Canberra: Commonwealth of Australia.

—— (2012b) *Foreign Investment Review Board – Annual Report*. Canberra: Foreign Investment Review Board.

—— (2012c) *Significant Investor Visa*. Canberra: Department of Immigration and Citizenship.

—— (2014a) Australian Treasury, Submission to the inquiry into foreign investment in residental real estate. Canberra: Submission to the House of Representatives Standing Committee on Economics.

—— (2014b) *Foreign Investment Review Board: Annual Report*. Canberra: Commonwealth Government.

Berry, M., Dalton, T. and Nelson, A. (2011) The impacts of the Global Financial crisis on housing and morgage markets in Australia: A view from the vulnerable. In: R. Forrest and N-M. Yip (eds) *Housing Markets and the Global Financial Crisis*. Cheltenham: Edward Elgar Publishing.

Brumby, J. (2011) Chinese investment an opportunity, not a threat. Australia-China Business Week.

Buckley, P. (2010) *Foreign Direct Investment, China and the World Economy*. Basingstoke: Palgrave Macmillan.

Buckley, P., Clegg, J., Cross, A., et al. (2010a) The determinants of Chinese outward foreign direct investment. In: P. Buckley (ed.) *Foreign Direct Investment, China and the World Economy*. Basingstoke: Palgrave Macmillan, 81–118.

Buckley, P., Cross, A., Tan, H., et al. (2010b) Historic and emergent trends in Chinese outward direct investment. In: P. Buckley (ed.) *Foreign Direct Investment, China and the World Economy*. Basingstoke: Palgrave Macmillan.

Chancellor, J. (2013) Pressing the right Chinese button for Australian real estate sales. Melbourne: Property Observer.

Coase, R. and Wang, N. (2013) *How China became Capitalist*, Basingstoke: Palgrave Macmillan.

Colic-Peisker, V., Robertson, S., Phipps, P., et al. (2012) Housing, employment and social cohesion in multicultural neighbourhoods 'in transition': A comparative case study from the City of Moreland. RMIT University.

Dorling, D. (2014) *Inequality and the 1%*, London: Verso.

Edgington, D.W. (1996) Japanese real estate investment in Canadian cities and regions, 1985–1993. *Le Géographe canadien* 40: 292–305.

Fincher, R. and Costello, L. (2003) Housing ethnicity: multicultural negotiation and housing the transnational student. In: B. Yeoh, M. Charney and C.K. Tong (eds) *Approaching Transnationalisms: Studies on Transnational Societies, Multicultural Contacts, and Imaginings of Home*. Boston: Kluwer Academic Publishers, 161–186.

—— (2005) Narratives of high-rise housing: placing the ethnicized newcomer in inner Melbourne. *Social & Cultural Geography* 6: 201–217.

Freudenburg, G. (2013) For the record: Gough Whitlam's Mission to China, 1971. Sydney: Whitlam Institute.

Gauder, M., Houssard, C. and Orsmond, D. (2014) Foreign investment in residential real estate. Sydney: Reserve Bank of Australia – Bulletin.

Grubisa, D. (2014) Real estate rescues: How to profit in real estate in the new economy. In: S. Zadel (ed.) *The New Way to Make Money in Property Fast!*. Sutherland: Zadel Property.

Hage, G. (1998) *White Nation: Fantasies of White Supremacy in a Multicultural Society*, Annandale: Pluto Press.
Hajdu, J. (2005) *Samurai in the Surf: The arrival of the Japanese on the Gold Coast in the 1980s*, Canberra: Pandanus Books.
Hay, I. (2013) *Geographies of the Super-Rich*, Northampton: Edward Elgar Publishing.
Ho, C. (2011) Respecting the presence of Others: School micropublics and everyday multiculturalism. *Journal of Intercultural Studies* 32: 603–619.
Hutchens, G. (2014) Tony Abbott says Australia benefited from foreign investment because it was 'unsettled' before the British. *The Sydney Morning Herald*, 3 July.
Jacques, M. (2012) *When China Rules the World: The End of the Western World and the Birth of a new Global Order*, New York: Penguin.
Javorcik, B., Özden, Ç., Spatareanu, M., et al. (2011) Migrant networks and foreign direct investment. *Journal of Development Economics* 94: 231.
Jayasuriya, L. and Pookong, K. (1999) *Asianisation of Australia?: Some Facts about the Myths*, Melbourne: Melbourne University Press.
Kemeny, J. (1983) *The Great Australian Nightmare: A Critique of the Home-Ownership Ideology*, Melbourne: Georgian House.
Macquarie. (2013) Macquarie SIV Funds: For advisers and licensed migration agents only. Sydney/Melbourne/Brisbane: Macquarie.
Mitchell, K. (1993) Multiculturalism, or united colors of capitalism? *Antipode* 25: 263–294.
National Australia Bank. (2013) *Quarterly Australian Residential Property Survey: Q2 2013*. Sydney: National Australia Bank.
Ong, A. (2011) Worlding cities, or the art of being global. In: A. Roy and A. Ong (eds) *Worlding Cities: Asian Experiments and the Art of being Global*. Chichester: Wiley-Blackwell.
Paris, C. (2013) The homes of the super-rich: multiple residences, hyper-mobility and decoupling of prime residential housing in global cities. In: I. Hay (ed.) *Geographies of the Super-Rich*. Cheltenham: Edward Elgar.
Ray, B., Halseth, G. and Johnson, B. (1997) The Changing 'Face' of the Suburbs: Issues of Ethnicity and Residential Change in Suburban Vancouver. *International Journal of Urban and Regional Research* 21: 75–99.
Ren, X. (2013) *Urban China*, Cambridge: Polity Press.
Robinson, P. (1983) The Asianisation of Australia. *Sydney Morning Herald*, 15 February.
Rogers, D. (2015), 'Becoming a super-rich foreign real estate investor: globalising real estate data, publications and events', in R. Forrest, D. Wissink and S.Y. Koh (eds) *Cities and the Super-Rich: Real Estate, Elite Practices and Urban Political Economies*, Palgrave Macmillan, Basingstoke.
Rogers, D. and Bailey, N. (2013) Citizenship and housing: the provision of housing and practices of citizenship within global cities. *Referred Proceedings: 7th Australasian Housing Researchers Conference*. Esplanade Hotel Fremantle, Western Australia.
Rogers, D. and Darcy, M. (2014) Global city aspirations, graduated citizenship and public housing: analysing the consumer citizenships of neoliberalism. *Urban, Planning and Transport Research*: 1–17.

Rogers, D., Lee, C.L. and Yan, D. (2015) The politics of foreign investment in Australian housing: Chinese investors, translocal sales agents and local resistance. *Housing Studies*. iFirst.

Said, E. (1978) *Orientalism*, London: Vintage Books.

Schlesinger, L. (2012) Chinese and Indian design principles will shape Australia's property markets: Bernard Salt. *Property Observer*, 12 March (Melbourne).

—— (2013a) Asian governments in transition impact property investment appetite. *Property Observer*, 7 March (Melbourne).

—— (2013b) Chinese appetite for Australian residential property hits $5.4 billion as demand for luxury property rises. *Property Observer*, 18 July (Melbourne).

—— (2013c) LJ Hooker looks to sell more property to Chinese buyers with three-year marketing deal with international property listings portal Juwai.com. *Property Observer*, 13 May (Melbourne).

Scott, R. (2002) The changing world of Chinese enterprise: An institutional perspective. In: S. Tsui and C. Lau (eds) *Managment of Enterprises in the People's Republic of China*. Boston: Kluwer Academic Press, 59–78.

Standing Committee on Economics. (2014) Report on Foreign Investment in Residential Real Estate. Canberra: Commonwealth of Australia.

Tallman, S. and Shenkar, O. (1994) A managerial decision model of international cooperative venture formation. *Journal of International Business Studies* 25: 91–113.

Taylor, A. (2012) Four tips to help you sell Australian property to Chinese buyers. *Property Observer*, 11 December (Melbourne).

Walsh, A. (2012) Tony Abbott moves to limit Chinese sovereign investment in Australia. *Property Observer*, 25 July (Melbourne).

—— (2013a) Knight Frank launches significant investor visa team ahead of Chinese investment influx. *Property Observer*, 1 April (Melbourne).

—— (2013b) Landmark Harcourt rural to market properties direct to Chinese. *Property Observer*, 7 August (Melbourne).

Wang, F. (2013) *2013 Beijing International Property & Investment Expo*. Available at: http://www.beijingexhibition.com/.

Wu, F., Xu, J. and Gar-On Yeh, A. (2007) *Urban Development in Post-reform China: State, Market, and Space*, Abingdon: Routledge.

Xiao, I. (2013) Tips for getting the most from Chinese property expos. *Property Observer*, 11 June (Melbourne).

Ye, J. and Sun, C. (2011) The impact of the finacial crisis on China's housing market. In: Forrest, R. and Yip, N-M. (eds) *Housing Markets and the Global Financial Crisis*. Cheltenham: Edward Elgar Publishing.

Yip, N-M. (2011) Business nearly as usual: The Global Financial Crisis and its impacts on households in Hong Kong. In: R. Forrest and N-M. Yip (eds) *Housing markets and the Global Financial Crisis*. Cheltenham: Edward Elgar Publishing.

Zhou, C. (2013) Chinese investors developing appetite for Sydney real estate. *ABC NEWS*. Sydney.

Index

AALCs (Active Adult Lifestyle
    Communities) 105, 106–7, 108–9,
    111–15, 116
  Golden Crest Manors *108*, **109**, 110,
    112, 115
  Halcyon Waters *108*, **109**, 109–10, 112,
    115
Aboriginal and Torres Strait Islander
    Council, *see* ATSIC
Aboriginal Australians 8, 74–5, **77**, 77–9,
    80, 81, 82–3
  housing discrimination 42, 43–4, 45
Aboriginal Rental Housing Program, *see*
    ARHP
Accommodating Everyone Inquiry 44–5, 46
Active Adult Lifestyle Communities, *see*
    AALCs
affordability 6, 7–9, 39, 89, 90, 91, 111–12,
    117, 122, 184
  NAHA 143, 187, 188–9, 190, 199
  NRAS 187, 190, 195, 198, 199
agent flexibility 50, **50**
agent interaction 51, **51**
aging in place 105, 106, 107–8, 110,
    112–13, 114, 115
AHURI (Australian Housing and Urban
    Research Institute) 14
'alternative dreamers' 98
apartments 6, 9, 122–3, 124, 125, 126, 127,
    128, 130–131, 132, 133
ARHP (Aboriginal Rental Housing
    Program) 79
ATSIC (Aboriginal and Torres Strait
    Islander Council) 79
Australian economy 2, 5, 10, 15, 156–7
Australian households 2, 3, 6, 7–8, 66–7,
    89–90, 91, 101–2, 139
Australian housing 1, 3–4, 6–9, 10, 15–16,
    90–91, 101–2, 122, 232–3
Australian Housing and Urban Research
    Institute, *see* AHURI

Australian housing research 11, 14, 21,
    92–3, 101
Australian society 2–3, 5, 8, 12, 122, 205,
    221

baby boomers 7, 60, 63, 105, 106, 107,
    110–111, 113, 115–16, 117, 222–3;
    see also AALCs; aging in place
Bonnyrigg Estate (NSW) *176*, 181–2
'boomerang phenomenon' 22, 23
Brisbane 24–5, 26, **27**, 29, **30**, **31**, **32**

CAG (Commonwealth Additional Grant)
    154–5
Carlton Estate (Victoria) 181
Challenging Racism Project 46, **47**
CHAs (Community Housing Associations)
    190n4, 191, 195, 197, 198
China 222, 223, 224–6, 227, 232
Chinese investors 221, 222, 223, 224,
    227–8, 230, 231–2
CHIP (Community Housing and
    Infrastructure Project) 79–80
CHPs (Community Housing Providers) 12,
    188, 189–91, 193–5, 196, 198, 199,
    200
cities 4–5, 6, 8, 9, 15, 23, 30, 34
climate change 9, 15, 57, 59, 60, 61, 67
Closing the Gap strategy 74
COAG (Council of Australian
    Governments) 80, 167, 187, 197
'comfort traders' 97
Common Ground Camperdown program,
    Sydney 211
Commonwealth Additional Grant, *see*
    CAG
Commonwealth State Housing Agreement,
    see CSHA
communal areas 112–13
community housing 12, 187, 188, 189–91,
    192, 193–5, 197–8, 199, 200–201

Indigenous Australians 74, 79–80, 81
Community Housing and Infrastructure
    Project, *see* CHIP
Community Housing Associations, *see*
    CHAs
Community Housing Providers, *see* CHPs
Council of Australian Governments, *see*
    COAG
CSHA (Commonwealth State Housing
    Agreement) 10, 12, 79, 168, 175,
    177–8

densification 3, 4, 8, 9, 12
downshifting 9, 89–90, 93–101, *94*, *96*, 102

energy use 57, 58, 59, 60, 61, 63
environment 4, 9, 57, 58–9, 60, 61, 63,
    65–6, 67, 100
EOCWA (Equal Opportunity Commission
    of Western Australia) 43–4, 45, 48
ESS (Economic Security Strategy) 157,
    159, 169
ethnic discrimination 8, 49–52, 53
EU (European Union) 40, **41**, 42
'exit strategists' 99

FDI (foreign direct investment) 8, 222,
    223, 224, 227–8, 229, 232, 233
FHOGs (First Home Owner Grants)
    11, 153–6, *158*, 158–61, *159*, *160*,
    162–6, 167–8, 169
    house prices 160, 162, 165–8, *166*
    Melbourne *163*, 163–5
    new dwellings **162**, 162–3, 164–5, 168
    Victoria 158, 159, *159*, 160–161, **161**,
    162, **162**, 168
Finding a Place Inquiry 43–4
FIRB (Foreign Investment Review Board)
    224, 227, 228
first home buyers 154, 157
    FHOGs 11, 153–6, *158*, 158–61, *159*,
    160, 162–6, 167–8, 169
foreign direct investment, *see* FDI

gatekeepers 64, 214
GFC (Global Financial Crisis) 12, 156,
    157, 178, 181, 187, 189, 195, 197,
    224

FHOGs 11, 154, 167, 168, 169
Gold Coast City region 107, 108–9
Golden Crest Manors *108*, **109**, 110, 112, 115

Halcyon Waters *108*, **109**, 109–10, 112, 115
Helensvale *108*, 109, **109**, 110, 112, 115
Henderson Commission of Inquiry into
    Poverty 177
home-leaving young adults 22, 26–7, 34
Home Savings Grant Program 154
home space 3, 9, 57, 58, 62, 64, 65
Homeground, Melbourne 210–211
homelessness 12–13, 73, 146–7, 205, 206,
    207–8, 210, 212, 215, 217
homeownership 6–7, 8, 10, 11, 73, 90, 92,
    95, 121, 122, 143
    FHOGs 153, 154, 158, *159*, *160*, 165,
    167–8, 169
    see also downshifting; multigenerational
    households
house prices 6, 7, 30, 90, 145, 149
    FHOGs 160, 162, 165–8, *166*
    Victoria 165–6, *166*, 167
household size 22, 29, 33, 64
households 6, 62–4, 65, 66–7, 91–3, 101–2
housing consumption 13, 29, 89, 90, 91–3,
    101, 102, 233
housing cost 39, 73, 102
housing debt 91, 100, 167
housing discrimination 39–40, 42–8, **46**,
    49–52, **50**, **51**, **52**, 53–4
    Aboriginal Australians 42, 43–4, 45
    EU 40, **41**, 42
    immigrants 8, 39, 40, *42*, 42–3, 44–6,
    46
    Indigenous Australians 8, 39, 73–4
    racism 40, 42, 46, **47**, 53
    refugees 41–2, 45–6
housing estates 175–7, *176*, 178–9, 180–
    182, 183–4
'Housing First' programs 13, 205–6,
    208–11, 212–18
housing inequality 8, 39–40, 168
housing market 6–7, 140–141, 145, 157,
    167, 222, 224, 226, 227–8, 233
housing pathways 92–3, 101
housing policy 1, 5, 10–14, 15, 142–8, 149,
    157, 173, 199, 226–7, 233

INDEX

FHOGs 153–6, 159–60, 168, 169
   Indigenous Australians 74, 75, 79–81, 83–4
housing production 13, 101, 102, 117, 165, 228, 231
housing supply 9, 154, 156, 165, 228
housing wealth 6, 7
HUD (Department of Housing and Urban Development) studies 40, 53

ICHOs (Indigenous community housing organisations) 79–80, 81
immigrants 6, 23, 26, 221
   housing discrimination 8, 39, 40, *42*, 42–3, 44–6, **46**
Indigenous Australians 46, 73, 76–7
   Aboriginal Australians 8, 74–5, **77**, 77–9, 80, 81, 82–3
   community housing 74, 79–80, 81
   housing discrimination 8, 39, 73–4
   housing policy 74, 75, 79–81, 83–4
   overcrowded households 73, 78
Indigenous community housing organisations, *see* ICHOs
Indigenous housing 8, 73–4, 78, 79–81, 82, 83, 84, 222
information provision 50–51, **51**
investment property 7, 8, 149, 221, 223, 225, 226, 227, 228–9, 230–231
   Chinese investors 221, 222, 223, 224, 227–8, 230, 231–2
   rental housing 140–141, 145, 148

Keynes economic system 2, 10, 11, 14, 153, 155, 157, 168, 175

'lucky ones' 97

Melbourne 122–3, 125–6, 127
   FHOGs *163*, 163–5
Menzies Government 10
mobility 15, 78–9, 82–3
multigenerational households 8, 21–2, 23–5, 26–9, **27**, 30–33, **31, 32**, 34–5, 64

NAHA (National Affordable Housing Agreement) 143, 187, 188–9, 190, 199

National Partnership Agreements, *see* NPAs
National Rental Affordability Scheme, *see* NRAS
NBESP (Nation Building Economic Stimulus Plan) 187–8, 190, 191, 195
NBJP (Nation Building and Jobs Plan) 157, 191
negative gearing 132, 144–6, 149
neighbourhoods 107, 113–14, 179, 180, 181, 183
Nerang *108*, **109**, 110, 112, 115
new dwellings **162**, 162–3, 164–5, 168
Northern Territory Emergency Intervention, *see* NTER
NPAs (National Partnership Agreements) 80, 81, 82, 190
NRAS (National Rental Affordability Scheme) 187, 190, 195, 198, 199
NSW (New South Wales) 188, 191, 192–3, 195–7, 199
NTER (Northern Territory Emergency Intervention) 80, 82
nuclear family 2–3, 5

OHS (Occupational Health and Safety) 130–131
overcrowded households 73, 78, *78*
owner building 95–6, 97, 101
owner corporations 123–4, 125, 126, 128, 129–30, 131–3

paired testing 40, 41, 48, 53
   RAs (Research Assistants) 48–9, 53
   agent flexibility 50, **50**
   agent interaction 51, **51**
   information provision 50–51, **51**
   renting encouragement 52, **52**
   renting requirements 52, **52**
physical activities 114–15, 116
population aging 6, 15, 22, 105, 108, 116–17
poverty 143, 146, 173, 177, 179, 180, 182, 183
private rental sector 8, 12, 139, 140–141, 142–8, 149
Project 40, Sydney 210, 211
public housing 12, 43, 74, 76–7, 173, 174–5, 177–8, 179–80, 182–3, 200, 223

housing estates 175–7, *176*, 178–9, 180–182, 183–4

RA (Rent Assistance) 142–4, 149
racism 40, 42, 46, **47**, 53
Radburn style estate *176*, 176–7
real estate tourism 230
recognition theory 75–6, 82, 83
recycling 57, 59, 61
refugees 41–2, 45–6
rental housing 2, 6, 7, 11–12, 73–4, 122, 142, 182
   housing discrimination 42–8, 49–52, **50, 51, 52**, 53–4
   private sector 8, 12, 139, 140–141, 142–8, 149
   strata titled property 121–2, 123–5, 126–33
renting encouragement 52, **52**
renting requirements 52, **52**
residential tenancies reform 146–8, 149
resource use 9, 57, 58, 59–60, 62, 63, 65, 67
retirement 7, 63–4, 107, 108, 111

safety 106, 107–8, 113–14, 117
security 106, 107–8, 113, 114, 117
SHI (Social Housing Initiative) 12, 187, 188, 190, 192–3, 197, 198–9, 200
   community housing 193–5, 197–8, 199, 200–201
   NSW 188, 191, 192–3, 195–7, 199
single parent households 6, 99
single person households 6, 21, 22, 34

social housing 12, 75, 81, 84, 169, 174, 178, 187–90, 192
   affordability 89, 111–12, 184
   community housing 190–191, 193–5, 197–8, 199, 200–201
   NSW 188, 191, 192–3, 195–7, 199
   SHI 12, 187, 188, 190, 192–3, 197, 198–9, 200
Social Housing Initiative, *see* SHI
strata titled property 121–2, 123–5, 126–33
'street to home' 208, 210–211
'Street to Home', Parramatta 211, 212, 213
Stretton, Hugh 1, 2–5, 9, 10–11, 12, 13–14, 15
suburbanisation 3–4
sustainability 57–8, 58–9, 61, 61–2, 63, 65–6, 67
Sydney 24–5, 26, **27**, 29, 30, **30, 31, 32**, 33, 34

Toronto, Canada 40–1
tourist accommodation 126–8, 132

United States 39, 40, 53, 209–10
urban areas 3, 4, 6, 8, 9, 11, 34, 61–2, 164, 179, 189

Victoria
   FHOGs 158, *159*, 159, 160–161, **161**, 162, **162**, 168
   house prices 165–6, *166*, 167
   strata titled property 123, 125, 128, 132

Way 2 Home, Sydney 211, 212
Whitlam Government 2, 3, 11